Mongolian Independence and the British

Geopolitics and Diplomacy in High Asia, 1911–1916

MATTEO MIELE

E-INTERNATIONAL
RELATIONS
PUBLISHING

E-International Relations
Bristol, England
2022

ISBN: 978-1-910814-64-2

This book is published under a Creative Commons CC BY-NC 4.0 license. You are free to:

- **Share** – copy and redistribute the material in any medium or format.

- **Adapt** – remix, transform, and build upon the material.

Under the following terms:

- **Attribution** – You must give appropriate credit to the author(s) and publisher, provide a link to the license and indicate if changes were made. You may do so in any reasonable manner, but not in any way that suggests the licensor endorses you or your use.

- **Non-Commercial** – You may not use the material for commercial purposes.

Any of the above conditions can be waived if you get permission. Please contact info@e-ir.info for any such enquiries, including for licensing and translation requests. Other than the terms noted above, there are no restrictions placed on the use and dissemination of this book for student learning materials or scholarly use.

Production: Michael Tang
Cover Image: Evgeniyqw/Shutterstock

A catalogue record for this book is available from the British Library.

E-International Relations

Editor-in-Chief and Publisher: Stephen McGlinchey
Books Editor: Bill Kakenmaster
Editorial Assistance: Franny Klatt, Adeleke Olumide Ogunnoiki, Farah Saleem Düzakman.

E-International Relations is the world's leading International Relations website. Our daily publications feature expert articles, reviews and interviews – as well as student learning resources. The website is run by a non-profit organisation based in Bristol, England and staffed by an all-volunteer team of students and academics. In addition to our website content, E-International Relations publishes a range of books. As E-International Relations is committed to open access in the fullest sense, free electronic versions of our books, including this one, are available at https://www.e-ir.info

A ma grand-mère Maria Piccardo

Abstract

This work focuses on some High Asian diplomatic, geopolitical and trade issues, from the point of view of the British Empire, in the period between the last phase of the Ch'ing dynasty and the early years of the Chinese Republic. In particular, the significance for the British of Mongolian independence in the geopolitical dimension of Tibet will be analyzed within the framework of the international equilibrium system that had originated from the Anglo-Russian Agreement of 1907. The geopolitical role of Tibet, whose peaks represented one of the great geographical defenses of the British Raj, was in fact necessarily called into question by the fall of the Ch'ing Empire and by the declaration of independence, at the end of 1911, of Mongolia, a country strongly linked for religious, cultural, and historical reasons to the Land of Snows but connected for political and economic reasons to Russia. The research, therefore, reconstructs the British attempt to use the relationship between Outer Mongolia and Russia to its advantage, in a sort of exchange necessary to make Saint Petersburg accept the Simla Convention of 1914 – finally signed by the British and Tibetans without the Chinese – and which came into conflict with what had been decided between the Russians and the British in 1907. As it was possible to study through archival documents, largely preserved in The National Archives, London, Kew, the Foreign Office could not find an agreement with Russia on this basis alone, but through a much broader diplomatic negotiation that has, therefore, been reconstructed in detail.

About the author

Matteo Miele (Frosinone, 1984) is an Affiliated Assistant Professor at the Center for Southeast Asian Studies (CSEAS) of Kyoto University and a Fellow of the Royal Asiatic Society of Great Britain and Ireland. Between August 2011 and July 2012, he was a Lecturer at the Sherubtse College, Royal University of Bhutan. He received his Ph.D. (Dottorato di Ricerca) from the University of Pisa in 2014.

Acknowledgements

I would like to thank in the first place my parents, my brother, and my grandmother Maria Piccardo for their love and support. Thanks to Nittayaporn Prompanya for her friendship, help and the long and pleasant conversations.

A significant thanks to the Center for Southeast Asian Studies (CSEAS) of Kyoto University and in particular to my old friend Yoshio Akamatsu, Ryota Sakamoto, Satoru Kobayashi, Kazuo Ando and Osamu Kozan for their great support. This work was in part supported by JSPS KAKENHI Grant Number 17F17306. Indeed, between 1 November 2017 and 31 October 2019, I was a JSPS International Research Fellow at the Kokoro Research Center, Kyoto University. Thanks to Seiji Kumagai, my host researcher when I was working at the Kokoro Research Center, and to Miguel Alvarez Ortega (Kyoto University).

This work represents a translated and revised part of my doctoral dissertation defended at the University of Pisa in July 2014. Therefore, I want to thank my then-tutor, Maurizio Vernassa. His numerous suggestions have represented important points of reference for me ever since, not yet twenty-years-old, I had the good fortune to meet him in Pisa.

The year spent in the Kingdom of Bhutan as a lecturer at the Sherubtse College was an extremely fruitful period. The meetings with various personalities of the institutions of the kingdom, first of all His Majesty Jigme Khesar Namgyel Wangchuck, the long and interesting conversations with the director, Singye Namgyel, with students, colleagues, and friends of the College, the hours of study spent in the Sherubtse College Library, the research conducted at the Trashi Yangtse dzong with Namkha Wangdi and Kawang Chhimi Dorji: all these moments have been enormously fruitful for my human and intellectual growth. Thanks therefore to all of them and in particular to Sarbajeet Mukherjee and Madhuchhanda Chakraborty, who took care of me as a younger brother. Thanks to Pankaj Thapa and his family. Thanks to my fraternal friend Namkha Wangdi who helped me in research, study and above all, together with his family, allowed me to fully understand the traditional kindness of Bhutan. Of course, a big thanks goes to my students. In addition to Namkha, special thanks go to my teacher of Classical Tibetan, Singye Wangdi, and to my student at Sherubtse College, Rinchen Dawa, for their help in understanding Tibetan texts. Thanks to Fabian Sanders with whom I continued to study the Classical Tibetan language in Italy.

For suggestions and help in the complex bibliographic research, a heartfelt thanks to my uncle Armando Delicato, to my dear friend Xia Feng, always ready to clarify my doubts in front of a Chinese text, and to my student Inchu Dorji.

Thanks to Maitrayee Deka (University of Essex) for the numerous and helpful writing tips, continued support, and deep friendship. Thanks to Rino Casella (University of Pisa) for his strong and old friendship. Thanks to Roy Smith (Nottingham Trent University), Enrica Lemmi (University of Pisa), Erberto Lo Bue (University of Bologna), Pier Giorgio Borbone (University of Pisa), Bruno Mazzoni (University of Pisa), Giuseppe Dell'Agata (University of Pisa), Emanuela Panattoni (University of Pisa), Paulo Donoso Johnson (Pontificia Universidad Católica de Valparaíso), Giorgio Belli and Sumiyabazar Choimboroljav for their valuable advice.

I obviously thank the staff of the libraries of the University of Pisa, Kyoto University, in particular the CSEAS Library, The National Archives (London, Kew), and the Tibetan Buddhist Resource Center (Cambridge, MA), in particular Kelsang Lhamo.

Thanks to Jo Sakai, Oana Loredana Scorus (Kansai University and Konan University) and Kozo Tamari for their friendship and help in Kyoto.

Thanks to Heather Campbell for her careful and meticulous proofreading.

Finally, special thanks to Stephen McGlinchey and the E-International Relations team for their care, attention and professionalism.

TRANSLITERATIONS AND TRANSCRIPTIONS

In this text I have tried to provide a scientific transliteration (or transcription for Chinese and Japanese) for each place name, as well as person. This part of the work was one of the most complex. In particular, for place names, various atlases of the time and geographical maps were consulted to try to identify each village or mountain pass mentioned. In the few cases where it was not possible to find the reference in the local language, it was decided to leave the name as transcribed in the documents and therefore highlighted by the quotation marks.

Transliteration of Tibetan

For Tibetan I used the transliteration system proposed by Turrell V. Wylie in 1959.[1] Since Tibetan spelling is particularly complex, for reasons of legibility, I inserted a hyphen between the syllables of the proper nouns within the text. This arrangement has not been adopted for technical terms and bibliographic notes. It should be borne in mind that the documents of the time use a phonetic transcription of Tibetan and therefore are often very distant from scientific transliteration.

Phonetic transcription of Chinese

For Chinese I preferred to use the Wade-Giles transcription system, developed by Thomas Francis Wade and Herbert Giles,[2] because – although less intuitive and less widespread today than Pinyin in the academic field – it is closer to the transcriptions found in the documents. However, in some cases, the transcriptions are accompanied by traditional Chinese characters.

Transliteration of Persian

For the names of people and places relating to Persia, Afghanistan and – with some exceptions – Central Asia, I have relied on the Persian language which is transliterated according to the BGN/PCGN 1958 System for the Romanization of Persian (updated 2019).

For the choice of short vowels, I consulted 'A. DEHKHODĀ, *Loghat-nāmeh*, Tehrān 1998 and □. 'AMĪD, *Farhang-e 'Amid*, Tehrān 1342 [1962-1963]. Often the pronunciation between the Persian language of Iran and the Persian language of Afghanistan differs. For Afghan toponyms I followed the rules valid for the Persian of Iran.

Indian place names

The toponyms of India are reproduced according to the common English form of the time. Occasionally, a scientific transliteration based on Persian, the pre-British court language, is provided in brackets. For the areas of Tibetan culture Tibetan transliteration is also indicated.

Central Asian place names

The toponyms of Central Asia follow the transliteration from Persian and/or the common transcription in English.

Other languages

Korean is transliterated following the Yale romanization system for Korean.[3] Japanese is transcribed according to the Hepburn system (*Hebon-shiki rōmaji*).

Transliteration of Russian

For Russian I adopted the scheme of the United States Board on Geographic Names (BGN) and of the Permanent Committee on Geographical Names for British Official Use (PCGN), the BGN/PCGN 1947 System (updated June 2019):

А а	a	К к	k	Ц ц	ts
Б б	b	Л л	l	Ч ч	ch
В в	v	М м	m	Ш ш	sh
Г г	g	Н н	n	Щ щ	shch
Д д	d	О о	o	Ъ ъ	″
Е е	e, ye	П п	p	Ы ы	y
Ё ё	ë, yë	Р р	r	Ь ь	′
Ж ж	zh	С с	s	Ѣ ѣ*	ē
З з	z	Т т	t	Э э	e
И и	i	У у	u	Ю ю	yu
I i*	ī	Ф ф	f	Я я	ya
Й й	y	Х х	kh	Ѳ ѳ*	th
				V v*	î

*These letters were abolished by the spelling reform of 1918 and are not transliterated in the BGN/PCGN 1947 System but were still used in the years described in the book. I therefore added their transliteration.

Transliteration of Mongolian

For the Mongolian names I have essentially relied on the transcriptions present in the documents and on the names in modern Mongolian (*halh*) in Cyrillic, although the adoption of the Cyrillic alphabet is later than the years in question. Transliteration of Mongolian Cyrillic follows the BGN/PCGN System for Mongolian Cyrillic (BGN/PCGN 1964 System, updated June 2019):

А а	*a*	Л л	*l*	Х х	*h*
Б б	*b*	М м	*m*	Ц ц	*ts*
В в	*v*	Н н	*n*	Ч ч	*ch*
Г г	*g*	О о	*o*	Ш ш	*sh*
Д д	*d*	Ө ө	*ö*	Щ щ	*shch*
Е е	*yö*	П п	*p*	Ъ ъ	*'*
Ё ё	*yo*	Р р	*r*	Ы ы	*ï*
Ж ж	*j*	С с	*s*	Ь ь	*ĭ*
З з	*dz*	Т т	*t*	Э э	*e*
И и	*i*	У у	*u*	Ю ю	*yu*
Й й	*y*	Ү ү	*ü*	Я я	*ya*
К к	*k*	Ф ф	*f*		

ARCHIVAL DOCUMENTS AND BIBLIOGRAPHIC REFERENCES

Archival documents

The Foreign Office documents are kept in The National Archives, London, Kew (TNA). The India Office documents are instead kept at the British Library, London (BL).

Bibliographic references

For the Chinese and Japanese authors, the personal name was shortened, except for the texts in Chinese in which the full personal name was kept and placed, as in use in China, after the surname.

Acronyms

AMS	United States Army Map Service
BGN	United States Board on Geographic Names
BL	British Library, London
BSP	British and Foreign State Papers
FO	Foreign Office
GA	General Assembly of the United Nations
IOR	India Office Records
PCGN	Permanent Committee on Geographical Names for British Official Use
TNA	The National Archives, London, Kew

Endnotes

1 T. V. WYLIE, *A Standard System of Tibetan Transcription*, in: Harvard Journal of Asiatic Studies, Vol. 22, 1959, pp. 261-267.

2 H. A. GILES, *A Chinese-English Dictionary*, London 1892.

3 S. E. MARTIN, *A reference grammar of Korean*, Rutland, Vermont – Tokyo 1992, pp. 8-12.

Contents

Introduction	1
1. At the End of the Great Game	6
2. The End of the Manchu Dynasty and Tibetan Independence	43
3. London and Mongolian Independence	55
4. The Chinese Backdown	90
5. The Parallel Negotiation	104
6. The British and the Kyakhta Accords	159
Conclusions	174
Annexes	179
References	201
Note on Indexing	222

Gairīshchā afshtachinō yazamaide

We praise the mountains from which the waters flow

Haftan Yasht, Kardāh VIII
(*Khordeh Avestā*, The Trustees of the Parsi Panchayat Funds and Properties, Bombay 1993).

Introduction

The signing of the Anglo-Russian Agreement of 1907 is generally regarded as the end of the Great Game.[1] In St. Petersburg, the British and the Russians defined the geopolitical role of Persia, Afghanistan and Tibet, the three main arenas in which the two empires had challenged each other for decades. Persia was divided into three areas. The Russian sphere of influence lay in the north, the British sphere was in the south-east, and the rest of the country remained open to the interests of both. Afghanistan remained a British protectorate. The suzerainty of the Ch'ing dynasty was recognized over Tibet. Both European powers would not interfere in internal administration, nor would they send their own representatives to Lhasa or request concessions in the country. Therefore, the Land of the Snows had to remain out of the appetites of London and St. Petersburg; it was the third geographical bastion of the Raj, but under the protection of a Manchu power in agony.

This is the geopolitical framework that was to resolve that confrontation that had begun in the first half of the nineteenth century and which had involved epic feats, military campaigns, massacres and fantasies, engulfing men and women in the dust and snow of Asia. The summer of 1907 was to put an end to the fears and obsessions that had swept through British India for almost a century. Geoffrey Wheeler in his *Epilogue* to Gerald Morgan's text, *Anglo-Russian Rivalry in Central Asia: 1810–1895*, writes that:

> From the Anglo-Russian Convention of 1907 to the revolution of 1917 the Russian menace to India was virtually forgotten; but after the Conference of Eastern Peoples held in Baku in 1920, it reappeared in a new form – that of Communism.[2]

This view[3] remains a decidedly optimistic interpretation, when compared with other authors less inclined to move the resumption of confrontation so much later into the twentieth century.[4] In particular, the work of Jennifer Siegel is based on a different interpretative line; analyzing the overall picture of Anglo-Russian relations in Asia after 1907, she comes to hypothesize that there was a risk of a military clash between the two empires, which was then averted only because of the First World War.[5]

The work at hand essentially focuses on a part of the renewed confrontation between the two empires between the 1907 and the 1917 revolutions: that of the geopolitical consequences of 1911 Mongolian independence. The primary region on which the research focuses is High Asia. It is evident that the Chinese Revolution triggered again the complexities of the Anglo-Russian relationship in the region, at least on the diplomatic table. The breaking of the ties of the Manchu dynasty with Mongolia and Tibet moved the latter outside the framework in which it had been formally located four years earlier. On the throne of Urga sat a monk, Tibetan by birth. The close historical and cultural link between the two Buddhist countries became the key that could open the doors of Lhasa to the Russians. Russia was Mongolia's great ally, and on 3 November 3, 1912, the two countries signed an agreement of friendship and trade. The treaty between Tibet and Mongolia – with which the two countries recognized their full independence from China and guaranteed mutual aid from external and internal threats – was signed a few weeks later, in January 1913. In the same days a Mongol delegation went to the Russian capital. Mongolian monks and, perhaps, Russian weapons were moving towards Tibet. This work, therefore, aims to analyze the perspective of the British Empire with respect to the consequences of these profound political-international changes, thus following the traces of the birth of the modern independent Mongolian state. The institutional and geopolitical transformations initiated by the Hsin-hai Revolution in High Asia outlined the need and the opportunity for London to redefine its relationship with Lhasa as a barrier to the risks deriving from the Russo-Mongol alliance.

The first chapter, therefore, goes into the details of the – according to the traditional view – final phase of the Great Game. The role played by Tibet within the Anglo-Russian challenge is presented, as well as the British Expedition of 1903-1904 with the arrival of Younghusband in Lhasa and the flight of the Dalai Lama first to Mongolia and then to Peking. The Anglo-Russian Convention of 31 August 1907 is then presented in detail, as well as the difficulties and mistrust that had been a prelude to it, despite the downsizing of the Russian threat after the defeat in the recent war with Japan. Part of the chapter is dedicated to Bhutan, the Himalayan country, culturally linked to Tibet. In 1907 Bhutan became a hereditary monarchy under the Dbang-phyug dynasty. Sir O-rgyan-dbang-phyug – who in 1905 had been awarded the Order of the Indian Empire – ascended the throne. Three years later, in 1910, with the Treaty of Punakha, the Bhutanese accepted British guidance in their foreign policy. The last part of the chapter introduces readers to the historical relationship between the Manchu dynasty and Tibet.

The second chapter starts with the Hsin-hai Revolution of 1911 and the birth of the Republic of China on January 1, 1912, and the abdication of P'u-i, the child emperor. The second and last part of the chapter is dedicated to the Tibetan declaration of independence of 1913.

The third chapter enters more carefully into the discourse at the center of this book. If the first two chapters served in part to introduce the historical context preceding and contemporary to the events studied, this chapter is in fact dedicated to the Mongolian independence declared in December 1911. The geopolitical consequences of this event for British interests in Asia – only apparently marginal in the context of the history of the British Empire – are the reference point on which the work orbits. A rapid historical reconstruction of relations between Russians and Mongols in modern and contemporary times up to the months following independence is presented. The Russo-Mongol Agreement of November 3, 1912 is therefore analyzed in detail. A few weeks later, in January 1913, a Mongolian delegation arrived in St. Petersburg, on the same days in which, as explained, the Tibetan-Mongol treaty was signed. Furthermore, in February, a Tibetan delegation also arrived in the Russian capital.

The fourth chapter continues with the political and geopolitical consequences of Mongolian independence, starting with the Russo-Chinese Agreement of November 5, 1913 by which Peking recognized the internal autonomy, including in commercial and industrial matters, of Outer Mongolia. For the British, the events described in the previous chapters became evident signs of the need to redefine what was established in 1907.

The fifth chapter is therefore dedicated to the long negotiation undertaken, on behalf of Sir Edward Grey, by the British ambassador in St. Petersburg, George Buchanan with the Foreign Minister of the Russian Empire Sergey Sazonov. The negotiation moved almost parallel to the discussions undertaken in Simla by the British, Tibetans and Chinese and which would later lead to the Simla Convention of July 3, 1914, signed by the Tibetans and the British, but repudiated by the Chinese. Buchanan's work in the Russian capital was long and complex. As I will explain, it unfolded on several levels, overlapping the secret negotiations – which had to remain as such in order to avoid wider crises with the other countries involved – on the internal and public political needs. The negotiations in St. Petersburg had to be reconciled in time and content with the negotiations in Simla and could not compromise the other results obtained with the Anglo-Russian Agreement of 1907, in particular with respect to Afghanistan which remained at the center of the Tsar's geopolitical attentions. The discussions fluctuated in the political and commercial spheres; the economic damage suffered by the British in the new Mongolian state – due to the support that Urga enjoyed from St. Petersburg – were underlined to ease Russian claims. A few weeks after the signing of the Simla Convention, however, the First World War broke out, thus putting Central Asian differences in the background, while not completely extinguishing them.

The sixth chapter analyzes the British perspective with respect to the Russo-Mongol Agreement of 30 September 1914 in Kyakhta and the agreement signed in the same town on June 7, 1915, between the Russians, Mongols and Chinese. The chapter ends with 1916, the year before the February and October Revolutions and the fall of the Russian Empire. In January 1916, the Chinese had signed another agreement with the Mongols and Russians in Urga that transferred the Haalgan-Urga-Kyakhta telegraph line to the Mongolian government. In the same year, the Tibetans had expressed their willingness to purchase machine guns from Japan through the Japanese consul in Calcutta. The question could have been the opportunity to send an agent to Lhasa to discuss the issue. This possibility was contemplated by the Simla Convention and had been discussed in the negotiations between Buchanan and Sazanov, when the British agreed to have to request and obtain Russian consent on the matter. As will be seen, Grey preferred to avoid opening new issues with the Russians and Japanese in the midst of the world conflict.

The conclusions are a quick attempt to read the events described in a broader framework, within the history of East and Central Asia in the twentieth century in order to define more clearly the geopolitical – and not only political – dimension of Tibet and Mongolia.

Almost all the primary sources used in this work are British archival documents kept at The National Archives (London, Kew) and to a lesser extent at the British Library (London). The British perspective is at the heart of this work. In this way I want to present the point of view of a government that was certainly directly involved in the events relating to the independence of Tibet and Mongolia, but more distant on an ideological and cultural level than the current debate on the Tibetan question. Although a certain attention has been given by historiography to the relationship between Tibetans and the British in the years described, using the perspective of Mongolian independence within the framework of the interests of the British Empire in Asia can provide further elements for academic discussion. With this work I have no pretensions to cross over into other subjects such as political science. This is a history book. There are no theoretical claims and the same conclusions as mentioned are only a way to propose a more extensive historical and geopolitical location of the events described and at the same time an invitation to further reflection and research on the matter.

Endnotes

1 See S. C. BAILEY, 'Great Game', in: *Encyclopedia of the Age of Imperialism, 1800-1914*, edited by C. C. Hodge, Westport, Connecticut – London 2008.

2 G. WHEELER, *Epilogue*, in: G. MORGAN, *Anglo-Russian Rivalry in Central Asia: 1810-1895*, London 1981, p. 220.

3 On this interpretation see also R. JOHNSON, *Spying for Empire: The Great Game in Central and South Asia, 1757-1947*, London 2006.

4 See for example I. KLEIN, *The Anglo-Russian Convention and the Problem of Central Asia, 1907-1914*, in: Journal of British Studies, Vol. 11, No. 1 (Nov., 1971), pp. 126-147.

5 J. SIEGEL, *Endgame: Britain, Russia and the Final Struggle for Central Asia*, New York 2002.

1

At the End of the Great Game

Tibet in the Great Game

At the end of 1903, the British Expedition to Tibet began, headed for Lhasa and under the command of Francis Edward Younghusband. Younghusband, who had already distinguished himself at a young age for his explorations in High Asia,[1] was not the first Englishman to admire the Po-ta-la. This primacy had instead belonged to Thomas Manning, who had arrived in the Tibetan capital almost a century before Younghusband. Manning was born on November 8, 1772 in Broome, Norfolk.[2] After his studies in Cambridge, at Caius College, the young physician studied Chinese in France and, recommended by Sir Joseph Banks, president of the Royal Society, managed to embark on a ship of the East India Company in 1806; he reached Canton the following year and remained there until 1810, when he went to Calcutta to then head towards Tibet.[3] In Lhasa, Thomas Manning met the ninth dalai lama on December 17, 1811.[4] At the time, the latter was just a child; Lung-rtogs-rgya-mtsho, born in 1806, died at the age of nine in 1815.[5] The Tibetan words of the little monk were translated into Chinese to Manning's secretary, who finally translated them to the doctor in Latin.[6] The Englishman asked for books on the religion and ancient history of Tibet, as well as a lama to instruct him, but the request and the answer were lost in the intricate path of translations.[7] From the point of view of political analysis, interest in Manning's journey is, however, limited. He was acting neither on behalf of the government nor for the East India Company, but his personal success is certainly – and a *fortiori* – indisputable. Indeed, presenting Manning's biography, the British geographer and future president of the Royal Geographical Society, Clements Robert Markham, wrote in 1876:

> He appears to have received little or no aid from the Government; to have been left entirely to his own resources without official recognition of any kind, and all the credit of his extraordinary journey is solely due to himself.[8]

Before and after Manning's trip the official British missions to Tibet had obtained limited results, but – thanks, in particular, to adventurous spies whose stories touch on the fictional – had developed the knowledge of the British in the field of exploration.[9] The first British expedition to Tibet had been led by George Bogle in the 1770s,[10] in a geopolitical and economic context that was profoundly different from that of the beginning of 1904. There had not yet been the First Opium War (1839-1842) and the subsequent Treaty of Nanking (1842) which opened five Chinese ports and handed over the island of Hong Kong to the British.[11] Furthermore, at the time, Tibet could not yet be considered as a real target of the Russian Empire.

Unlike the eighteenth century, however, the international framework of High Asia between the end of the nineteenth and the beginning of the twentieth century, from the British point of view, hinged primarily on strategic and defensive issues (commercial matters were in third place). The decades immediately preceding the Younghusband Expedition had been filled with British fear of Russian operations in the region. As for Tibet, the Russian expedition of 1899-1901 led by Pëtr Kozlov[12] had been another demonstration of the risk: the Russians had arrived as far as Chab-mdo, the gateway to what was later called Outer Tibet.[13] Kozlov's expedition had come dangerously close to Lhasa and therefore to India, and although it failed in its goal of reaching the Tibetan capital, it was still enough to alarm the British. The Russo-Japanese War broke out only in February 1904, with Younghusband already on the way.

It is enough to follow the progressive Russian advance in Central Asia in the second half of the nineteenth century to realize the new geopolitical role of that region for British India and to understand the scene on which the Great Game unfolded. The three Islamic states east of the Caspian Sea had progressively fallen under the direct or indirect control of Russia. The city of Tāshkand (Russian: Tashkent), an important trading center of the Khanat of Khoqand, had been conquered by the tsarist troops in 1865[14] and formally annexed to the Russian Empire the following year.[15] In 1867, therefore, the city became the capital of a Russian Turkestan under the authority of a governor-general,[16] in the person of Konstantin Petrovich Kaufman.[17] In 1868 Samarkand (*Samarqand*) fell, conquered, together with the nearby Kattah-qūrghān (Russian: Kattakurgan), from the emir of Bokhara (*Bokhārā*) who also became a tributary of the tsar.[18] On September 28, 1873, Russia and Bokhara signed a friendship treaty.[19] That same year, a campaign against the Canat of Khiva (*Khīvah*)[20] forced the sovereign of the country to declare himself as a 'fidèle serviteur' of the Russian emperor:

> Séid Mouhamed Rahim Boghadour Khan se reconnaît fidèle serviteur de l'Empereur de toutes les Russies. Il renonce à

toutes relations amicales directes avec les Souverains et Khans voisins, et à la conclusion de toutes Conventions de Commerce ou autres avec eux ; il s'engage à n'entreprendre contre eux aucune opération de guerre à l'insu ou sans l'assentiment des autorités militaires supérieures Russes.[21]

The Canat of Kokand (*Khaūqand*) – already linked to Saint Petersburg since 1868 by a commercial treaty[22] – had been first invaded in 1875, resulting in the annexation of the north of the country,[23] and in March 1876 the last portion of territory still formally independent was incorporated into the lands of the tsar.[24]

A few weeks after the Russian complete conquest of the Canat of Kokand, on April 27, the British Parliament approved the Royal Titles Act of 1876,[25] on the basis of which, the next day, Queen Victoria issued a proclamation adding to her titles that of 'Indiæ Imperatrix'.[26] Almost twenty years earlier, in 1858, following the Sepoy Mutiny, control of India had passed from the East India Company to the Crown.[27]

Between 1878 and 1880 the British fought the Second Anglo-Afghan War.[28] On May 26, 1879, Pierre Louis Napoleon Cavagnari and the emir of Afghanistan, Moḥammad Ya'qūb Khān, signed the Treaty of Gandamak (*Gandomak*) by which the Asian country became a British protectorate (Article III) and a representative settled in Kabul (Article IV).[29] The appointed representative was in fact Cavagnari who had assumed the post in July 1879, but was killed, together with the escort and his collaborators, a few weeks later, in a tragic attack in Kabul, thus reopening the hostilities which ended only in 1880, with the exile of Ya'qūb Khān and the accession to the throne of 'Abd-al-Raḥmān Khān (*regnabat* 1880-1901).[30] The killing of Cavagnari clearly evoked the assassination of one of the most famous heroes of the Great Game, Alexander Burnes, killed by a mob on November 2, 1841 in the Afghan capital,[31] as well as that, a few weeks later, of William Hay Macnaghten, British envoy and minister at the court in Kabul.[32]

Between the end of 1880 and the beginning of 1881, the Russians won an important and dramatic victory over the Turkmens at Geog Teppeh (Russian: Gëkdepe) and then temporarily entered Persian territory.[33] The oasis of Ākhāl Tekkeh (Russian: Akhal-Teke) was therefore officially annexed by an edict of the tsar on 18 (6) May 1881.[34] On December 21, 1881, Persians and Russians signed a treaty in Tehrān that defined the border east of the Caspian Sea between Khorāsān and Ākhāl.[35] Furthermore, on February 12 (January 31) 1884, in 'Eshqābād (Russian: Ashkhabad), the leaders of the four Turkmen tribes of Marv (Russian: Merv) and twenty-four delegates, each on behalf of two thousand kibitkas («tents»), swore allegiance to the tsar, also in the name of the people.[36] The conquest of Marv opened the way to nearby Herāt and therefore to Afghanistan, while the British were involved in the war in Sudan. Indeed, the following year, the Russians arrived inside the Afghan territory, severely defeating the emir's military garrisoning the oasis of Panjdeh; open war between the Russians and the British was avoided also thanks to the conciliatory position taken by the emir, but the incident led at least to the definition of that part of the border between Afghanistan and Russia, preventing the further advance of the tsarist troops.[37]

During these years, British attention again turned to Tibet where the Chinese imperial authority was unable to enforce an international treaty signed with Great Britain. The case was in fact the Convention relating to Sikkim and Tibet of 1890.[38] The Kingdom of Sikkim was in the British sphere of influence. Indeed, on March 28, 1861, the Treaty of Tumlong had been signed between the British and Sikkimese. The document provided, among other things, the commitment of Sikkim to submit to British arbitration in the event of disputes with neighboring countries allied to the British (Article 17), the impossibility of ceding any portion of Sikkimese territory without the authorization of Great Britain (Article 19) and the prohibition of authorizing the presence of foreign forces in the kingdom 'without the sanction of the British Government' (Article 20).[39] Furthermore, according to the treaty: 'The whole military force of Sikkim shall join and afford every aid and facility to British Troops when employed in the Hills' (Article 18). The Convention of 1890 concerned, among other things, the definition of the border between the Kingdom of Sikkim and Tibet, and followed the alleged encroachment of Tibetan soldiers in 1886 to which the British had responded with the Expedition of 1888.[40] This treaty – as well as the subsequent Regulations, which were signed in Darjeeling on December 5, 1893[41] and which provided for the opening of a market for the British, with the consequent dispatch of agents in Ya-tung 亞東 (Tibetan: Gro-mo), in Tibetan territory – was not respected by the Tibetans.[42] The Chinese, as the British political agent in Sikkim, John Claude White, recalled, had 'no authority whatever':

> The Chinese have no authority whatever here. The Tibetans will not obey them, and the Chinese are afraid to give any orders. China is suzerain over Tibet only in name. This appears to be partly due to the Chinese Emperor always dealing very leniently with the Tibetans, and also that the Chinese have only some 500 soldiers in Tibet, and these are wretchedly armed with old swords, tridents and old muzzle-loading fowling-pieces. They are also without the elements of drill. The Chinese therefore, though rulers in name, have no power and can enforce no order; as an example, the Tibetans

were ordered by the Chinese to evacuate Lingtu, but flatly refused to obey the order. This makes negociation here most difficult, for though the Chinese agree to any proposal, they are quite unable to answer for the Tibetans, and the Tibetans, when spoken to, either shelter themselves behind the Chinese, or say they have no order to give any answer for Lhassa, and can only report. Thus it is absolutely impossible to get at any one, for he simply puts the blame on some higher authority who is not forthcoming. If the Chinese had any real power negociations would be comparatively easy, as there would only be one power to deal with. To quote another instance of Chinese impotence here. Mr. Taylor, though a Chinese official, a mandarin of the blue button, and a recipient of the double dragon, and though he wears Chinese clothes on official interviews, is prevented by the Tibetans from returning the calls of the other Chinese officials who live at Chema ; nor can any of his servants pass the Yatung barrier to purchase the necessaries of life, which he has to procure from either Gnatong or Darjeeling. The Chinese officials hate the Tibetans, and do not scruple openly to say so. This, I take it, is caused by the knowledge of their impotence, knowing full well that they have no real power, though to all outward appearance they receive a great deal of respect; the Tibetans, for instance, being made to hold a lower seat at receptions than the Chinese. [...] The Chinese are most friendly and willing to help, but are quite powerless as regards the Tibetans. [...] [T]he only way to deal with the Tibetan is to force his hand, and this can be done in the present instance by threatening to close the trade route by the Jeylap-la and to open up that by the Lachen valley.[43]

The British were thus faced with the dilemma of Tibet. The strategic and partly commercial importance of the Land of Snows had become very clear and of essential geopolitical and economic concern for the Raj, but the counterpart that had to guarantee compliance with the agreements, China, had proved to be completely inadequate. International law, which provided that a protectorate was, in the context of foreign policy, represented exclusively by the suzerain power, had to be rethought in new terms. First, the very idea of a *protectorate* was an unlikely adaptation. The British had applied legal schemes to complex religious and political mechanisms which, while having – perhaps – found similarities in the past, were totally misleading in the late nineteenth century. The limits to the emperor's power on the Roof of the World were of a different nature. There was, to begin with, a purely geographical discourse. Distances multiplied in the valleys of Tibet and on the

Himalayan passes. The mountains amplified the difficulties of movement, almost always making any claim on the plateau only nominal. This explains the Chinese interest today in the construction of a series of infrastructures capable of rapidly connecting the Tibetan Autonomous Region and the rest of the People's Republic of China. Already Sun Yat-sen,[44] as Director General of the National Railways after his resignation as president of the Republic of China, had in fact realized the importance of a railway network that was able to unite the east with the western regions that the Republic considered as its own territories.[45] According to Diana Lary '[a]lmost 100 years later, the present government of China is in the process of implementing part of Sun's scheme, a railway to Tibet'.[46] The difficulties of physical geography were then joined by a bond that was expressed in the relationship of *mchod yon*: the political leader, the emperor, guaranteed protection to one of his religious teachers, the dalai lama. In fact, the Ch'ing dynasty, although immersed in the Chinese cultural system, where political power was legitimized and expressed through Confucian models, remained a dynasty faithful to Tibetan Buddhism[47] and to its Manchu identity.[48]

Younghusband in Lhasa

Once attempts to find in imperial China an effective counterpart to define the border, ensure trade and exclude any Russian influence on Tibet had failed, for the British it was time to speak directly with the Tibetans. The task was entrusted to Francis Younghusband who therefore arrived in Lhasa on August 3, 1904[49] and who managed to sign a treaty with the Tibetans on September 7.[50] The dalai lama had fled the capital for Mongolia[51] before the British arrived and his seal was then affixed to the document by the regent, together with those of the Council of Ministers, of the three great Dge-lugs monasteries (Se-ra, Bras-spungs and Dga'-ldan)[52] and of the National Assembly.[53] The signature of the amban was missing, since he had to wait for approval from Peking.[54] With that document, the Tibetans recognized the Anglo-Chinese Convention of 1890 and, therefore, also the border with Sikkim (Article I). In addition to the trade mart of Ya-tung, already planned in 1893, a trade mart was also to be opened in Rgyal-rtse and Sgar-thog (Article II). Furthermore, Article IX established that, without British consent:

> (*a*) No portion of Tibetan territory shall be ceded, sold, leased, mortgaged or otherwise given for occupation, to any Foreign Power;
>
> (*b*) No such Power shall be permitted to intervene in Tibetan affairs;

(c) No Representatives or Agents of any Foreign Power shall be admitted to Tibet;

(d) No concessions for railways, roads, telegraphs, mining or other rights, shall be granted to any Foreign Power, or to the subject of any Foreign Power. In the event of consent to such concessions being granted, similar or equivalent concessions shall be granted to the British Government;

(e) No Tibetan, revenues, whether in kind or in cash, shall be pledged or assigned to any Foreign Power, or to the subject of any Foreign Power.

The British were entitled to an indemnity of £500,000, equivalent to 750,000 rupees (Article VI) and they would also continue to temporarily occupy the Chu-'bi valley, a Tibetan territory located between Bhutan to the east and Sikkim to the west, pending the payment of the indemnity 'and until the trade marts have been effectively opened for three years, whichever date may be the later'. In November 1904, according to a declaration appended to the Convention, the sum of the indemnity would then drop to 250,000 rupees, 'as an act of grace' by the viceroy of India, George Curzon, and the occupation of the Chu-'bi valley had therefore to 'cease after the due payment of three annual instalments of the said indemnity', the opening of the trade marts for at least three years 'and that, in the meantime, the Tibetans shall have faithfully complied with the terms of the said Convention in all other respects'.[55]

On a political level, the British Expedition to Sikkim and the Younghusband Expedition were also the clearest demonstrations of the end of Peking's pretensions. To be precise, there had been also another important precedent in 1842, when the Chinese did not protect Tibet from the attack of Gulab Sĩng.[56] Once again, the Ch'ing had not protected the country from the invader. Between 1886, the year of the Tibetan encroachment in Sikkim, and the arrival of Younghusband in Lhasa in 1904, the unrealistic task of the Manchu emperor was definitively concluded. Despite Peking's attempts to firmly control Tibet in the following years, the inability to first impose the outcomes of the 1890 treaty, the subsequent 1893 agreements and ultimately protect the country from British soldiers had made it clear to eyes of international politics and history that China was about to leave the scene. The declaration of independence of 1913 was only the formal seal that the thirteenth dalai lama wanted to give to this situation.

About two years after the Younghusband Expedition, on April 27, 1906, the British and Chinese signed another convention which partially confirmed the agreement signed at the Po-ta-la.[57] According to the text, the British undertook, in Article II, 'not to annex Tibetan territory or to interfere in the administration of Tibet', while the Chinese government 'undertakes not to permit any other foreign State to interfere with the territory or internal administration of Tibet'. The concessions defined in point 'd' of the aforementioned Article IX of the 1904 treaty would be denied to any state or subject of a state other than China.

Ancient ghosts

With the Anglo-Russian Convention of August 31, 1907 (August 18 according to the Russian calendar),[58] the borders of the Raj were finally secured from a possible Russian invasion. The anguish of a good part of the nineteenth century and the very first years of the twentieth century, and the fears that had forced the British to intervene in Tibet thus vanished that summer in Saint Petersburg. In reality, London had been reassured as early as September 1905 when the Treaty of Portsmouth had marked the Russian defeat in the war against a country, Japan, which had left its own Middle Ages not even half a century earlier.[59] Indeed, with that treaty:

> Le Gouvernement Impérial de Russie, reconnaissant que le Japon possède en Corée des intérêts prédominants politiques, militaires et économiques, s'engage à ne point intervenir ni mettre d'obstacles aux mesures de direction, de protection et de contrôle, que le Gouvernement Impérial du Japon pourrait considérer nécessaire de prendre en Corée [*Article II*].

As for Manchuria, the two countries

> s'engagent mutuellement: 1.–A évacuer complètement et simultanément la Manchourie à l'exception du territoire sur lequel s'étend le bail de la de la presqu'île de Liaotong, [...]; et 2.–A restituer entièrement et complètement à l'administration exclusive de la Chine toutes les parties de la Manchourie qui sont occupées maintenant par les troupes japonaises ou russes ou qui sont sous leur contrôle, à l'exception du territoires susmentionnés [*Article III*].

Saint Petersburg also ceded the southern part of Sakhalin Island to Japan 'et toutes les îles qui sont adjacentes' (Article IX) and, 'avec le consentement du Gouvernement de Chine, le bail de Port Arthur [*Chinese: Ya-se-kang* 亞瑟港],

de Talien [*Ta-lien* 大連] et de territoires et eaux adjacents' (Article V). In Portsmouth, the doubts and fears of those who had led the Raj in those last decades had been cleared up. Not of secondary importance, in the scheme of international relations that preceded the First World War, was the Entente Cordiale of 1904 between the British and the French[60] – the latter an ally of the Russians from the last decade of the nineteenth century – and before that the alliance signed by London and Tokyo in 1902[61] and then renewed in 1905.[62] When in 1906 – after a long wait – the Buryat monk Dorzhiyev was received by the tsar to implore for the defense of Tibet from the British, Nicholas II explained to his subject the difficulties of the moment due to the defeat at the hands of the Japanese.[63]

Between 1904 and 1907, decades seemed to have passed. The British elections of 1906 had sanctioned the victory of the Liberals and confirmed Henry Campbell-Bannerman, who had already been at 10 Downing Street since December 1905, as head of the government.[64] Within the new cabinet, Sir Edward Grey led the Foreign Office; on December 13, 1905, he informed the Russian ambassador in London of the desire to reach an agreement with Saint Petersburg and, on May 28, 1906, sent a new ambassador to Russia, Sir Arthur Nicolson.[65]

Yet ancient fears remained in certain political circles. Among the Conservatives there were, for example, those who, like Lord Percy (Henry Percy, 1871-1909), saw – still in the spring of 1907 – the division of Persia into different areas of influence as an opportunity for Saint Petersburg to build railways in the direction of the British zone and later renege on the agreement.[66] Sir Edward Grey was instead confident in the Agreement to improve relations between the two empires.[67] On the contrary, Grey feared the failure of the negotiations much more: in that case the British would have been forced to annex parts of Persia to avoid a Russian penetration towards Herāt and Sīstān.[68]

Another concern for the British was the dalai lama in Mongolia. It was not enough to have entered Lhasa: Thub-bstan-rgya-mtsho was still in Urga (current Ulaanbaatar) much closer to the Russian border than to the Raj. The fear was that the Russians wanted to use the thirteenth dalai lama as their agent in Tibet against the paṇ-chen bla-ma, considered by Saint Petersburg to be on the side of the British.[69] The tsar had sent a telegram to the dalai lama, but it was a simple eulogy of his religious role – this had still alarmed the Manchus who had threatened to depose the dalai lama in case of conspiracies with the Russians.[70]

The official explanation of the tsar's interest in the dalai lama, namely that of a Christian ruler who wanted to win the benevolence of his Buddhist subjects, continued, with a good deal of reason, not to convince the British.[71] Indeed, as Cecil Spring-Rice reminded Grey,

> [t]he total number of Buddhist subjects of the Empire must be under 600,000 out of 128,000,000 and his sympathy for the Jews and the Mahomedans among his subjects (who are numbered by millions) is not very pronounced.[72]

For the British to stand up as the 'temporal protector of the head centre of the Buddhist faith' could legitimize the tsar of all the Russias in the role of 'moral chief of the continent of Asia'[73] – an idea that Spring-Rice himself admitted to be 'chimerical but so was the idea of becoming the "Lord of the Pacific" of which he talked so much and which cost his Empire so dear'.[74] Spring-Rice's words do not suggest fear of a British defeat, which was quite improbable. More than anything else, it was the fear of the war itself. An agreement on Tibet was certainly necessary:

> I did not argue the question although it appears to be pretty plain that the Russians are likely to run the Dalai Lama as their agent against the Tashi Lama [pa -chen bla-ma] whom they regard as ours, and that therefore it would be as well to come to close quarters with them if possible and arrive at a clear definite and written understanding as to the policy of the two Governments in Thibet.[75]

To complicate the situation in Asia and further worry the British there was also the problem of xenophobic clashes in Persia – where the Constitutional Revolution broke out in 1905[76] – which could lead the Russians to send the army to defend their compatriots.[77]

The Russians, for their part, were worried that the Anglo-Japanese alliance, renewed in 1905, was hiding a secret pact for the defense of the Ottoman Empire from possible aggression.[78] A secret article of the alliance had arrived in the hands of Count Benkendorf (von Benckendorff), the Russian ambassador to London.[79] In reality it was a simple, probably German, fake.[80] At the same time, however, the Russians had signed, on July 30, 1907, an important agreement with the Japanese: in the public section of the treaty they undertook, among other things, to recognize the territorial integrity of their empires and of China.[81] In a secret convention they outlined their respective influences in Manchuria: the north was in the Russian sphere and the south in the Japanese one (Article I).[82] An 'Article additionnel' to the Convention established the boundaries of the two spheres of influence:

> La ligne de démarcation entre la Manchourie du Nord et la Manchourie du Sud mentionnée dans l'article I de la présente Convention est établie comme suit: Partant du point nord-ouest de la frontière russo-coréenne et formant une succession de lignes droites, la ligne va, en passant par Hunchun et la pointe de l'extrêmité nord du lac de Pirteng, à Hsiushuichan; de là elle suite le Soungari jusqu'à l'embouchure du Nunkiang, pour remonter ensuite le cours dece fleuve jusqu'à l'embouchure du fleuve Tolaho. A partir de ce point, la ligne suit le cours de ce fleuve jusqu'à son intersection avec le 122 méridien est de Greenwich.

Furthermore, the Japanese obtained the Russian commitment not to curb the 'développement' of Japanese-Korean relations – relations which, within three years, changed into the annexation of the Korean Empire (*Tayhanceykwuk* 大韓帝國) – in exchange for the Japanese guarantee to grant Russia the status of most favored nation in Korea (Article II). With Article III of the secret convention, perhaps the most important for the purposes of this study, the Russians had also managed to include Outer Mongolia in their sphere of influence:

> Le Gouvernement Impérial du Japon, reconnaissant dans la Mongolie extérieure les intérêts spéciaux de la Russie, s'engage à s'abstenir de toute ingérence qui puisse porter préjudice à ces intérêts.

Nobody trusted anyone yet. Even the dalai lama, as mentioned, had preferred to stay away from Lhasa, where in the past he had had to avoid several assassination attempts.[83] He had first settled in the Mongolian monastery of Gandan (Tibetan: *Dga' ldan dgon gyi nyi 'od*).[84] Even in Mongolia, however, he was not much loved by the hierarchy, or rather, by the top of the religious hierarchy in the country. The devotion he had received at the popular level had in fact fueled the jealousy of the rje-btsun dam-pa, and after several provocations of the latter, the dalai lama had moved to another monastery.[85] Moreover, the paṇ-chen bla-ma had traveled to India, leading the Chinese press to suspect the British intention of a replacement.[86] Furthermore, in 1905, meeting with the paṇ-chen bla-ma, the British trade agent in Rgyal-rtse, William Frederick O'Connor, had intended the possibility, for the British, of being able to favor the break between the two, decreeing the independence of the paṇ-chen bla-ma.[87] It is therefore not difficult to understand at this point why the Russians, as we have seen above, considered the paṇ-chen bla-ma an ally of London.[88] Later, however, following the rapprochement of the dalai lama to the British, the paṇ-chen bla-ma would show his sympathy for the Chinese.[89]

The Agreement of 1907

In Saint Petersburg, two years later, the three chapters of the history of the Great Game in Central Asia on which the British and Russians had clashed in the past decades ended. First, the Persian chapter. The Russian Empire had already conquered several Persian Caucasian regions, at the beginning of the nineteenth century with the treaties of Golestān (1813) and Torkmānchāy (1828).[90] According to the Anglo-Russian Agreement of 1907, Persia was divided into three areas. The first was in the center-north, under Russian influence, bounded by a line that, starting from Qaṣr-e Shīrīn – a Persian city on the border with the Ottoman Empire (today on the border with Iraq) – continued to south-east towards Eṣfahān and finally to Yazd, the ancient city with an important Zoroastrian community and built between the Dasht-e Lūt and the Dasht-e Kavīr. The boundary then went up towards the north-east, arriving first in Kākhk and ending at the point where the Persian frontier met the Russian (now Turkmen) and Afghan borders. The south-east of the country was under British influence, following the line that starting from the village of Gazīk, on the Afghan-Persian border, then continued towards Bīrjand and Kermān to end in Bandar 'Abbas, a coastal city on the Strait of Hormoz. All the rest of the Persian territory between the two aforementioned lines would be the subject of concessions for both the British and the Russians.

The second pillar of the agreement was Afghanistan which – as seen – was a British protectorate from the Second Anglo-Afghan War and remained so until 1919.[91] In 1905 a new treaty between the emir and the British had reaffirmed the role of London[92] and the 1907 Convention provided for the continuation of British influence, but not in an anti-Russian function. Saint Petersburg agreed to have political relations with Kabul only through London, but the Russian and Afghan border authorities could have direct relations for local matters. Furthermore, the Russians would enjoy the same commercial privileges accorded to the British and the Indians.

Finally, Tibet. As widely seen, the Land of the Snows (*Gangs can*) had been the third and final scenario of the Great Game. Apparently immobile, in the seventeenth century the fifth dalai lama had managed, with the help of the Mongols of Güsh haan, to take power and then, among various events which will be explained shortly, the country had been incorporated, at the beginning of eighteenth century into the complex system of the Ch'ing Empire. Its local leaders and the Manchus wanted to make it a kingdom sealed within its own insurmountable peaks,[93] as the subsequent literary tradition continued to present it to the West. The 1907 Agreement recognized Peking's suzerainty over Lhasa, and, therefore, its role as intermediary for Tibet's international relations, while the British and the Russians would refrain from interfering in the internal administration of the country, from sending representatives to the capital and requesting concessions of any kind. The British, however, did not renounce the direct relationship between British trade agents and the Tibetan authorities, as had been established in 1904 by the Anglo-Tibetan Convention imposed during the Younghusband Expedition and reaffirmed in 1906 in another agreement with the Manchu authorities. The possibility was also guaranteed to the Buddhist subjects of His British Majesty or of the tsar of All the Russias, to have direct contact with the dalai lama or with other teachers, exclusively for religious reasons. Finally, the British reaffirmed their intention to withdraw from the Chu-'bi valley at the end of the payment by Tibet of three annual installments of 250,000 rupees.

A vital problem of the difference between sovereignty – that is, absolute and direct control over a territory which is an integral part of the state – and suzerainty – i.e., the representation in foreign policy of another country which maintains full internal autonomy – was linked to the fact that for China, in the last period of the Ch'ing, there was no such distinction and the British themselves, in negotiating the 1906 Agreement, had been careful not to clarify the question to their Chinese counterparts. According to G. E. Morrison:

> A discussion at the time of the negotiation of this Agreement took place in England as to whether China was the suzerain or sovereign power in Tibet. China recognises no such distinction. She claims to be the sovereign power. In the negotiations which led to the signature of the Adhesion Agreement, no reference whatever was made to her being [the][94] suzerain power. You can get the confirmation of this statement from C. W. Campbell, whom you know well, and who was present at every one of the discussions that took place between the Chinese and Sir Ernest Satow prior the signature of the agreement.[95]

The question, in fact unresolved, resulted in the broader and more articulated difficulty of understanding the relationship between Peking and Lhasa and between the Manchu emperor and the dalai lama, in the complexity of matching the legal view of Western international relations with the Eastern one. This dichotomy exploded, with all the force of its contradiction in the 1950s, but already now had to deal with the political history of the dying Ch'ing Empire and of High Asia.

The birth of the Bhutanese monarchy and the Treaty of Punakha

The British withdrew from the Chu-'bi valley on February 8, 1908[96] after the war indemnity was paid not by the Tibetan authorities, but by the Ch'ing.[97] On April 20, 1908, the new trade regulations were signed in Calcutta, amending those of 1893.[98] The commitment made by the British and Russians in the 1907 agreement, in fact, 'ne modifie pas non plus les engagements assumés par la Grande-Bretagne et la Chine en vertu de l'Article I de la dite Convention de 1906' (Article II, Arrangement concernant le Thibet) and Article I of the 1906 Convention had stipulated that:

> The Convention concluded on September 7th 1904 by Great Britain and Tibet, the texts of which in English and Chinese are attached to the present Convention as an annexe, is hereby confirmed, subject to the modification stated in the declaration appended thereto, and both of the High Contracting Parties engage to take at all times such steps as may be necessary to secure the due fulfilment of the terms specified therein.[99]

In the 1908 agreement, in addition to the English and Chinese signatures, there was also that of the Tibetan delegate and the text was written in three languages.

In the meantime, however, on the thirteenth day of the eleventh month of the earth-monkey year, i.e. December 17, 1907, Bhutan, east of the Chu-'bi valley, had become a hereditary monarchy under the Dbang-phyug dynasty and O-rgyan-dbang-phyug (Ugyen Wangchuck) had ascended the throne.[100]

Bhutan had been born as an independent country in the first half of the 17th century, founded by a Tibetan lama of the 'brug-pa school, known as the zhabs-drung, Ngag-dbang-rnam-rgyal. This school is a branch of the Bka 'brgyud pa school. Bhutan takes its endonym from the Drukpa school: *'Brug yul* (Druk yul), or *Country of the 'brug pa school*, which is often translated *Land of the thunder dragon* based on the meaning of the name of the school.[101] The country was, therefore, structured in the complex dual system of government (*chos srid gnyis ldan*): power was shared between the head of the monastic-religious system, the rje mkhan-po, and the head of the secular sphere, the 'Brug sde-srid, but the country was led at the top by the zhabs-drung and – formally – also by his successors.[102] This form of government typical of the Tibetan cultural area formally resisted the birth of the secular monarchy in 1907 and the democratic reforms initiated in the 1950s by the third king of Bhutan and carried out by the fourth and fifth monarchs with the entry into force of the Supreme Constitution of Bhutan in 2008 (*'Brug gi rtsa khrims chen mo*).[103]

The British East India Company and the Brug sde-srid of Bhutan signed a first treaty in 1774, followed by a British mission and a trade agreement negotiated by George Bogle.[104] George Bogle's mission was later followed by other British missions[105] and in 1863 Ashley Eden, later chief commissioner and lieutenant-governor in Burma,[106] was sent to the Himalayan country. The Bhutanese forced him to sign a treaty, written in Tibetan, without being able to participate in any real negotiations. Eden added the words 'Under Compulsion' to his signature and after these events the Anglo-Bhutanese War broke out (1864-1865).[107] This war ended with the Treaty of Sinchula of 1865.[108]

Twenty years later, in 1885, O-rgyan-dbang-phyug, allied with the dpon-slob of Spa-ro and the rdzong-dpon of Dbang-'dus-pho-brang, had defeated the two rdzong-dpon of Spu-na-kha and Thim-phu and the other rivals in the battle of Lcang-gling-mi-thang (*Lcang-gling-mi-thang-gi dmag-'dzing*).[109] During the Younghusband Expedition, O-rgyan-dbang-phyug had been the mediator between the British and the Tibetans. Actually, the mediator role of O-rgyan-dbang-phyug, although known and certainly fundamental, had not been officially sanctioned by the British, unlike the Tibetans instead.[110] In 1905 he was awarded the Order of the Indian Empire.[111] At his election as first king of Bhutan (Druk gyalpo, *'Brug rgyal-po*), the Raj was represented by the political agent in Sikkim, John Claude White, together with Major Rennick and an official from the Political Department.[112] In 1910, forty-five years after the Treaty of Sinchula, the Kingdom signed the Treaty of Punakha, accepting the British guide in its foreign policy, while maintaining full and uninterrupted independence.[113] The British thus welded their bond with this Tibetan Buddhist Himalayan kingdom.

The Manchus and Tibet

As mentioned earlier, one of Britain's concerns was the absolute weakness of Chinese authority in Tibet. The decline of the Manchu rulers was evident in international relations by the long series of treaties – later considered by nationalists and communists as «unequal» (不平等條約 *pu p'ing teng t'iao yüeh*)[114] – inaugurated in Nanking in 1842. On the internal level, however, the crisis of the throne was demonstrated by the many rebellions, the best known of which is the one that led to the establishment of the T'ai-p'ing celestial kingdom.[115] However, in lands even further away than those ravaged by the rebels and their imperial or Western executioners, the confrontation between local power and imperial authority was a different matter. Even in Tibet the crisis of imperial power was reshaping the institutional balance that had governed relations between the Manchu emperors and the dalai lama since the first half of the 1700s. There was actually an even older link between the emperor and the Land of the Snows, already established in medieval times by the Mongol dynasty, in the relationship of *mchod yon*.[116] The interpretation of this relationship is at the center of the current debate on the legitimacy of the Chinese occupation of Tibet: it is understood in a political way, which is the thesis of pro-Chinese historiography,[117] or according to a purely religious view of a relationship between the emperor offering protection to his teacher – in the case of the Ch'ing and the dalai lama – which is the position of historiography close to the Tibetan Central Authority.[118] This bond, however, still existed in the Ch'ing period, but let us proceed in order, briefly reviewing the history of this relationship.

According to tradition, Buddhism was introduced to Tibet by Srong-btsan-sgam-po in the seventh century.[119] Chinese influence in Tibet also began with Srong-btsan-sgam-po, thanks to the marriage between the Tibetan ruler and a princess sent to him by T'ai-tsung, emperor of the T'ang dynasty.[120] Alongside his Chinese wife, a Nepalese wife would also contribute to the propagation of Buddhist teaching in Tibet.[121] In the mythical genealogy of 'manifestations' (Sanskrit: *nirmā akāya*, Tibetan: *sprul sku*) of Avalokiteśvara (Tibetan: *Spyan-ras-gzigs*), the Tibetans also include Srong-btsan-sgam-po. According to *Rgyal rabs gsal ba'i me long*, written in the fourteenth century, Srong-btsan-sgam-po's Nepalese wife and Chinese wife are born respectively from the light emitted by the right eye and the left eye of Avalokiteśvara, while Srong-btsan-sgam-po from the light emitted by the heart.[122] A second spread of Buddhism dating back to the eleventh century is due – to a large extent – to the Indian monk Atīśa and to the translators among whom Rin-chen-bzang-po stands out.[123] The oldest schools of Tibetan Buddhism, also known as Schools of the Red Hats, are the rnying-ma-pa, the bka'-brgyud-pa, the sa-skya-pa and the jo-nang pa.[124] At the decline of the Mongol dynasty, when power in Tibet had long been administered by the Sa-skya-pa School, albeit in a political context of evident Mongol sovereignty,[125] the control over the country was assumed by Byang-chub-rgyal-mtshan: he founded the Phag-mo-gru-pa dynasty, put an end to the Sa-skya-pa's rule around the middle of the fourteenth century and his authority was recognized by the dying power of the Yüan dynasty.[126] The Mongol ruler thus maintained only a formal role.[127]

The relationship between Tibet and China was therefore a relationship between Tibetans and the Yüan rulers, which was thus interrupted with the end of the Mongol dynasty, despite the unrealistic claims of the Ming emperors.[128] The idea of a continuation of that bond during the Ming era finds the first evident denial in the very birth of that bond: the Mongols had in fact conquered Tibet before the conquest of China.[129] It would actually be complex for China to claim authority over a territory that had been part of an empire before China itself became – as a conquered territory and not as the conquering power – part of that same empire. It is therefore only with the Ch'ing dynasty that the link between the emperor and Tibet re-emerges, but in a different form. The Manchu rulers had extended their influence over Tibet, ruled by the dalai lamas from 1642, at the beginning of the 18th century, a few years after the death of the sixth dalai lama Tshangs-dbyangs-rgya-mtsho (1683-1706); before that, the School of the Yellow Hats had renewed the Tibetan-Mongol link through the alliance between the third dalai lama and Altan han.

The dge-lugs-pa, also called Yellow School or School of the Yellow Hats, was founded by Tsong-kha-pa (1357-1419) in an attempt to restore a more rigid observance of monastic discipline ('dul ba) among the religious, first of all respecting the rule of celibacy and, consequently, the succession of masters was entrusted to the system of «manifestations».[130] When Bsod-nams-rgya-mtsho met Altan han in 1578, near Lake Kokonor (Mtsho sngon po), he was still only an eminent master of the Yellow School. There, the Mongolian lord granted him the golden seal on which was engraved (in Mongolian) his new title: rdo rje 'chang tā la'i bla ma rgyal, i.e. the Tibetan word for «master» bla-ma associated with the Mongolian word dalai (transcribed in Tibetan tā-la'i), «ocean», which corresponds to the Tibetan rgya-mtsho.[131] Thus, the link between the Yellow Hats and the Mongols was solidified with the conversion to Buddhism of Altan han. In less than seventy years the link, although with other protagonists, dissolved the knots of political disputes on the Roof of the World in favor of the Yellow Hats. The relationship between Tibetan Buddhists and Mongolian leaders was not a new one. The novelty was in the school. Bsod-nams-rgya-mtsho was therefore the third dalai lama since the title was also extended to his two predecessors namely Dge-'dun-grub (1391-1475) and Dge-'dun-rgya-mtsho (1475-1542).[132] Bsod-nams-rgya-mtsho, however, failed to achieve political supremacy and instead died in Mongolia where his successor was traced to Yon-tan-rgya-mtsho (1589-1617), a Mongolian and nephew of Altan han.[133] Only with Ngag-dbang-blo-bzang-rgya-mtsho (1617-1682), the Great Fifth, as remembered among the Tibetans, the dalai lama became the political leader of Tibet, when in 1642 Güsh haan, chief of the Hoshuud Mongols, donated to him central and eastern Tibet after the defeat, in 1641, of a bon prince and, the following year, the capitulation of the Gtsang, karma-pa allies.[134] Parallel to the political victory, the religious dimension evolved and the dalai lama was now identified as another «manifestation» of Avalokiteśvara.[135]

The sixth dalai lama, Tshangs-dbyangs-rgya-mtsho, however, was little inclined to religious life, preferring beer and female companions: he chose to engage – it must be said, with remarkable results – in the composition of love poems.[136] For these reasons he had come into conflict with Sangs-rgyas-rgya-mtsho, the regent and son of the fifth dalai lama and who had led Tibet after the latter's death in 1682, a death that the son had kept hidden until 1697.[137] In 1705 the Hoshuud troops of Lhazan han (Tibetan: Lha-bzang), heir of Güsh han, entered Lhasa and killed the regent.[138] The son of the fifth dalai lama had resigned from his post as regent in 1703 after the sixth dalai lama had renounced his vows, but he had still unofficially maintained power.[139] Tibet thus became, in 1710, a tributary state of the Manchu emperor after the latter had recognized the son of Lhazan han as the legitimate sixth dalai lama.[140] Tshangs-dbyangs-rgya-mtsho, who died in 1706[141] during the journey to China that had been imposed on him by the Hoshuud Mongols[142] (although a secret biography says he survived and lived for several decades in Mongolia[143]), continued to be recognized as the legitimate dalai lama by the Tibetan religious world, while the seventh dalai lama was identified in Blo-bzang-bskal-bzang-rgya-mtsho (1708-1757).[144] The seventh dalai lama was born in the late summer of 1708, in Khams, near the monastery of Li-thang.[145]

Therefore, not recognizing the legitimacy of the son of Lhazan han and looking with suspicion at the interest, or perhaps – as van Schaik believes – only the respect, for the Christian religion of Lhazan han, the dge-lugs-pa relied on the Dzungars who were faithful to the Yellow School and who conquered Lhasa in 1717.[146] Revealing themselves as cruel and intolerant rulers even towards their own religious school, it was therefore the task of Emperor K'ang-hsi (*regnabat* 1661-1722) to restore order in Lhasa and triumphantly install Blo-bzang-bskal-bzang-rgya-mtsho on the throne in 1720.[147] However, the power of the latter was ephemeral and the withdrawal of the imperial troops ordered by Emperor Yung-cheng in 1723 led to the civil war of 1727-1728.[148] The conflict brought to the throne a Gtsang noble, Pho-lha-nas, who reigned over Tibet with imperial recognition.[149] His successor, who ascended to the throne in 1747, was killed by the imperial ambans in 1750.[150] The assassination was followed by the lynching of the ambans by the population.[151] The Manchu dynasty, therefore, decided to support again the seventh dalai lama and his school.[152]

The first amban in the country had been appointed in 1727 by Yung-cheng and, according to Kolmaš, a total of 173 ambans were appointed from that year to 1912.[153] Tibet, as well as other areas on the outskirts of the Empire, was afforded a status of substantial autonomy, at least until the early twentieth century. The Tibetan political-religious traditions remained essentially disconnected from the Chinese ones in a particular institutional mosaic that was mutually accepted and which guaranteed the maintenance of their own historical paths both in Lhasa, but also in Peking.[154] Gray Tuttle rightly gives the example of the exam system for recruiting officials of the imperial administration in China which was not extended to Tibet and, likewise, the *sprul-sku* system was not applied in China.[155] Furthermore, up to the years immediately preceding the proclamation of the Republic, the imperial court, for Inner Asian issues, relied on Manchu and Mongolian officials and maintained a sort of segregation among the different ethnic groups.[156]

As mentioned previously, a radical change in the imperial approach to Tibetan affairs occurred, however, at the beginning of the twentieth century, within the broader institutional change in China. The reform programs implemented by the Ch'ing dynasty after the Boxer Rebellion[157] also involved Tibet and – as will be discussed later – Mongolia. As early as 1905, in Khams, in eastern Tibet, the attempt to strengthen Chinese authority over the region had sparked a rebellion which was then suffocated in blood by Chao Erh-feng.[158] A specific program for the Chinese colonization of the region was drawn up by Chang Yin-t'ang 張蔭棠, the Chinese vice-amban in Tibet between 1906 and 1908.[159] Articulated in nineteen points, the plan provided for a broad process of modernization of the Land of Snows and is a clear example of the intentions and the new direction the Empire wanted to follow.[160] The imperial administration, according to this project, had to be enormously strengthened compared to the marginal role it had played in previous centuries and, particularly important, represented by Han officials. Instead, the power of the dalai lama had to be reduced within the new institutional structure and subjected to the control of a Han official for secular issues. The plan also outlined the deployment of six thousand soldiers to Tibet awaiting the formation and training of a Tibetan militia ('民兵'). The project was a clear colonial plan; indeed, Chang Yin-t'ang defined Tibet, in the last point, as a «colony» ('殖民地').[161] The Chinese historian Ya Han-chang 牙含章 admitted in his text on the biographies of the fourteen dalai lamas the similarity between the Chinese action in Tibet at the beginning of the twentieth century with the British colonization of India.[162] According to the plan, there was also a need to create schools to spread the Chinese language in Tibet.[163]

The Dalai Lama in Peking

About two years after Chang Yin-t'ang had been appointed vice-amban of Lhasa, the thirteenth dalai lama, Thub-bstan-rgya-mtsho, arrived in Peking on September 28, 1908.[164] In the imperial capital he met the Emperor Kuang-hsü and the Empress Dowager Tz'u-hsi, as well as several Western diplomats – including the British ambassador, John Jordan – and the prince of Sikkim.[165] On October 20, in his meeting with Jordan, the dalai lama inaugurated a new path of friendship with the British, the ancient enemies, asking the diplomat to express his friendship to Edward VII:[166]

> Some time ago, he said, events had occurred which were not of his creating ; they belonged to the past, and it was his sincere desire that peace and amity should exist between the two neighbouring countries. He desired the Minister to report these words to the King-Emperor.[167]

King Edward responded favorably a few weeks later when the dalai lama was already on his way to Tibet.[168]

The audience with Emperor Kuang-hsü, initially scheduled for October 6, was then postponed to October 14.[169] To mark his submission to imperial power, Tz'u-hsi had decided to assign to the dalai lama a new and clear title: 'the Loyally Submissive Vice-gerent'[170] – four characters to be added to the oldest title that Emperor Shun-chih had granted to the Great Fifth in 1654, 'the Great, Good, Self-existent Buddha of Heaven'.[171] Thus the full title of the dalai lama, in Chinese characters, became '誠順贊化西天大善自在佛'.[172] Kuang-hsü died a month later probably poisoned on the orders of Tz'u-hsi and the next day the empress dowager also died.[173] The thirteenth dalai lama left Peking on the morning of December 21, 1908,[174] while Dorzhiyev left on December 23, heading first to Transbaikalia and then to Saint Petersburg, with the aim of settling in the Russian capital and building monasteries.[175] Thub-bstan-rgya-mtsho, on the other hand, went first to A-mdo, to the dge-lugs monastery of Sku-'bum (*Sku 'bum byams pa gling*) where he had to wait for imperial permission to reach Lhasa.[176] Thub-bstan-rgya-mtsho returned to his capital only on December 25, 1909.[177] A few weeks later, faced with the danger of falling into the hands of the Chinese troops who had invaded the country, he had to flee again and, this time, take refuge in India.[178]

Endnotes

1 British Library, London (further only BL), IOR/L/PS/20/150, Report of a mission to the northern frontier of Kashmir in 1889 by Captain F. E. Younghusband, Calcutta 1890; F. E. YOUNGHUSBAND, *The Heart of a Continent: A Narrative of Travels in Manchuria, across the Gobi Desert, through the Himalayas, the Pamirs, and Chitral, 1884-1894*, London 1896. On Younghusband see, inter alia, P. FRENCH, *Younghusband: The Last Great Imperial Adventurer*, London 2004.

2 C. R. MARKHAM, *Narratives of the Mission of George Bogle to Tibet, and of the Journey of Thomas Manning to Lhasa*, London 1876, p. clv.

3 MARKHAM 1876, pp. clv-clviii.

4 MARKHAM 1876, p. 263. The story of his journey was published and edited in MARKHAM 1876, pp. 213-295.

5 L. PETECH, *The Dalai-Lamas and Regents of Tibet: A Chronological Study*, in: T'oung Pao, Vol. 47, Livr. 3/5, 1959, p. 374.

6 MARKHAM 1876, pp. 265-266.

7 MARKHAM 1876, p. 266.

8 MARKHAM 1876, p. clviii.

9 On this see: A. LAMB, *Britain and Chinese Central Asia: The Road to Lhasa, 1767 to 1905,* London 1960; P. HOPKIRK, *Trespassers on the Roof of the World: The Secret Exploration of Tibet*, New York 1995.

10 See MARKHAM 1876, pp. 1-210.

11 The text of the Treaty of Nanking in English and Chinese, with a declaration by the Viceroy of India (in English and Chinese translation) is in *Treaties, Conventions, etc., between China and Foreign States*, Vol. I, Second Edition, published by Order of the Inspector General of Customs, Shanghai 1917, pp. 351-356.

12 On Pëtr Kuz'mich Kozlov see A. I. ANDREYEV – T. I. YUSUPOVA, *Petr Kuzmich Kozlov (1863–1935)*, in: *The Quest for Forbidden Lands:*

Nikolai Przhevalskii and his Followers on Inner Asian Tracks, edited by A. Andreyev, M. Baskhanov and T. Yusupova, Leiden – Boston 2018, pp. 212-254.

13 The National Archives, London, Kew (further only TNA), FO 17/1746, (Inclosure in No. 1), Extract from the " Saint Petersburgh Viedmosti " of March 24 (April 6), 1903, f. 10 (pp. 1-2). The extract of the report in its English translation was sent by Sir Charles Stewart Scott, British ambassador to Saint Petersburg, to the British Foreign Secretary, Lansdowne (TNA, FO 17/1746, No. 1, Sir Charles S. Scott to the Marquess of Lansdowne, f. 5).

14 BL, IOR/L/PS/18/C69/5, Russian advances in Asia, 1873, War Office, Topographical Department, 1873, p. 11. On the Russian colonization of the city see J. SAHADEO, *Russian Colonial Society in Tashkent: 1865-1923*, Bloomington – Indianapolis 2007.

15 BL, IOR/L/PS/18/C69/5, Russian advances in Asia, 1873, War Office, Topographical Department, 1873, pp. 23-25.

16 M. DE BULMERINCQ [*August von Bulmerincq*], *Le passé de la Russie depuis les temps les plus reculés jusqu'à la paix de San-Stefano 1878*, Bruxelles 1881, p. 313.

17 F. H. SKRINE – E. D. ROSS, T*he Heart of Asia: A History of Russian Turkestan and the Central Asian Khanates from the Earliest Times*, London 1899, p. 253.

18 BL, IOR/L/PS/18/C69/5, Russian advances in Asia, 1873, War Office, Topographical Department, 1873, pp. 28-30.

19 BL, IOR/L/PS/20/RUS/3, Russian abstract, No. XXVIII, Translation in English of the Russian version of a Treaty of Friendship concluded between Russia and Bokhara, at Shar, dated 28th September 1873, 9th August 1878, pp. 79-81 (pp. 1-3).

20 BL, IOR/L/PS/18/C69/6, Russian advances in Asia, No. II, 1873-4-5, War Office, Quartermaster General's Department, Intelligence Branch, 1877, pp. 3-30.

21 C. 919, *Correspondence respecting Central Asia*, London 1874, Conditions de Paix proposées par le Commandant-en-chef de l'Armée d'Opérations contre le Khiva, l'Aide-de-camp Géneral de Kaufmann I, et

acceptées par le Khan de Khiva, Séid Mouhamed Rahim Boghadour Khan. An English translation of the treaty is in BL, IOR/L/PS/20/RUS1, No. LXV, Treaty of Peace between Russia and Khiva, August 12 (24), 1873, pp. 257-260 (pp. 1-4).

22   BL, IOR/L/PS/18/C69/5, Russian advances in Asia, 1873, War Office, Topographical Department, 1873 (Appendix VII, Our Commercial Treaties with the Khanates of Central Asia, From the "Messagier Officiel," 31st October (12th November) 1872), pp. 66-67.

23   BL, IOR/L/PS/18/C69/6, Russian advances in Asia, No. II, 1873-4-5, War Office, Quartermaster General's Department, Intelligence Branch, 1877, pp. 55-62.

24   BL, IOR/L/PS/18/C69/7, Russian advances in Asia, No. III, 1876, 1877, 1878, War Office, Quartermaster General's Department, Intelligence Branch, 1882, pp. 4-5.

25   Act of the British Parliament, to enable Her Most Gracious Majesty to make an addition to the Royal Style and Titles appertaining to the Imperial Crown of the United Kingdom and its Dependencies, April 27, 1876, the full text is in *British and Foreign State Papers* (further only BSP), Vol. 67, p. 539.

26   BRITISH PROCLAMATION, respecting the Alteration of Her Majesty's Style and Titles, Windsor, April 28, 1876, the full text is in BSP, Vol. 67, pp. 547-549.

27   ACT of the British Parliament, "for the better Government of India.", August 2, 1858, the full text is in BSP, Vol. 49, pp. 742-761.

28   Intelligence Branch Army Head-Quarters, India (produced in the), *The Second Afghan War, 1878-1880: Abridged Official Account*, London 1908.

29   The English-language full text of the treaty is in BSP, Vol. 70, pp. 49-52.

30   On the Second Anglo-Afghan war see also: H. HENSMAN, *The Afghan War of 1879-80*, London 1881; A. FORBES, *The Afghan Wars: 1839-42 and 1878-80*, London 1892, pp. 159-327. On Cavagnari see K. P. DEY, *The Life and career of Major Sir Louis Cavagnari, C.S.I., British envoy at Cabul, together with a brief outline of the Second Afghan War*, Calcutta 1881. For a political history of Afghanistan in the second half of the nineteenth century see M. H. KAKAR, *A political and diplomatic history of Afghanistan, 1863-1901*, Leiden 2006.

31   J. A. NORRIS, *The First Afghan War: 1838-1842*, Cambridge 1967, pp. 365-366. His best known work is A. BURNES, *Travels into Bokhara ; Being an account of a journey from India to Cabool, Tartary and Persia ; Also, narrative of a voyage on the Indus from the sea to Lahore*, 3 vols, London 1834. The literary fruit of Burnes' trade mission to Kabul on behalf of the then governor-general of India George Eden in 1836-1838 is A. BURNES, *Cabool: a personal narrative of a journey to, and residence in that city, in the years 1836, 7, and 8*, London 1843.

32   Entry «Macnaghten, Sir William Hay», in: *Dictionary of National Biography*, edited by S. Lee, Vol. XXXV, New York – London 1893.

33   BL, IOR/L/PS/18/C32, Report on the North-Eastern Frontier of Persia and the Tekeh Turkomans, 4th July 1881, by C. E. Stewart, Lieutenant-Colonel, Bengal Staff Corps, ff. 120-121, pp. 32-33; BL, IOR/L/MIL/17/14/84, Siege and assault of Denghil-Tépé: General Skobeleff's report, translated from the Russian in the Intelligence Branch of the Quarter-Master General's Department: Horse Guards, War Office, by Lt J. J. Leverson, R. E., London 1881.

34   BL, IOR/L/PS/18/C78, The Russians in Akhal, March 1882, f. 40, p. 32.

35   On this document see *The New Russo-Persian Frontier East of the Caspian Sea*, in: Proceedings of the Royal Geographical Society and Monthly Record of Geography, Vol. 4, No. 4 (Apr., 1882), pp. 213-219.

36   BL, IOR/L/PS/18/C41/5, Correspondence respecting the occupation of Merv by Russia and her proceedings on the Khorassan Frontier of Persia, written by A.W.M. [*Adolphus Warburton Moore*], Political and Secret department, 15th August 1884, f. 110/106, p. 1.

37   See KAKAR 2006, pp. 200-209.

38   C. 7312, *Convention between Great Britain and China relating to Sikkim and Tibet. Signed at Calcutta, March 17, 1890. With Regulations appended thereto, signed at Darjeeling, December 5, 1893*, London 1894, Convention between Great Britain and China relating to Sikkim and Tibet, pp. 1-3. The Chinese text is in *Treaties, Conventions, etc., between China and Foreign States* 1917, pp. 513-515.

39   Full text of the treaty: C. U. AITCHISON, *A Collection of Treaties, Engagements, and Sanads relating to India and Neighbouring Countries*, Vol. I, Calcutta 1892, pp. 165-170.

40 BL, IOR/L/MIL/17/12/60, Report on the Sikhim Expedition: From January 1888 to January 1890, prepared (under the orders of the Quarter Master General in India) by Lieutenant C. J. Markham, in the Intelligence Branch, Calcutta 1890.

41 C. 7312, *Convention between Great Britain and China relating to Sikkim and Tibet. Signed at Calcutta, March 17, 1890. With Regulations appended thereto, signed at Darjeeling, December 5, 1893*, London 1894, Regulations regarding Trade, Communication, and Pasturage, to be appended to the Sikkim-Tibet Convention of 1890, pp. 3-5. The Chinese text is in: *Treaties, Conventions, etc., between China and Foreign States* 1917, pp. 516-519.

42 F. YOUNGHUSBAND, *India and Tibet. A history of the relations which have subsisted between the two countries from the time of Warren Hastings to 1910; with a particular account of the mission to Lhasa in 1904*, London 1910, pp. 54-60.

43 BL, Mss Eur F197/103, Cd. 1920, *East India (Tibet). Papers relating to Tibet*, London 1904, Annexure 2 to Enclosure 1 in No. 13, Letter from J. C. White, Esq., Political Officer, Sikkim, to the Commissioner, Rajshahi Division, dated Yatung, the 9th June, 1894. (Extract.), p. 30.

44 Transcription of the Cantonese name by which the first president of the Republic of China is known in the West. One of the names by which he is best known in China is Sun Chung-shan 孫中山. On his different names see M.-C. BERGÈRE, *Sun Yat-sen*, translated by J. Lloyd, Stanford, California 1998, pp. vii-viii.

45 D. LARY, *China's Republic*, Cambridge, UK – New York 2007, p. 47.

46 LARY 2007, p. 47.

47 See R. J. SMITH, *The Qing Dynasty and traditional Chinese culture*, Lanham 2015, pp. 72-81 and pp. 250-251.

48 See: E. S. RAWSKI, *The Last Emperors: A Social History of Qing Imperial Institutions*, Berkeley – Los Angeles – London 1998; P. K. CROSSLEY – E. S. RAWSKI, *A Profile of The Manchu Language in Ch'ing History*, in. Harvard Journal of Asiatic Studies, Vol. 53, No. 1 (Jun., 1993), pp. 63-102. Among other important works in support, albeit with different nuances, of the preservation of the Manchu identity by the Ch'ing dynasty see: P. K. CROSSLEY, *A Translucent Mirror: History and Identity in Qing Imperial*

Ideology, Berkeley 1999; M. C. ELLIOTT, *The Manchu Way: The Eight Banners and Ethnic Identity in Late Imperial China*, Stanford 2001; and the numerous studies published within *New Qing Imperial History: The Making of Inner Asian Empire at Qing Chengde*, edited by J. A. Millward, R. W. Dunnell, M. C. Elliott, P. Forêt, London 2004.

49   TNA, FO 535/4, Inclosure in No. 39, of India to Mr. Brodrick, August 6, 1904, p. 77.

50   TNA, FO 535/4, Inclosure in No. 82, of India to Mr. Brodrick, September 12, 1904, p. 137. For an overview of Anglo-Tibetan relations after the Younghusband Expedition up to Indian independence see A. MCKAY, *Tibet and the British Raj: the frontier cadre, 1904-1947*, Richmond 1997.

51   On this see U. E. BULAG, *Introduction: The 13th Dalai Lama in Mongolia, or the Dawn of Inner Asian modernity*, in: *The Thirteenth Dalai Lama on the Run (1904-1906): Archival Documents from Mongolia*, edited by S. Chuluun and U. E. Bulag, Leiden – Boston 2013, pp. 1-25.

52   On these monasteries see M. C. GOLDSTEIN, *A History of Modern Tibet, 1913-1951: The demise of the Lamaist State*, Berkeley – Los Angeles – London 1989, pp. 24-30.

53   TNA, FO 17/1751, Telegram from Viceroy (to India Office); dated 10th September 1904, f. 392; YOUNGHUSBAND 1910, p. 304. Full text of the treaty (English version): BL, IOR/L/PS/20/259, Cd. 5240, *East India (Tibet). Further papers relating to Tibet* [In continuation of Cd. 2370], London 1910, No. 1, Convention between Great Britain and Tibet, signed at Lhasa on the 7th September, 1904, pp. 1-3 (Annexure 1 and Annexure 2, p. 4). The Chinese text, with declaration of the Viceroy of India (in English and Chinese translation), is in *Treaties, Conventions, etc., between China and Foreign States* 1917, pp. 655-660.

54   TNA, FO 17/1751, Telegram from Viceroy, September 10, 1904, f. 392

55   BL, IOR/L/PS/20/259, Cd. 5240, *East India (Tibet). Further papers relating to Tibet* [In continuation of Cd. 2370], London 1910, Annexure 1 to No. 1, Declaration signed by His Excellency the Viceroy and Governor-General of India and appended to the ratified Convention of 7th September, 1904, November 11, 1904, p. 4.

56   See M. C. VAN WALT VAN PRAAG, *The Status of Tibet: History, Rights, and Prospects in International Law*, Boulder 1987, pp. 22-23.

57 Cd. 3088, *Convention between Great Britain and China respecting Tibet. Signed at Peking, April 27, 1906*, London 1906. Chinese text: *Treaties, Conventions, etc., between China and Foreign States* 1917, pp. 652-654.

58 TNA, FO 535/10, Enclosure 1 in No. 49, Convention, 18 (31) August 1907, pp. 31-35. The French text of the Convention is in the Annexes.

59 Full text of the treaty: 韓國二關スル條約及法令 / 統監府編纂, カンコク ニ カンスル ジョウヤク オヨビ ホウレイ, [京城] 1906, Traité de paix entre le Japon et la Russie, pp. 39-56. On the Russo-Japanese War see *Official history (naval and military) of the Russo-Japanese war*, Vols I-III, prepared by the Historical section of the Committee of imperial defence, London 1910-1920.

60 Cd. 2383, *Convention between the United Kingdom and France respecting Newfoundland, and West and Central Africa, Signed at London, April 8, 1904*, London 1905; Cd. 2384, *Declaration between the United Kingdom and France respecting Egypt and Morocco. Signed at London, April 8, 1904*, London 1905; Cd. 2385, *Declaration between the United Kingdom and France concerning Siam, Madagascar, and the New Hebrides, Signed at London, April 8, 1904*, London 1905.

61 Cd. 914, *Agreement between the United Kingdom and Japan relative to China and Corea. Signed at London, January 30, 1902*, London 1902.

62 Cd. 2735, *Agreement between the United Kingdom and Japan. Signed at London, August 12, 1905*, London 1905. Another agreement between the two countries was signed in 1911 (Cd. 5735, *Agreement between the United Kingdom and Japan. Signed at London, July 13, 1911*, London 1911). On relations between London and Tokyo at the beginning of the twentieth century see *The Anglo-Japanese Alliance, 1902-1922*, edited by P. P. O'Brien, London – New York 2004.

63 S. VAN SCHAIK, *Tibet: A History*, New Delhi 2012, pp. 219-220.

64 For a biography of Henry Campbell-Bannerman see R. HATTERSLEY, *Campbell-Bannerman*, London 2006.

65 B. WILLIAMS, *Great Britain and Russia, 1905 to the 1907 Convention*, in: *British Foreign Policy under Sir Edward Grey*, edited by F. H. Hinsley, Cambridge 1977, p. 133. For a biography of Sir Edward Grey see K. ROBBINS, *Sir Edward Grey: A Biography of Lord Grey of Fallodon*, London 1971.

66 TNA, FO 800/72, Copy of letter from Sir E. Grey to Sir A. Nicolson, Saint Petersburg, 1 May 1907, f. 283.

67 TNA, FO 800/72, Copy of letter from Sir E. Grey to Sir A. Nicolson, Saint Petersburg, 1 May 1907, f. 283.

68 TNA, FO 800/72, Copy of letter from Sir E. Grey to Sir A. Nicolson, Saint Petersburg, 1 May 1907, f. 283.

69 TNA, FO 800/72, Cecil Spring-Rice to Sir Edward Grey, April 10, 1906, f. 98; TNA, FO 800/72, Cecil Spring-Rice to Sir Edward Grey, April 12, 1906, f. 102. On the ninth paṇ-chen bla-ma see F. JAGOU, *Le 9e Panchen Lama (1883-1937): enjeu des relations sino-tibétaines*, Paris 2004.

70 VAN SCHAIK 2012, p. 220. The text of the telegram, in English, is in C. BELL, *Portrait of the Dalai Lama*, London 1946, p. 68.

71 TNA, FO 800/72, Cecil Spring-Rice to Sir Edward Grey, May 2, 1906, ff. 114-115.

72 TNA, FO 800/72, Cecil Spring-Rice to Sir Edward Grey, May 2, 1906, f. 114.

73 TNA, FO 800/72, Cecil Spring-Rice to Sir Edward Grey, May 2, 1906, ff. 114-115.

74 TNA, FO 800/72, Cecil Spring-Rice to Sir Edward Grey, May 2, 1906, f. 115.

75 TNA, FO 800/72, Cecil Spring-Rice to Sir Edward Grey, April 10, 1906, ff. 98-99.

76 On the Persian Constitutional Revolution see: J. AFARY, *The Iranian Constitutional Revolution, 1906-1911: Grassroots Democracy, Social Democracy and the Origins of Feminism*, New York 1996; M. BAYAT, *Iran's First Revolution: Shi'ism and the Constitutional Revolution of 1905-1909*, New York 1991.

77 TNA, FO 800/72, Cecil Spring-Rice to Sir Edward Grey, April 12, 1906, f. 102.

78 TNA, FO 800/72, Sir Edward Grey to Spring-Rice, March 26th, 1906, ff. 84-85.

79 TNA, FO 800/72, Sir Edward Grey to Spring-Rice, March 26th, 1906, ff. 84-85; TNA, FO 800/72, Télégramme de Musurus Pasha au Premier Secrétaire du Sultan en date du 29 Janvier. 1906, ff. 86-87.

80 TNA, FO 800/72, Sir Edward Grey to Spring-Rice, March 26th, 1906, ff. 84-85; TNA, FO 800/72, Cecil Spring-Rice to Sir Edward Grey, April 10, 1906, f. 98.

81 The French text of the treaty is in *Traités et conventions entre l'Empire du Japon et les puissances étrangères*, Première Partie - Traités, Ministère des affaires étrangères, Tokyo 1908, pp. 606-607. Japanese text of the treaty: 日露協約 Nichi-Ro Kyōyaku [*Japanese-Russian Agreement*], in: 官報 Kanpō, August 15, 1907. On this treaty see M. MATSUI, *The Russo-Japanese Agreement of 1907: Its Causes and the Progress of Negotiations*, in: Modern Asian Studies, Vol. 6, No. 1, 1972, pp. 33-48. On Russo-Japanese relations in this period see P. BERTON, *Russo-Japanese Relations, 1905-17: From Enemies to Allies,* London – New York 2012.

82 The text of the secret Convention in original French (photocopy) and English translation is in E. B. PRICE, *The Russo-Japanese Treaties of 1907-1916 Concerning Manchuria and Mongolia*, Baltimore 1933, pp. 107-111.

83 VAN SCHAIK 2012, pp. 220-221.

84 ZHWA SGAB PA DBANG PHYUG BDE LDAN, *Bod kyi srid don rgyal rabs*, Vol. II, Kalimpong 1976, pp. 133-134.

85 ZHWA SGAB PA DBANG PHYUG BDE LDAN, Vol. II 1976, pp. 135-136.

86 GOLDSTEIN 1989, p. 62.

87 GOLDSTEIN 1989, p. 62.

88 TNA, FO 800/72, Cecil Spring Rice to Sir Edward Grey, April 10, 1906, ff. 98-99.

89 GOLDSTEIN 1989, pp. 62-64.

90 On these treaties, as well as on relations between Russia and Persia during that period see M. ATKIN, *Russia and Iran: 1780-1828*, Minneapolis 1980. Russian text of the Treaty of Golestān: *Договоры Россiи съ Востокомъ: Политическiе и торговые*, Собралъ и издал Т. Юзефовичь, С. Петербургъ 1869, pp. 208-214. Russian text of the Treaty of Torkmānchāy: *Полное собранiе законовъ Россiйской имперiи*, Томъ: III, 1828, Санктпетербургъ 1830, N. 1794, Февраля 10. Трактат, заключенный между Его Величествомъ Императоромъ Всероссiйскимъ и Его Величеством Шахомъ Персидскимъ, pp. 125-130. On the Russian conquest of the Caucasus see J. F. BADDELEY, *The Russian conquest of the Caucasus*, London – New York – Bombay – Calcutta 1908.

91 On the third Anglo-Afghan war see: BL, IOR/R/12/LIB/106, *The Third Afghan War 1919*. Official account, compiled in the General Staff Branch, Army Headquarters, Government of India, Calcutta 1926; P. SYKES, *A History of Afghanistan*, Vol. II, London 1940, pp. 270-282; G. N. MOLESWORTH, *Afghanistan 1919. An Account of operations in the Third Afghan War*, Bombay 1962. On Afghanistan during Amānollāh Khān's reign see L. POULLADA, *Reform and rebellion in Afghanistan, 1919-1929: King Amanullah's failure to modernize a tribal society*, Ithaca 1973. Text of the 1921 treaty: Cmd. 1786, *Treaty between British and Afghan Governments. Signed at Kabul, November 22, 1921*, London 1922.

92 BL, Mss Eur F131/5, Cd. 2534, *Treaty between the British Government and the Amir of Afghanistan, Dated 21 March 1905, with papers relating thereto*, London 1905, No. 8, Translation of Treaty signed at Kabul on the 21st March, 1905, p. 9.

93 D. L. SNELLGROVE – H. E. RICHARDSON, *A Cultural History of Tibet*, Boulder 1980, pp. 227-228; M. T. KAPSTEIN, *Early Twentieth-Century Tibetan Encounters with the West*, in: *Sources of Tibetan Tradition*, edited by K. R. Schaeffer, M. T. Kapstein and G. Tuttle, New York 2013, p. 703.

94 '[the]' was added by the editor of the book.

95 *The Correspondence of G. E. Morrison*, Vol. II: 1912-1920, edited by H. Lo, New York 2013, n. 541, G. E. Morrison to H. A. Gwynne, September 1912, p. 28.

96 TNA, FO 535/11, Inclosure in No. 42, Government of India to Mr. Morley, February 12, 1908, p. 27.

97 TNA, FO 535/11, Inclosure in No. 28, Government of India to Mr. Morley, January 27, 1908, p. 20 (3rd installment); VAN WALT VAN PRAAG 1987, p. 40; YA HAN-CHANG 牙含章, *Ta lai la ma chuan* 达赖喇嘛传, Pei-ching 北京 1984, p. 188.

98 Cd. 4450, *Regulations respecting Trade in Tibet (amending those of December 5, 1893) concluded between the United Kingdom, China, and Tibet. Signed at Calcutta, April 20, 1908*, London 1908. Chinese text: *Treaties, Conventions, etc., between China and Foreign States* 1917, pp. 661-668.

99 Cd. 3088, *Convention between Great Britain and China respecting Tibet. Signed at Peking, April 27, 1906*, London 1906.

100 The text of the Gyenja (*Gan rgya*), the agreement with which the hereditary monarchy was established in Bhutan, is in DAM CHOS LHUN GRUB, '*Brug brgyud 'dzin gyi rgyal mchog dang pa mi dbang o rgyan dbang phyug mchog gi rtogs brjod*, Thimphu 2008, pp. 176-178 (transcription) and p. 180 (reproduction of the original text). On the birth of the Bhutanese monarchy see M. ARIS, *The Raven Crown: The Origins of Buddhist Monarchy in Bhutan*, Chicago 2005. For a history of Bhutan see: M. ARIS, *Bhutan: The Early History of a Himalayan Kingdom*, Warminster, England 1979; K. PHUNTSHO, *The History of Bhutan*, Noida 2013.

101 ARIS 2005, p. 24.

102 See R. W. WHITECROSS, *Buddhism and Constitutions in Bhutan*, in: *Buddhism and Law: An Introduction*, edited by R. R. French and M. A. Nathan, New York 2014, pp. 355-357. On the birth of Bhutan and the medieval theocracy see Y. IMAEDA, *Histoire médiévale du Bhoutan: établissement et évolution de la théocratie des 'Brug pa*, Tokyo 2011. On Bhutanese law see: WHITECROSS 2014, pp. 350-367; M. WINDISCHGRAETZ – R. WANGDI, *The Black-Slate Edict of Punakha Dzong*, Thimphu 2019. On the dual system of government see N. C. SINHA, *Chhos Srid Gnyis Ldan*, in: Bulletin of Tibetology, V, 3, 1968, pp. 13-27.

103 On the constitution of Bhutan see L. DUBGYUR, *The Wheel of Laws: An Insight into the Origin of Buddhist Kingship, Constitution and Judicial Independence in Bhutan*, Thimphu 2015.

104 See: N. SINGH, *Bhutan: A Kingdom in the Himalayas*, New Delhi 1972, pp. 30-32; A. DEB, *George Bogle's Treaty with Bhutan (1775)*, in: Bulletin of

Tibetology, 8, 1, 1971, pp. 5-14; for the texts of the 1774 treaty and the Bogle's agreement see SINGH 1972, pp. 177-179.

105 See BL, IOR/L/PS/20/D4, *Political Missions to Bootan*, Calcutta 1865; on relations between Bhutan and neighboring states see also F. POMMARET, *Ancient Trade Partners: Bhutan, Cooch Bihar and Assam (17th to 19th centuries)*, in: Journal of Bhutan Studies, Vol. 2, No. 1, Summer 2000, pp. 30-53.

106 *The India Office List for 1893*, London 1893, p. 28 and p. 30.

107 The English translation of the treaty signed by Eden with the Bhutanese can be found in D. H. E. SUNDER, *Survey and Settlement of the Western Duars in the District of Jalpaiguri, 1889 – 1895*, Calcutta 1895, pp. 30-31.

108 For the complete text of the Treaty of Sinchula see A. J. PEASLEE, *Constitutions of Nations*, Vol. I, Concord 1950, pp. 145-147.

109 On this period see: PHUNTSHO 2013, pp. 485-492; J. C. WHITE, *Sikhim & Bhutan: Twenty-One Years on the North-East Frontier. 1887-1908*, London 1909, pp. 131-134.

110 TNA, FO 535/4, Inclosure 2 in No. 22, Mr. Walsh to Colonel Younghusband, June 12, 1904: (A.) Letter from the Dalai Lama to the Tongsa Penlop, sent by Lama Se-kong Tulku, dated April 28, 1904, pp. 45-46 [*English translation*]; TNA, FO 535/4, Inclosure 2 in No. 22, Mr. Walsh to Colonel Younghusband, June 12, 1904: (B.) Letter from the Thibetan Council (" Ka-sha "), to the Tongsa Penlop, dated January 19, 1904, pp. 46-47 [English translation]; TNA, FO 535/4, Inclosure 1 in No. 14, Mr. Walsh to Colonel Younghusband, June 3, 1904, p. 24; TNA, FO 535/3, Inclosure 9 in No. 94, Government of India to Mr. Walsh, May 26, 1904, p. 142.

111 WHITE 1909, pp. 140-144.

112 BL, IOR/L/PS/20/211, Summary of Principal Events in 1907, Simla 1908, p. 45.

113 Full text of the Treaty of Punakha: PEASLEE 1950, pp. 147-148.

114 On the question of the definition of these treaties see D. WANG, *China's unequal treaties: narrating national history*, Lanham 2005.

115 On the rebellions in China see P. A. KUHN, *Rebellion and its enemies in late imperial China: militarization and social structure, 1796-1864*, Cambridge, Mass. 1980. In particular, on the revolt of the T'ai-p'ing see S. TENG, *The Taiping rebellion and the Western powers*, Oxford 1971. On China's international relations between the first and second half of the nineteenth century, up to the Second Opium War see H. B. MORSE, *The international relations of the Chinese Empire*, Vol. [I]: The period of conflict, 1834-1860, London 1910.

116 See: L. PETECH, *Central Tibet and the Mongols: The Yüan-Sa-skya Period of Tibetan History*, Roma 1990; D. S. RUEGG, *Mchod yon, yon mchod and mchod gnas / yon gnas: On the historiography and semantics of a Tibetan religio-social and religio-political concept*, in: *Tibetan History and Language: Studies dedicated to Uray Géza on his seventieth birthday*, edited by E. Steinkellner, Wien 1991, pp. 441-454.

117 For example WANG CHIA-WEI 王家伟 – NI-MA-CHIEN-TSAN 尼玛坚赞, *Chung kuo Hsi tsang te li shih ti wei* 中国西藏的历史地位, Pei-ching 北京 1997, pp. 16-24.

118 *The Mongols and Tibet: A Historical Assessment of Relations Between the Mongol Empire and Tibet*, Department of Information and International Relations (DIIR), Central Tibetan Administration, Dharamsala 1996, pp. 22-25.

119 G. TUCCI, *Le religioni del Tibet*, Roma 1976, pp. 15-16.

120 L. PETECH, *Il Tibet*, in: *Nuova storia universale dei popoli e delle civiltà*, Vol. XX: Asia Centrale e Giappone, edited by M. Bussagli, L. Petech and M. Muccioli, Torino 1981, p. 246.

121 ZHWA SGAB PA DBANG PHYUG BDE LDAN, *Bod kyi srid don rgyal rabs*, Vol. I, Kalimpong 1976, pp. 146-147.

122 SA SKYA BSOD NAMS RGYAL MTSHAN, *Rgyal rabs gsal ba'i me long*, Pe cin 2002, pp. 62-66.

123 On this see G. TUCCI, *Indo-Tibetica*, Vol. II: Rin c'en bza□ po e la rinascita del buddhismo nel Tibet intorno al Mille, Roma 1933; TUCCI 1976, pp. 35-48.

124 On the different schools of Tibetan Buddhism see TUCCI 1976, pp. 71-143.

125 L. PETECH, *Il Tibet*, in: *Le civiltà dell'Oriente. Storia, letteratura, religioni, filosofia, scienze e arte*, Vol. I: Storia, under the direction of G. Tucci, Firenze – Roma 1965, p. 1129.

126 PETECH, *Il Tibet* 1965, p. 1130. On Byang-chub-rgyal-mtshan see W. D. SHAKAPA (Tsepon), *The Rise of Changchub Gyaltsen and the Phagmo Drupa Period*, in: Bulletin of Tibetology, 1, 1981, pp. 23-33.

127 VAN WALT VAN PRAAG 1987, p. 6.

128 PETECH, *Il Tibet* 1965, p. 1130. On the relationship between Ming dynasty and Tibet see T. V. WYLIE, *Lama Tribute in the Ming Dynasty*, in: *Tibetan Studies in Honour of Hugh Richardson: Proceedings of the International Seminar on Tibetan Studies, Oxford 1979*, edited by M. Aris and A. S. S. Kyi, Warminster, England 1980, pp. 335-340. Wylie's essay also focuses on the position of Chinese historiography in this regard.

129 On this see: VAN WALT VAN PRAAG 1987, pp. 6-7; J. POWERS, *Introduction to Tibetan Buddhism*, Ithaca – Boulder 2007, p. 160.

130 PETECH 1981, pp. 268-269; on Tsong-kha-pa see *Life and Teachings of Tsong Khapa*, edited by R. A. F. Thurman, Dharamsala 2006.

131 ZHWA SGAB PA DBANG PHYUG BDE LDAN, Vol. I 1976, p. 376; H. RICHARDSON, *The Dalai Lamas*, in: *The History of Tibet*, Vol. II, edited by A. McKay, London – New York 2003, p. 557.

132 In this work for the dates of birth and death of the dalai lamas, as well as of the regents, I refer to PETECH 1959.

133 PETECH 1981, pp. 272-273.

134 PETECH 1981, p. 276; PETECH, *Il Tibet* 1965, p. 1132.

135 On the question see Y. ISHIHAMA, *On the Dissemination of the Belief in the Dalai Lama as a Manifestation of the Bodhisattva Avalokiteśvara*, in: *The History of Tibet*, Vol. II, edited by A. McKay, London – New York 2003, pp. 538-553.

136 See TSÀN-YAN-GHIA-TSÒ (VI Dalai Lama), *Canti d'amore*, edited by E. Lo Bue, Palermo 1993.

137 PETECH, *Il Tibet* 1965, p. 1134.

138 G. TUCCI, *Tibetan painted scrolls*, Vol. I, Roma 1949, p. 77.

139 PETECH 1959, pp. 380-381.

140 PETECH, *Il Tibet* 1965, p. 1134.

141 TUCCI 1949, p. 78.

142 PETECH, *Il Tibet* 1965, p. 1134.

143 See N. L. DARGYE, *La biografia segreta del Sesto Dalai Lama, 1683–1706 (1746)*, edited and translated by E. Rispoli, Milano 1999.

144 PETECH, *Il Tibet* 1965, p. 1134; PETECH 1959, pp. 372-373.

145 PETECH 1959, p. 373.

146 VAN SCHAIK 2012, pp. 167-169.

147 VAN SCHAIK 2012, pp. 169-170; L. PETECH, *China and Tibet in the early 18th century*, Leiden 1950, p. 61.

148 PETECH, *Il Tibet* 1965, p. 1135.

149 PETECH, *Il Tibet* 1965, p. 1135.

150 PETECH, *Il Tibet* 1965, p. 1136.

151 PETECH, *Il Tibet* 1965, p. 1136.

152 PETECH, *Il Tibet* 1965, p. 1136.

153 The paper written by Kolmaš also lists all the names of the ambans in Tibet (J. KOLMAŠ, *The Ambans and Assistant Ambans of Tibet (1727-1912). Some statistical observations*, in: *The History of Tibet,* Vol. II, edited by A. McKay, London – New York 2003, pp. 602-614).

154 G. TUTTLE, *Tibetan Buddhists in the Making of Modern China*, New York 2005, pp. 16-17.

155 TUTTLE 2005, p. 17.

156 TUTTLE 2005, pp. 28-33; KOLMAŠ 2003, p. 605.

157 On this period see C. ICHIKO, *Political and institutional reform, 1901-11*, in: *The Cambridge History of China*, edited by D. Twitchett and J. K. Fairbank (general editors), Vol. 11: Late Ch'ing 1800-1911, Part 2, edited by J. K. Fairbank and K. Liu, New York 1980, pp. 375-415.

158 See E. SPERLING, *The Chinese Venture in K'am, 1904-1911*, and the Role of Chao Erh-feng, in: *The History of Tibet*, Vol. III, edited by A. McKay, London – New York 2003, p. 62-91.

159 KOLMAŠ 2003, p. 613.

160 The nineteen points of Chang's program are published in YA HAN-CHANG 牙含章 1984, pp. 192-194.

161 YA HAN-CHANG 牙含章 1984, p. 194.

162 YA HAN-CHANG 牙含章 1984, p. 195.

163 YA HAN-CHANG 牙含章 1984, p. 193.

164 TNA, FO 535/11, No. 112, Sir J. Jordan to Sir Edward Grey, September 30, 1908, p. 96.

165 TNA, FO 535/12, Inclosure 1 in No. 7, Memorandum respecting an Interview between the Dalai Lama and the Maharaj Kumar of Sikkim, held at the Yellow Temple, Peking, on November 25, 1908, pp. 9-10.

166 The report of the meeting is in the memorandum written by S. F. Mayers: TNA, FO 535/11, Inclosure in No. 117, Memorandum by Mr. Mayers, pp. 102-103.

167 TNA, FO 535/11, Inclosure in No. 117, Memorandum by Mr. Mayers, p. 103.

168 TNA, FO 535/12, No. 1, Sir Edward Grey to Sir J. Jordan, January 4, 1909, p. 1.

169 TNA, FO 535/11, No. 99, Sir J. Jordan to Sir Edward Grey, October 12, 1908, p. 99. The visit and its political and religious meanings have been analyzed with particular attention in F. JAGOU, *The Thirteenth Dalai Lama's Visit to Beijing in 1908: In Search of a New Kind of Chaplain-Donor Relationship*, in: *Buddhism Between Tibet and China*, edited by M. T. Kapstein, Boston 2009, pp. 349-378.

170 TNA, FO 535/11, Inclosure 1 in No. 121, Extract from the "Peking Gazette" of November 3, 1908, Imperial Decree issued in the name of the Empress Dowager, p. 105.

171 TNA, FO 535/11, Inclosure 1 in No. 121, Extract from the "Peking Gazette" of November 3, 1908, Imperial Decree issued in the name of the Empress Dowager, p. 105; TNA, FO 535/11, No. 121, Sir J. Jordan to Sir Edward Grey, September 30, 1908, p. 104.

172 WANG CHIA-WEI 王家伟 – NI-MA-CHIEN-TSAN 尼玛坚赞 1997, p. 83.

173 P. K. CROSSLEY, *The Wobbling Pivot: China since 1800; An Interpretive History*, New York 2010, p. 141.

174 TNA, FO 535/11, No. 119, Sir J. Jordan to Sir Edward Grey, December 21, 1908, p. 104.

175 TNA, FO 535/12, No. 8, Sir J. Jordan to Sir Edward Grey, December 23, 1908, p. 11.

176 TNA, FO 535/11, No. 119, Sir J. Jordan to Sir Edward Grey, December 21, 1908, p. 104.

177 TNA, FO 535/13, Enclosure in No. 2, Government of India to Viscount Morley, January 12, 1910, p. 2.

178 TNA, FO 535/13, Enclosure in No. 30*, Government of India to Viscount Morley. (Communicated by India Office, March 2, 1910), March 2, 1910, p. 22*.

2

The End of the Manchu Dynasty and Tibetan Independence

The Republic

On January 1, 1912, the Republic of China was proclaimed.[1] The Hsin-hai Revolution, which had commenced on October 10, 1911, quickly put an end to the Empire, but at the same time the institutional changes broke those ancient ties that had held together diverse territories. From the point of view of the newly formed Republic of China, however, the end of the Ch'ing dynasty did not mean the end of the unity of the Empire's regions. New independent countries were firmly denied by the Provisional Constitution of the Republic of China of March 1912[2] which assigned five members of the Senate (*Ts'an i yüan* 參議院) to each province, Inner and Outer Mongolia and Tibet, while Ch'ing-hai – which largely corresponds to the Tibetan A-mdo – was entitled to a senator (Article 18). The indissolubility of the territory of the former Ch'ing Empire was therefore recognized, ignoring Mongolian independence that had been declared a few months earlier. The flag of the Republic itself had to symbolize this unity: each colored strip was associated with the country's main ethnic groups, namely the Hans (red), the Manchus (yellow), the Mongols (blue), the Muslims (white) and the Tibetans (black).[3] The anti-Manchu republicans thus preserved the concept of the unity of the «five races» (*wu tsu* 五族), but as understood in the last year of the dynasty, ignoring that in its original meaning, at the time of Ch'ien-lung, this view represented a rigid separation, albeit under the authority of the emperor.[4] This change of perspective questioned the very idea of China; it was a further step along the path started with the Opium Wars and directed towards the transformation of China into a modern state. New China, in addition to relating to other countries on a formally equal level, was now building a different administrative, institutional, and even social order. However, it had been a *de facto* one-sided transformation, also because the Manchus themselves had been decidedly reluctant to take part in this metamorphosis during the Empire.[5] Above all, however, at the fall of the dynasty, there was no acceptance of the Republic by the Tibetans and the Mongols, regardless of the new roles that each minority now had to play.

The end of the Manchu dynasty: renunciations and conditions

P'u-i, a child and the last emperor of the Ch'ing dynasty and of China – if we exclude the Yüan Shih-k'ai's pathetic attempt at restoration – abdicated on the twenty-fifth day of the twelfth month of his third year of reign (Hsuan-tung 宣統, this was the name of P'u-yi as the reigning emperor), that is, February 12, 1912,[6] a few days after he was six years old. The signature on the document, in the name of the adopted son, had been affixed by the empress mother, Lung-yü, who still on December 28 had tried a last desperate option of an edict for the convening of a National Convention.[7] Before mid-January 1912, the secretary of Yüan Shih-k'ai had informed Jordan that the probable abdication was imminent.[8] In fact, it seems that Mongolian independence – declared a few weeks earlier and which will be discussed later – was decisive in writing the word end to the millenary imperial history of China and to the centuries-old Manchu dynasty.[9] The text of the abdication called for the unity of the Manchu, Han, Mongol, Hui and Tibetan territories in «one great Republic of China» ('總期人民安堵海宇乂安仍合滿漢蒙回藏五族完全領土為一大中華民國'). Another document also defined the terms relating to the treatment and guarantees due to P'u-i, the Ch'ing dynasty and also to ethnic groups.[10] The little child was assured, among other things, the maintenance of the *tsun hao* 尊號, the imperial name ('尊號仍存不廢'), the treatment reserved by the authorities of the Republic for a foreign sovereign ('中華民國以待各外國君主之禮相待') and a series of guarantees and privileges, including four million tael each year, which were later converted into four million yüan, provided by the Republic ('歲用四百萬兩俟改鑄新幣後改為四百萬元此款由中華民國撥用'), and the residence in the Summer Palace, after temporary accommodation in the Imperial Palace within the Forbidden City. The Republic also ensured the protection of the ancestral temple and tombs of the dynasty ('其宗廟陵寢永遠奉祀由中華民國酌設衛兵妥慎保護'). The violation of this promise in the 1920s[11] – among the many offenses of the republican government – was perhaps the most tragic outrage for the young P'u-i.[12] A second part of the agreement, as mentioned, concerned the members of the imperial family: they were guaranteed their titles ('清王公世爵概仍其舊'), were equated with other citizens of the Republic as regards «public rights and private rights» ('清皇族對於中華民國國家之公權及私權與國民同等'), exempt from military service ('清皇族免當兵之義務') and their private properties were to be protected ('清皇族私產一體保護'). As for the «conditions for the treatment of Manchu, Mongolian, Hui and Tibetan ethnic groups» ('關於滿蒙回藏各族待遇之條件'), the Republic assured «equality with the Hans» ('與漢人平等'), as well as the protection of private property ('保護其私有財產'), the preservation of the aristocracy ('王公世爵概仍其舊'), the commitment to guarantee sustenance for those nobles in difficulty and for the members of the Eight Banners, the abolition of the previous limitations relating to residence and profession, with consequent freedom to register in any county of the Republic; finally «Manchu, Mongolian, Hui and Tibetan have the freedom to adhere to their ancestral religions» ('滿蒙回藏原有之宗教聽其自由信仰'). Another edict, among those of February 12, in its final part, in addition to wishing everyone happiness under the new republican regime, also invited Mongols, Tibetans, Muslims and Manchus to erase the ancient divisions and to continue to respect the law.[13]

The water-buffalo year. The Declaration of Independence

On February 7, 1913, Tibet celebrated the *lo-gsar*, the Tibetan New Year.[14] Thus the water-buffalo year began. About two weeks earlier, on the sixteenth day of the twelfth month of the year of the water-rat (January 23, 1913), while a very strong wind was blowing over Lhasa, the dalai lama, after the Tibetans had managed to defeat the Chinese soldiers, had returned to the Po-ta-la.[15] As seen, Thub-bstan-rgya-mtsho had to flee his capital again, in February 1910, escaping from the Chinese troops who had invaded Tibet.[16] It had been the last, tragic and ephemeral attempt of a dying imperial power. A clear description of the return of the dalai lama to Lhasa comes from a letter written by Haji Ghulam Muhammad, the chief of the Ladakhi traders in Lhasa and sent to the British agent in Rgyal-rtse.[17] Here is an extract of its English translation:[18]

> On the 16th of the 12th month (23rd January, 1913), on the occasion when the Dalai Lama entered the Potala, all the Thibetan officials, the Gurkhas, the Muhammadans and the heads of the different monasteries went to receive his Holiness the Dalai Lama at a place called Luding (near Drepung monastery). The Dalai Lamas came riding in Mongolian dress accompanied by twelve attendants. All the troops and the people there saluted him. His Holiness then changed into a Lama's dress at Luding and blessed the people in a tent. All the Thibetan, Gurkha and Muhammadan officials were allowed to sit in his presence. At 12 o'clock his Holiness entered his palanquin. When he was going towards the Potala, a very strong wind arose and the thousands of people, who were waiting to see him, were unfortunately unable to obtain a view of him.
>
> On the 18th (25th January, 1913), a quarrel took place between the Thapin[19] troops and the Gya-dzong[20] troops.

Thinking that there might be a serious fight, Lheding Depon went to stop the quarrel. The Gya-dzong troops threw stones at him (Lheding Depon), and he ran away. On the 19th (26th January, 1913), three Gya-dzong soldiers killed one Thupin soldier by striking him with the back of their swords.

On the 22nd (29th January, 1913), the Thibetan Government posted police in Lhassa city and at the Sho (below Potala).

The Thibetan Government have punished Rampa Shap-pe[21] and Kalon Lama Temang Chho-trak by degrading them two grades below their former rank, and by fining them [...].

Both of them have been retained in Thibetan Government service.

On the 29th (3rd February, 1913), the Thibetan Government arrested seven men of Tengyeling monastery[22] and imprisoned them. All the rest of the monks of Tengyeling monastery have been sent to different estates and monasteries where they will be kept under surveillance.

The 1st of the 1st month (7th February, 1913), was the New Year. On the 2nd (8th February, 1913), all the Thibetan, Muhammadan and Gurkha officials went to the Potala to offer their scarves as usual. The new year's arrangements were made as in previous years by the Thibetan Government.

On the 3rd (9th February, 1913), I went to pay my respects to Lonchen Chhang-khyim (Tre-kang). He informed me that the Thibetans are now the masters of Thibet. The foreign Powers, viz., Great Britain, Russia, Japan, France, and Germany, have recognised the independence of Thibet. Moreover, Russia, Japan and Great Britain are helping the Thibetans. As the country which immediately borders on Thibet is British, the Thibetans are confident of being supported by the British, and therefore they rely solely on the British Government. From what he (Lonchen) said it appears that the Thibetans have received intimation from Russia to the effect that the Russian Government has addressed the British Government with a view to affording help to the Thibetans, as the nearest country to Thibet is British.

The Thibetans have received a communication from the Chinese President, to the effect that the Thibetans and Chinese should preserve their friendship as before, and that he (President) proposes to send an official to discuss matters. Thibetan Government have replied to the President saying that the Dalai Lama does not desire the titles conferred on him by China. Although Thibet and China were previously on terms of mutual friendship, on account of the relationship of the priest and the Lay, lately they have not been on good terms. The Thibetans have now regained their power, and the Yellow sect religion is prospering. If a Chinese representative comes to discuss matters with the Thibetan Government he must not come by the original route (*i.e.*, by land), as they cannot allow him to do so. If a Chinese representative is sent by the sea route (*i.e.*, through India), a representative of the Thibetan Government can be sent to Darjeeling to discuss matters. The Thibetans cannot allow Chinese representatives to enter Thibet.

It is proposed to concentrate in Lhassa city annually, at the great yearly festival (held in 1st month, *i.e.*, about February) 1,000 monks from each of the three great monasteries. On the 3rd (9th February, 1913), 1,000 monks from the Sera, and 1,000 from the Ganden monastery reached Lhassa, but none came from Drepung monastery as the monks of Drepung monastery are not on friendly terms with the Sera and Ganden monks. The head of the Drepung monastery requested that he might be excused from attending the festivals, but on the 4th (11th [*sic,* 10th *recte*] February, 1913), the leave applied for was refused. In the meantime, the monks of the Sera and Ganden monasteries began the celebration of the festival. On the 5th (11th February, 1913), a She-ugo (a temporary monk magistrate) of Drepung came to Lhassa (with the Drepung monks) and celebrated the festival. On this account the Sera and Ganden monks did not attend two ceremonies on that date. On the 6th (12th February, 1913), the Sera and Ganden monks were ordered by the Thibetan Government to attend the festivals and to perform the ceremonies. They then attended the festival and ceremonies. All the people in the city are in anxiety, for there is every likelihood of friction between the monks.

On October 28, 1912, Chinese president Yüan Shih-k'ai, probably in an extreme attempt to give himself and China some authority over Tibet, had reassigned the title to the dalai lama,[23] which the Ch'ing had – with little real effect – formally revoked.[24] The British were well aware of the inconsistency of that revocation on a religious level.[25] The Manchus themselves had cited the precedent of the replacement of the sixth dalai lama[26] and that replacement, as seen, was never recognized by the Tibetans. The dalai lama refused the title by the new Chinese head of state[27] and declared the independence of Tibet on the eighth day of the first month of 1913.[28] That text which has actually been considered as a declaration of independence is something different. As Luciano Petech rightly points out, in fact,

> il Dalai-Lama si limitò a riassumere con un proclama il governo del paese, ma non completò mai l'ultimo passo dichiarandone l'indipendenza, forse perché le categorie del diritto internazionale non avevano alcun significato per la mentalità tibetana.[29]

Precisely, in the proclamation the dalai lama reaffirmed his role in Tibet and recalled the main historical points, from the period of Mongol domination to the beginning of the twentieth century, from the ancient relationship based on the principle of *mchod yon*, up to the recent Chinese invasion of the country, with the consequent flight of the ruler to India, followed by the Tibetan victory.[30] Finally, the religious and social duties of the Tibetans were indicated.[31] Independence was simply a fact. Petech wrote: 'Egli regnò come se l'alta sovranità cinese non esistesse; né gli interessava il fatto che essa venisse sempre riconosciuta *de jure* da tutte le grandi potenze'.[32]

On the Tibetan Declaration of Independence

The collapse of the Manchu dynasty in China between the end of 1911 and the beginning of 1912 had meant breaking the imperial tradition which, among various events, had governed the country since the unification by Ch'in Shih-huang in the third century BC. The fault that passed through the historical, cultural, and philosophical events produced the earthquakes that destroyed the foundations of the dynasty, together with Western and Japanese penetration. Although expanded over the centuries, the confrontation between systems of thought could not fail to create fractures which often left out dynamics that were repeated throughout the nineteenth century with their explosive vitality, giving way to a long series of tragic rebellions.

Certainly, the collapse of the Ch'ing dynasty had broken the relationship between Lhasa and Peking. Formally, the link, as previously noted, was between the dalai lama and his protector and lay disciple, that is, the emperor. So this should already be enough to explain the meaning of the thirteenth dalai lama's Declaration of Independence. However, another reflection must also be added to this reasoning. The Chinese repression in the last years of the Empire carried out by Chao Erh-feng and the policy of sinization of Tibet were naturally part of a broader mechanism centered on a new idea of empire. Until the first half of the nineteenth century the Chinese Empire was truly the Middle Kingdom, in the sense that it existed in a system of international relations, largely limited to East, Southeast and Inner Asia, which certainly placed it at the cultural, economic, and diplomatic center of that world. Therefore, the relationship with Tibet or with other peripheral countries, whether they were tributaries or not, was also explained within that system. The *mchod yon* bond was sufficient, as it had been for the Mongol predecessors, to explain the relationship between Lhasa and Peking. The case of the second half of the nineteenth century and the first decade of the twentieth century was different. Tibet had been abandoned and the very cause of the Younghusband Expedition was precisely the British need to establish a direct communication between the Raj and Tibet given the inability of the Manchus to exercise their own suzerainty and therefore to impose anything on the Tibetans. The defense of the road to Lhasa, traveled by the troops of the most powerful empire of the time, had been left in the hands of a small, almost medieval army. So, in what capacity could the empire still compare itself to a protective power? The answer was given, precisely, in the titles. A title was assigned, as we have seen, to the dalai lama who, in 1908, after centuries of substantial autonomy, became the 'the Loyally Submissive Vice-gerent',[33] an *ad hoc* creation of the dynasty to formally retain its role. At the same time, moreover, the Ch'ing had tried to claim a new title 'Emperor of China and Tibet', which the British refused to accept.[34] This was a betrayal of Chinese history. «China» in Chinese is simply 中國 Chung-kuo the «Middle (中) Country (國)».[35] A country that over the millennia recognized, through its own name, its centrality in the world, now implored the recognition of a title from the West.

In a certain sense, therefore, the Western political view – rather than the collapse of the dynasty – broke that link between Peking and Lhasa; it could survive, conveniently for both sides, only in the traditional Chinese and Tibetan system of relations. When one of the two parties tried to impose itself on the other, the bond was deprived of its historical and cultural foundation. From this point of view, republican China's fatuous claims on Tibet and the concrete invasion of the People's Republic of China are nothing more than the natural continuation of that idea about Tibet drawn by the dying Ch'ing Empire. And so, while deciphering the declaration of independence of Tibet, we must consider also this Chinese understanding of its new role in a wider world. It is the drama of the empires that extend over the whole world and mark their borders with the *hic sunt leones*. When those borders open, however, the impact is devastating for traditional structures. Tibet immediately before the declaration of independence was for China nothing more than an attempt to reason according to a Western scheme, given the failure of the Eastern one. However, if Peking was seeking – paradoxically – on the peaks of the Himālaya a European legitimacy for its institutions, Lhasa, in addition to not being willing to indulge such political mirages, also rejected the same model that Westerners had imported. For the thirteenth dalai lama, as well as for his successor until the Communist invasion, there were still lions in the rest of the world.

A final consideration concerns the very figure of Thub-bstan-rgya-mtsho. At the time of the declaration of independence, he was thirty-seven. A rare case. The other successors of the Great Fifth had either lived too little or had not actually exercised power except for an extremely limited time.[36] The ninth dalai lama had died as a child and his immediate successors passed away still very young.[37] The eighth dalai lama, Byams-spel-rgya-mtsho, born in 1758 died in 1804, but had ruled the country only between 1786 and 1788.[38] Thub-bstan-rgya-mtsho was attempting to restore the authority that many of his predecessors had hardly touched. It was the very institution of the dalai lama that for too long had been relegated to a formal office. The collapse of the empire on the one hand and an adult dalai lama on the other were two conditions which, when combined, gave Tibet the possibility of achieving independence under the Yellow School.

Endnotes

1   See, among others: LARY 2007, pp. 14-79; R. MITTER, 1911: *The Unanchored Chinese Revolution*, in: The China Quarterly, No. 208 (December 2011), pp. 1009-1020; G. WANG, *To Reform a Revolution: Under the Righteous Mandate*, in: Dædalus, Vol. 122, no. 2, 1993, pp. 71-94.

2   The full text of the constitution is in the appendix (附錄) of KAO LAO 高勞, *Hsin-hai ke-ming shih* 辛亥革命史, Shang-hai 上海 12 [1923], pp. 59-68.

3   A. MA LYNN, *Muslims in China*, translated by P. Lan Lin and C. Fang, Indianapolis 2004, p. 45.

4   TUTTLE 2005, pp. 59-61.

5   TUTTLE 2005, pp. 60-61.

6   The text of the act of abdication is in Lin shih kung pao 臨時公報, 辛亥年十二月二十六日 (February 13, 1912), Pei-ching 北京 1912, pp. 003-004.

7   M. DILLON, *China: A Modern History*, London – New York 2012, p. 147.

8   TNA, FO 405/208, No. 67, Sir J. Jordan to Sir Edward Grey, January 14, 1912, p. 100.

9   This according to information obtained from the Japanese government: TNA, FO 405/208, No. 69, Sir C. MacDonald to Sir Edward Grey, January 16, 1912, p. 101.

10   Full text: Lin shih kung pao 臨時公報, 辛亥年十二月二十六日 (February 13, 1912), Pei-ching 北京 1912, pp. 005-007.

11   E. J. M. RHOADS, *Manchus and Han: ethnic relations and political power in late Qing and early Republican China, 1861-1928*, Seattle – London 2000, pp. 250-251.

12   See R. F. JOHNSTON, *Twilight in the Forbidden City*, New York 1934, pp. 444-445.

13   Lin shih kung pao 臨時公報, 辛亥年十二月二十六日 (February 13, 1912), Pei-ching 北京 1912, pp. 04-05.

14 TNA, FO 535/16, Enclosure 3 in No. 181, Letter addressed to British Trade Agent, Gyantse, p. 157 the letter, dated February 14, 1913, was written by Haji Ghulam Muhammad, who was the chief of the Ladakhi traders in Lhasa, as explained in TNA, FO 535/16, Enclosure 2 in No. 181, British Trade Agent, Gyantse, to Government of India, February 21, 1913, p. 156.

15 TNA, FO 535/16, Enclosure 3 in No. 181, Letter addressed to British Trade Agent, Gyantse, pp. 156-158.

16 TNA, FO 535/13, Enclosure in No. 30*, Government of India to Viscount Morley. (Communicated by India Office, March 2, 1910), March 2, 1910, p. 22*. On the dalai lama in India see BELL 1946, pp. 82-130.

17 TNA, FO 535/16, Enclosure 2 in No. 181, British Trade Agent, Gyantse, to Government of India, February 21, 1913, p. 156.

18 Full text: TNA, FO 535/16, Enclosure 3 in No. 181, Letter addressed to British Trade Agent, Gyantse, p. 156-158.

19 According to a footnote to the translation: 'New troops composed of men of mixed Chinese and Thibetan parentage', TNA, FO 535/16, Enclosure 3 in No. 181, Letter addressed to British Trade Agent, Gyantse, p. 157.

20 According to a footnote to the translation: 'The old regular troops', TNA, FO 535/16, Enclosure 3 in No. 181, Letter addressed to British Trade Agent, Gyantse, p. 157.

21 According to a footnote to the translation: 'These are two Shap-pes whom the Thibetan Government imprisoned for being pro-Chinese', TNA, FO 535/16, Enclosure 3 in No. 181, Letter addressed to British Trade Agent, Gyantse, p. 157.

22 Bstan-rgyas-gling monastery had suffered a long siege by the Tibetans because it housed Chinese soldiers. In 1913 it was destroyed (GOLDSTEIN 1989, pp. 63-64 and p. 109).

23 Chinese text of the decree: *Chung kuo Hsi tsang she hui li shih tzu liao* 中国西藏社会历史资料, edited by Chin Hui 金晖, Jen I-nung 任一农 and Ma Nai-hui 马鼐辉, Pei-ching 北京 1994, p. 38. For its English translation see Presidential Mandate of October 28, 1912 (Translated from the Government Gazette), published in E. TEICHMAN, *Travels of a Consular Officer in Eastern Tibet, Together with a History of the Relations between China, Tibet and India*, Cambridge 1922, pp. 17-18.

24 TNA, FO 535/13, No. 21, Translation of Telegram from Wai-wu Pu, dated the 25th instant, received in London on the evening of the same day.- (Communicated by Chinese Minister, February 26, 1910.), p. 18; TNA, FO 535/13, Enclosure in No. 50, Wai-wu Pu to Sir J. Jordan, March 9, 1910, p. 50. Text of the proclamation in Chinese: YA HAN-CHANG 牙含章 1984, pp. 230-231.

25 TNA, FO 535/13, Enclosure in No. 23, Government of India to Viscount Morley, February 27, 1910, p. 19.

26 TNA, FO 535/13, Enclosure in No. 50, Wai-wu Pu to Sir J. Jordan, March 9, 1910, p. 51.

27 ZHWA SGAB PA DBANG PHYUG BDE LDAN, Vol. II 1976, p. 219.

28 The full text of the Tibetan declaration of independence in Tibetan is in ZHWA SGAB PA DBANG PHYUG BDE LDAN, Vol. II 1976, pp. 219-223.

29 PETECH 1981, p. 298.

30 ZHWA SGAB PA DBANG PHYUG BDE LDAN, Vol. II 1976, pp. 219-221.

31 ZHWA SGAB PA DBANG PHYUG BDE LDAN, Vol. II 1976, pp. 221-223.

32 PETECH 1981, p. 298.

33 TNA, FO 535/11, Inclosure 1 in No. 121, Extract from the "Peking Gazette" of November 3, 1908, Imperial Decree issued in the name of the Empress Dowager, p. 105.

34 TNA, FO 535/11, No. 115, Sir J. Jordan to Sir Edward Grey, October 15, 1908, p. 100.

35 Originally the term designated the area of fiefdoms around the domain of the Chou kings (Eastern Chou period), A. CHENG, *Storia del pensiero cinese*, Vol. I: Dalle origini allo «studio del Mistero», Italian translation by A. Crisma, Torino 2000, p. 41.

36 PETECH 1959, pp. 372-376.

37 PETECH 1959, pp. 374-376.

38 PETECH 1959, pp. 373-374.

3

London and Mongolian Independence

The Game, again

The current Mongolian state (*Mongol uls*) covers over one and a half million square kilometers with a population, in 2020, of just over three million inhabitants.[1] Geographically, however, the country represents only a part of the wider national and cultural identity of the Buddhist Mongols, who are also present in the People's Republic of China, in particular in the Autonomous Region of Inner Mongolia. Another ancient presence, although numerically very limited, is represented by the Mongols of Hsin-chiang.[2] Still others live in Russia, in particular in Buryatia and Kalmykia. The Mongols of Kalmykia moved from Zungaria in the seventeenth century. Kalmykia remained a khanate until 1771, when many Mongols returned to Zungaria and the country was fully integrated into Russia by Catherine II.[3]

In the historical analysis of British geopolitical designs of the early twentieth century, Outer Mongolia – apparently – should have a peripheral role. The country was too far from the geographic heart of Britain's interests in Asia. Indeed, those interests traveled the routes of the Indian Ocean and, through the vital Strait of Malacca and therefore Singapore, arrived in southern China, where the British imperial tradition was embodied in the colony of Hong Kong. The commercial dimension of a country with one of the lowest population densities in the world was certainly negligible: in 1920, shortly after the period examined in this research, the total population was estimated between two and five million inhabitants over the entire Mongolian territory (Inner and Outer Mongolia).[4] The 1950 data, that is a few tens of years after the period analyzed by this work, refer to a total population of about 780,000 inhabitants in independent Mongolia alone.[5] Even regarding the defense of India – from a strategic point of view – the geographical position of Mongolia was secondary.

Yet, as I will try to explain, Outer Mongolia, freed from the yoke of the Ch'ing Empire, reopened the geopolitical confrontation of Great Britain and Russia in High Asia, particularly in Tibet, although the previous years had witnessed the development of international relations that had placed the United Kingdom and Russia on the same side. 'Russian action in Mongolia does not, I imagine, directly concern Great Britain, but indirectly it is of very great consequence indeed' explained George Ernest Morrison, an ex-correspondent from Peking for *The Times* and an adviser to Yüan Shih-k'ai, writing to Dudley D. Braham, in February 1913.[6]

Then in what terms can we speak of a new geopolitical confrontation? Probably a further analysis should be added to the then framework of international relations, to explain the importance of a region so far from Calcutta and Delhi. Mongolia — as has already been seen — was (and is) strongly linked to Tibet by cultural and religious ties. Changes in Urga had different consequences on the relations of the Western powers with Lhasa. Thinking in terms of historical and geopolitical analysis necessarily means placing a country in its own geographical and cultural context. The description made by the Italian orientalist Alessandro Bausani on the centrality of the religious element (even in a text dedicated to Persia) is very effective:

> In great traditional civilizations [...] the different cultural components interweave; art and religion, law and politics are not pieces of a mosaic but are closely blended into a single organism dominated and permeated by the most important of all motifs, religion.[7]

Such a discourse is even more valid for countries where religious hierarchies, over the centuries, assumed a pre-eminent position to the point of coinciding with the very idea of political power and established a theocracy. Lhasa was, from this point of view, the religious and consequently political center for a Tibetan Buddhist region that met with British objectives. As Charles Bell wrote in 1924: 'race and religion are the strongest of ties, especially in the East'.[8] Add to this the return of the dalai lama to Lhasa and the declaration of independence of Tibet in 1913. The end – and fragmentation – of the Ch'ing Empire was the novelty that intervened in these regions on the issues defined by the Anglo-Russian Convention in 1907. Walter Langley, assistant under-secretary of state for Foreign Affairs,[9] wrote to the India Office in March 1913 in this regard:

> Recent information from Peking and India has tended to confirm the impression that a large increase of Russian influence in Thibet is to be apprehended in the near future,

while the course of events since 1907, culminating in the practical acquisition of independence by the Thibetans, and in the conclusion of treaties by Mongolia with Russia and Thibet respectively, would seem to have distinctly altered the *status quo* in Thibet, and both Russian and British relations towards that country.[10]

Therefore, Mongolian independence reopened, in the British view, the game: that country could become the key to open the doors of Lhasa to the Russians. The British also feared, for example, the many Mongolian monks who moved to Tibetan monasteries.[11] Russian weapons were probably sent to Tibet by the Mongols.[12]

Let us therefore proceed in order, thus highlighting the historical-political path of independent Outer Mongolia and the dimension that it assumed in the geopolitical interests of the British Empire.

Mongolian independence

In Tibet, the thirteenth dalai lama declared independence – as seen – at the beginning of 1913. In Outer Mongolia, independence had been declared even before the official end of the empire, in December 1911. The leader of the Yellow School in Mongolia was the khal-kha rje-btsun dam-pa, in Mongolian: bogd jivzundamba hutagt haan bogd jivzundamba hutagt haan. Hutagt (Tibetan: *ho thog tu*), in Chinese: *hu-t'u-k'o-t'u* 呼圖克圖, is a title reserved for the highest leaders of Tibetan Buddhism.[13] Ngag-dbang-blo-bzang-chos-kyi-nyi-ma-bstan-'dzin-dbang-phyug, Tibetan by birth, was the eighth in a sprul sku line that is traced back to the seventeenth century, to Blo-bzang-bstan-pa'i-rgyal-mtshan (1635-1723), son of a Halh prince, Gombodorj.[14] In the sequence of what were considered «manifestations» of Bde-mchog, in addition to the rje-btsun dam-pa, the jo-nang master Tā-ra-nā-tha (1575-1634), who died in Mongolia in 1634: the first rje-btsun dam-pa Blo-bzang-bstan-pa'i-rgyal-mtshan, also called Zanabazar, was regarded as his subsequent rebirth by the dalai lama and paṇ-chen bla-ma.[15] Zanabazar is also remembered for his extraordinary artistic work and for having created the «soyombo» scripture, whose first grapheme, also called «soyombo», became since 1911 one of the main symbols of independence and Mongolian identity, even during the communist period, and is still – among other things – on the flag and in the national emblem of the current Republic.[16] The Mongolian capital was originally a monastery for Zanabazar founded in 1639.[17]

On December 1, there was the formal declaration and a few weeks later – on December 29 – the eighth rje-btsun dam-pa Ngag-dbang-blo-bzang-chos-kyi-nyi-ma-bstan-'dzin-dbang-phyug ascended the throne as bogd haan.[18] His government was made up of five ministries: internal affairs, foreign affairs, military affairs, justice and finance.[19] The ministers were Tserenchimed (Internal Affairs), Handdorj (Foreign Affairs), Namsray (Justice), Gombosüren (Military Affairs), and Chagdaryaj (Finance).[20] The name *Ih Mongol Uls* was resurrected by some Mongolian historians, thus underlining the link of the new country with the ancient medieval empire created by Chingis haan.[21] The Chinese soldiers in Mongolia, unpaid because of the revolution, mutinied.[22] The link between the Manchu dynasty and the Mongols was to be considered dissolved and there was, according to the Mongols, no continuation of this link to the Republic of China that was about to be born.[23] In 1688 the Halh princes had asked the Manchu Emperor K'ang-hsi for protection against Galdan, the haan of the Oyrat Mongols, who was later defeated in 1690.[24] In 1691, the princes therefore recognized the emperor's authority.[25] As with Tibet later, that recognition did not imply the full annexation to China; the bond was a relationship between emperor and princes, and not between Mongolia and China. Indeed, according to Luciano Petech:

> Il vassallaggio accettato nel 1691 dai principi Qalqa della Mongolia Esterna era un rapporto personale fra di essi e la dinastia manciù. Durante i secoli XVIII e XIX i capi mongoli obbedirono all'imperatore manciù come avevano obbedito e pagato tributo al loro *qa'an*. Dal 1719 fu loro vietato di avere rapporti diretti con le potenze straniere. Ciò voleva dire che le relazioni col vicino russo venivano trattate dal governo di Pechino. Queste relazioni vennero poi regolate col trattato di Kiakhta del 1860. Gli imperatori in linea di massima non intervennero negli affari del paese, rispettando tutti i diritti dell'aristocrazia mongola.[26]

Only from the beginning of the twentieth century, from 1902 to be precise, did the Ch'ing dynasty authorize the Chinese (Han) colonization of Outer Mongolia, which had been banned before then.[27] Even in Mongolia, as seen for Tibet, the «New Policy» (新政 *hsin cheng*), inaugurated in 1901, was implemented.[28] In 1906, a Bureau for the Colonization of Mongolia was born.[29] Therefore, colonization, at the time of independence, was still just beginning and the Chinese had settled only in the fertile valley between Urga and Kyakhta.[30] To encourage the sinization there was also the action of Sando (in Chinese 三多 *San-to*), the last amban of Urga, who – still in 1911 – had opened another bureau for colonization.[31] Sando, an anti-Russian, had arrived in Urga in March 1910.[32] Certainly his management of power, his harshness and disrespect towards the Mongols – despite being of Mongolian origin himself[33] –as well as his greed to tax the population, had contributed greatly to the end of the centuries-old bond with the Ch'ing. Indeed, according to T. A. Rustad, a Norwegian who worked for the British and American Tobacco Company:

> The mongols have got horses that every year they dedicate to the Living-God. These horses are brought into Urga during the summer festival, when horse-racing etc takes place. Well the *Amban* with his soldiers took these horses by force from the mongols and branded them with his own brand saying that they were to be used only by the army hereafter. Well you can imagine what effect that had on the mongols, who are very religious, in their way. The *amban* taxed every little bit that the mongols produced and needed. The building of the barraks near Urga, just about 3 miles to the East of the town was also done with mongol money. There were some fine trees in a certain valley near Urga that the mongols thought a lot of. Well the first thing the *Amban* did was to cut down these trees and use them in the barrack buildings. The *Amban* in fact did everything that he knew the Mongols did not like. He sat on them, properly speaking. Treated them just like animals, not as well as he treated his own overfed ponies. The mongols are very peaceful people, but this was more than any human being could stand. Those that had any valuables were put in prison and what they had was taken away from them. I have heard hundred of stories of how he managed to get what they had [...]. Well the behaviour of the *Amban* was the cause of the Mongol rising against the government of China.[34]

G. E. Morrison simply accused the two high imperial officials of the cruelty in Mongolia (by Sando) and in Tibet (by Chang Yin-t'ang); in short, according to him, it was simply a matter of personal responsibility, as if there had not been a broader plan of colonization and total submission of territories for centuries completely autonomous from the central imperial power.[35] Morrison's opinion must obviously be filtered and understood in his role as adviser to Yüan Shih-k'ai. The British ambassador Jordan did not have great sympathy towards the adviser, considering him – according to Morrison himself – essentially Chinese ('My chief difficulty is the hostility of Sir John Jordan who appears to regard me as a Chinese').[36]

In Inner Mongolia, Han colonization had begun as early as 1840.[37] By 1913, there were 82,000 Chinese in the district of T'ao-nan 洮南, while Mongols were just 23,000.[38] Sinization, however, meant not only colonization in the lands of the Mongols, but also and above all a cultural and social process, a radical change in the traditional lifestyle, since one of the fundamental lines of demarcation between Chinese and Mongols was the nomadic lifestyle: of the 23,000 Mongols in the district of T'ao-nan, 4,000 had become farmers.[39] Furthermore, the Mongols were removed from the fertile lands – which the Chinese kept for themselves – and only the arid highlands remained to raise their livestock.[40] With loans at usury rates, the Mongolian tribes were losing land and livestock to the newcomers[41] and at the same time the Mongols' hatred of the Chinese was fueled.[42] The Chinese government also banned the Mongols from obtaining loans from the Russians.[43] Basically, the attempt by the Chinese was to make Mongolia a Chinese province in all respects. Similar projects also involved Tibet. Indeed, Wen Tsung-yao 溫宗堯, after his removal from the post of junior amban of Lhasa in 1910,[44] prepared a plan for Tibet for the practical transformation of Tibet into a Chinese province, although not formally calling it in that way: '不必遽改為行省，而當以治行省之道治之'.[45] It is useful to remember, in this regard, that even today Outer Tibet and Inner Mongolia are not formally «provinces» (省 sheng) of the People's Republic of China, but «autonomous regions» (tzu chih ch'ü 自治區 / 自治区).

The Russians and Mongolia

In the days following the Mongol declaration of independence in 1911, the role of Russia was also being decided. In 1854, at the height of the Revolt of the T'ai-p'ing, certain of the end of the Ch'ing dynasty, Nikolay Murav'yëv-Amurskiy (1809-1881) had explained to the Russian government the need to avoid Chinese dominion over Mongolia after the end of the Manchu rule.[46] At the time, Murav'yëv-Amurskiy was the Governor General of Eastern Siberia.[47] In the seventeenth century the Russians had sent several missions to the Mongols with the aim of convincing the princes to recognize the tsar's authority, without, however, obtaining real results, with the exception – perhaps – of Altan han Ombo Erdene.[48] The difficulties increased in the second half of the seventeenth century, with border incidents and Mongolian incursions into Siberia.[49] Only in 1689, under the pressure of Chinese troops, did the Treaty of Nerchinsk establish the border between the two empires along the Argun' and Shilka rivers and the Stanovoy mountain range, excluding the Russians from the Amur region.[50] Between 1858 and 1860, other treaties extended the borders of the Russian Empire at the expense of the Ch'ing empire, towards Central Asia and the regions of Amur, Priamur'ye and Ussuri.[51] The hero of the conquest of the new territories was precisely Murav'yëv-Amurskiy.[52] His 1854 proposal on Mongolia had won some favor in the government; a special commission had espoused his ultimate goal to extend Russian influence over Mongolia, albeit in a peaceful way.[53] The Russian caution, however, about a possible subjugation of Mongolia and Manchuria, as protectorates, stemmed from a possible Western reaction: in response, other powers could annex other territories – for example Korea – as explained by the Amur Commission to the tsar in 1861.[54] The following year, however, the same commission expressed its favor, in the event of the fall of the Ch'ing dynasty, for the independence of Mongolia and Manchuria, thus clarifying the next Russian policy on the issue.[55]

On January 11, 1912, with an official communiqué, Saint Petersburg responded positively to the request of the Chinese and Mongols for mediation, but placed as a precondition the absence of Chinese officials, soldiers or settlers in Mongolia.[56] Naturally, the Chinese, for their part, had asked for Russian help with the aim of averting the full independence of the country.[57] The Russians could try to persuade the Mongols not to permanently abandon their ties with China, but in the event of full independence, Saint Petersburg had to establish business relations with Mongolia, given the country's commercial interests.[58] Sergey Sazonov, Russian foreign minister, however, immediately explained to the Chinese ambassador in Saint Petersburg that the communiqué did not mean a Russian attempt to annex Mongolia, but only to ensure real autonomy for the Mongols.[59] At the same time Sazonov told Sir George Buchanan, the British ambassador to Saint Petersburg, that Russia did not want to establish a protectorate over Urga.[60] Indeed, to such a proposal, previously made by some Mongol princes, Russia had already given a negative answer.[61] Shchekin, the Russian chargé d'affaires in China, also told Jordan that the only Russian goal was the autonomy of Mongolia and not independence.[62]

Mongolian military actions in 1912

On January 15, 1912, the Mongols had occupied the Chinese city of Haylaar (Hai-la-erh 海拉爾), in Manchuria – today in the Autonomous Region of Inner Mongolia, near the Russian border – put the tao-t'ai on the run and also proclaimed the independence of the border area between Outer Mongolia and Manchuria, between Haylaar and Man-chou-li 滿洲里.[63] In fact, the fall of the Chinese city of Haylaar was followed by a march to the west which saw the assault on the Dalai nuur.[64] On February 2, the Chinese sector of Man-chou-li was attacked.[65] The Mongol military successes concerned cities today in Chinese territory, in the Autonomous Region of Inner Mongolia.

The collapse of Manchu imperial power, with the Chinese troops who – as mentioned above – had mutinied and were now dedicated to banditry, necessarily had to push the Russians to act directly to preserve their commercial interests.[66] According to Henry Edward Sly, the British consul in Harbin,[67] the Russians themselves pushed the Mongols to intervene in Manchuria.[68] And actually several clues supported that idea. The formal neutrality of the Russians, invoked by the Chinese and Mongols as mediators to resolve the crisis, was contradicted by the Russian weapons used by the

Mongols in their operations in Manchuria and the bullets found on the ground were also Russian.[69] Saint Petersburg officially recognized the legitimacy of Chinese claims on the region just conquered by the Mongols in Manchuria.[70] In the meantime, however, before attacking the Chinese sector of Man-chou-li, the Mongols were in the city's Russian barracks and returned there after the operation.[71] Furthermore, the body of a Russian officer had been found on Chinese territory.[72] There were, therefore, without a shadow of a doubt, direct actions by the Russian authorities in the area, actions that Konovalov, former head of the Imperial Maritime Customs at Harbin, in a conversation with his old friend Sly, had dismissed as 'blunders'.[73] General Martinov had given the order and at the end of March 1912 he alone was considered responsible and therefore punished.[74] Basically, as Jordan wrote to Grey,

> it would appear that General Martinof, in command of the Chinese Eastern Railway Guards, has been made the scapegoat for what M. Konovalof described as a " blunder " on the part of the Russian authorities on this occasion.[75]

Indeed, the area of the Mongol attacks was also located within the largest Russian sphere of influence that Saint Petersburg had agreed with Tokyo in the aforementioned secret convention of 1907, later confirmed in another secret agreement of 1910.[76]

Meanwhile, according to a memorandum drawn up by the military attaché of the British Embassy in Peking sent by Sir John Jordan to Sir Edward Grey, in August 1912,[77] in the district of T'ao-nan 洮南, there had been an uprising of a part of the eastern Mongolian tribes and those tribes then moved towards Ch'ih-feng 赤峰 (in Mongolian: Ulaanhad), in the province of Chih-li,[78] causing some skirmishes between the Chinese and the Mongols the following winter.[79] The 'Talikangai' district was occupied by a thousand Mongols from eastern Mongolia (south of Haylaar) who had left Urga at the end of January and by another six hundred from the capital of Outer Mongolia, who also had left at the end of January and were well received by the Mongolian inhabitants of the district.[80] The thousand people from eastern Mongolia were actually under the orders of a raider who had helped the Russians in the Russo-Japanese conflict.[81] These soldiers were to be joined by four thousand men from Uliastay (today in the Republic of Mongolia), who also gathered in Urga before proceeding to Talikangai in February.[82]

In response to the attacks, the Chinese had strengthened the garrisons along the Mongolian border, for a total of between 30 and 40,000 soldiers.[83] Half of these (15-20,000 soldiers), under the command of the Military Governor of Jehol, were located in the north-east, from Jehol[84] to the borders of Inner

Mongolia and Manchuria.[85] Between 10 and 12,000 men instead defended the territory that went from Doloon nuur towards the southwest, up to Haalgan[86] and the prefecture (*fu* 府) of Ta-t'ung 大同,[87] and were under the command of the military governor of Haalgan.[88] The remaining 5 or 6,000 men were located within a radius of 50 miles around the city of Kuei-hua-ch'eng 歸化城 and were taking orders from the military governor of that city.[89]

These garrisons were mostly composed of less than 500 soldiers, therefore exposed to the violence of the nomads.[90] These few men had to face the fast Mongolian gangs, able to travel, with camels, 30 miles a day and without difficulty in obtaining horses and provisions.[91] For weapons, on the other hand, the Mongols clearly relied on the Russians; it seemed that the Mongol deputation in Saint Petersburg had ordered, in 1911, 5,000 old pattern rifles, 500 of which had been delivered to Urga in 1912[92] and the Russians had always supplied three batteries of quick-firing guns and twenty machine guns.[93]

The Russo-Mongol agreement of November 3, 1912 and the Mongolian delegation in Saint Petersburg

On November 3, 1912 (October 21 of the Russian calendar) Russia and Mongolia signed an agreement of friendship and trade in Urga.[94] The French translation of the text, based on the Chinese version and printed in H. Triepel, *Nouveau Recueil Général de Traités et autres actes relatifs aux rapports de droit international*, Troisiéme Série, Tome VII, Leipzig 1913, states that:

> Pour permettre à la Mongolie de conserver sa situation actuelle d'indépendance, la Mongolie a le droit de former une armée nationale, et le gouvernement chinois ne pourra envoyer en Mongolie ni soldats ni colons.

Anyway, according to the German translation of the Russian text printed in the same book:

> Die kaiserlich russische Regierung erweist der Mongolei ihre Hilfe bei der Aufrechterhaltung der von ihr eingeführten autonomen Ordnung wie auch des Rechts, ihr nationales Heer zu unterhalten und nicht zuzulassen, dass ihr Territorium von chinesischen Truppen betreten und von Chinesen kolonisiert werde.

Russia thus recognized Mongolia – although its independence was recognized only in Chinese – and also guaranteed itself a long series of rights and privileges aimed at strengthening its political, economic and commercial role, as well as the status of most favored nation in Mongolia. In fact, the second point of the document reads: 'Aucune puissance ne peut avoir en Mongolie des droits et privilèges plus grands que ceux des Russes'. Furthermore, according to the third point:

> Si le gouvernement mongol estime nécessaire de faire un traité avec le gouvernement chinois ou un autre gouvernement étranger, ce traité devra d'abord être approuvé par la Russie et rien, dans ce traité, ne pourra être en opposition avec le présent traité.

Furthermore, as seen, according to the German translation of the Russian text, Russia was directly committed to the protection of Mongolian autonomy.

A few weeks after the agreement, in January 1913, a Mongolian delegation of sixteen went to Saint Petersburg as a sign of gratitude for the Russian recognition of independence.[95] The mission was led by Handdorj, the Mongolian foreign minister,[96] a pro-Russian man, and was accompanied by Yakov Parfent'yevich Shishmarëv, the Russian consul-general in Urga.[97] Also Tserenchimed – who held the post of minister of the interior[98] – and Haysan Bayantömöriyn joined the mission.[99] On January 23 the delegation was received by the tsar in Tsarskoye Selo and the next day by the minister of war, General Vladimir Sukhomlinov, to whom the Mongolian representatives asked for modern weapons and instructors to defend themselves from the Chinese, obtaining positive responses from both Sukhomlinov and the tsar.[100] The position of the Mongols with respect to the extent of their territories was different from that of Great Britain and Russia. In a conversation with the editor of the Russian newspaper *Novoye Vremya*, published on January 31, 1913, the members of the delegation argued that their idea of Mongolia coincided with all the lands inhabited by Mongols and, therefore, also Inner Mongolia had to fall under the authority of the new state and the task of the mission was also to persuade the Russians on this point.[101] However, the Mongols had not answered the question of whether they had succeeded.[102]

The Mongols also asked for a meeting with the ambassadors of France and Great Britain, allies of Russia in the Triple Entente, but not with those of Germany and Austria-Hungary, surprising Sazonov with their knowledge of European affairs.[103] Both the British and French ambassadors, however, declined the invitation.[104] At the center, of course, was the question of the recognition of Mongolian independence, to which the British preferred the word 'autonomy' under the Chinese suzerainty.[105] This position was formally shared by Sazonov in his conversations with the British ambassador, citing, as an explanation of the Mongolian claims, the lack of distinction, in the

Mongolian language, between the term «autonomy» and the term «independence».[106] Mongolia had asked Great Britain to recognize its independence and to enter into a trade treaty with a letter from the Mongolian Foreign Board addressed to the Foreign Office and delivered to the British consulate in Harbin on December 13, 1912.[107] The letter officially announced that the bogd haan was now the monarch of the country.[108] 'I do not propose that any reply should be made to this communication' had written Edward Grey to Buchanan in Saint Petersburg.[109] The Mongolian foreign minister had also approached Yüan Shih-k'ai's Political Advisor Morrison to have the address of the British diplomat Charles William Campbell in London to help him obtain London's recognition and also to hire Campbell himself as an advisor.[110] A doubt regarding the effects of independence was related to the economic effects. It was not clear at this point of the status of British rights with respect to Outer Mongolia. The country's independence had not yet been recognized by the United Kingdom, nor of course by the newly formed Republic of China.[111] The British Board of Trade therefore wondered whether the rights acquired by the previous treaties signed with China should be considered unaltered, considering Outer Mongolia still as part of the Republic.[112] Alongside the issue of Mongolia's international status, the British refusal to meet the delegation was explained by not wanting to create unnecessary misunderstandings with Russia regarding British interests in the region,[113] but this aspect will be analyzed more carefully later. The economic and commercial question was secondary; there was instead a political and geopolitical point, a broader reading of the Mongolian question for the interests of the British Empire in Tibet. The mission in Saint Petersburg ended in March, after obtaining an agreement for the Russian supply of ammunition for the Mongolian army.[114]

The Tibetan-Mongolian mutual recognition and the Tibetan delegation in Saint Petersburg

On January 17, 1913, the Russian foreign minister delivered to George Buchanan a memorandum about an agreement, signed in the name of the dalai lama by Dorzhiyev, with which Urga and Lhasa mutually recognized their independence from Peking.[115] The copy of this treaty was then delivered by the Russian government to Buchanan together with a dispatch from the Russian actual state councillor in Urga, Ivan Yakovlevich Korostovets.[116] The treaty was signed in Urga on January 11, 1913.[117] The 1912 Treaty with Russia was taken as a model for the Tibetan-Mongolian treaty.[118] The treaty consisted of just nine articles. In the first two articles the two rulers mutually recognized and approved the creation of the two states. Article 3, on the other hand, provided for cooperation between Urga and Lhasa in favor of Buddhism, while Article 4 ensured mutual help against external and internal dangers. Article 5 guaranteed support for travelers from one country to another, whether they were pilgrims or on a state visit. Article 6 guaranteed the continuation of mutual commercial relations as well as the openings of industrial plants.

By signing this treaty, both countries, therefore, openly rejected the concept of Chinese suzerainty, and reaffirmed their full independence in matters of foreign policy. In the preamble, Lhasa and Urga made clear to the world their liberation from the Manchu yoke, but also their separation from China. Western diplomats of the time expressed several doubts about the validity of the treaty: first of all, there was no formal authorization of Dorzhiyev – a Buryat and subject of the tsar – to sign a treaty in the name of the sovereign of Tibet.[119] Sazonov doubted that Dorzhiyev was legitimated in this sense[120] and Korostovets himself, in his dispatch from Urga, considered the signatories lacking legal authority, denying the treaty validity in terms of international law, but still recognizing its substance and also the usefulness of the agreement: China now had to witness the rapprochement between two leaders whose private relationship had been particularly difficult in the past.[121] In fact, it seems that the rje-btsun dam-pa did not like the popularity of the dalai lama during his stay in Mongolia. According to Zhwa-sgab-pa-dbang-phyug-bde-ldan, the rje-btsun dam-pa offended Thub-bstan-rgya-mtsho on various occasions, even forcing him to change his residence.[122] The dalai lama himself criticized the rje-btsun dam-pa in the meeting held in Peking with the prince of Sikkim, Srid-skyong-sprul-sku-rnam-rgyal.[123] Another interesting description comes from a report written by A. Rose, of the Embassy in Peking, after the conversation with Frans August Larson.[124] On March 10, 1913, Jordan sent the report to Sir Edward Grey.[125] The bogd haan,

> is described as a weak man, almost always intoxicated with the champagne which he obtains from France, owning a modern-furnished and luxurious palace, but preferring to sit on the carpets of his tent.

He was highly respected by lay and religious. He had a wife: Dondogdulam. A. Rose wrote:

> Larson describes her as a vigorous woman, with strong business instincts, and two shops of her own in Urga. She has not only induced the Lama Church to recognize her, but she has been granted the rank of a reincarnation, little, if any lower than that of the Bogdo himself. Larson considers her as a decided factor in the situation. It is interesting to know that she is the advocate of the Chinese cause in Urga.

The report is also interesting as a further source to see the military situation. According to the text, in Urga the Russians were training two thousand Mongol soldiers, four thousand were the reservists, while in the city there were six hundred Cossacks. The number of Chinese present in Haalgan was not clear: according to some there were 45,000 men, while Larson estimated them to be between ten and fifteen thousand. 'The Commander-in-Chief of the Mongol army' instead it is defined as a 'robber chief', an elderly opium addict who owed his popularity to raids during the Russo-Japanese War.

Formally, also for the British government 'in the absence of evidence as to the legal rights of the signatories,' the Tibetan-Mongolian agreement 'does not possess any political significance'.[126] However, Dorzhiyev had personally explained to Korostovets that the treaty was an idea of the dalai lama himself.[127] On February 10, 1913, the British ambassador to Peking, Sir John Jordan, communicated to Sir Edward Grey that

> [*i*]t appears that the Dalai Lama took the initiative in negotiating this compact which formally declares the separation from China and the independence of Thibet and Mongolia. The two States agree to uphold the Buddhist religion and to assist each other against external or internal dangers.[128]

Feeling doubtful, on March 9, 1913, the Government of India wrote to the secretary of state for India, Robert Crewe-Milnes:

> We think that, while we are waiting for text of agreement, political officer in Sikkim should be instructed to write to Dalai Lama informing him that His Majesty's Government, having heard a report that the agreement has been concluded, wish to know whether it was authorised by his Holiness, and, if so, what are the terms of the agreement.[129]

The political agent in Sikkim at the time was Charles Alfred Bell who, therefore, sent a communication of the British trade agent, the Anglo-Sikkimese[130] David Macdonald, according to whose sources, the dalai lama had not actually authorized to sign a treaty between the two countries:[131]

> I have the honour to state that the first-named person " Ku-char Tsan-shib Khen-chen Lob-sang Ngak-wang " is the notorious Buriat Dorjieff.

2. The second-named person " Dro-nyer Ngak-wang Chho-dzin " has been stationed at Urga to look after the many Thibetans who are residing there.

3. The third person " Ye-she-gyam-tso " is a monk official who is in charge of the bank belonging to the Dalai Lama at Urga.

4. The fourth person " Gen-dün-gyal-tsan " is a clerk to Ye-she-gyam-tso.

5. I learn on good authority, that the Dalai Lama has not authorised the above-named persons to sign a treaty between Thibet and Mongolia. Thibetans declare that the Mongolians are the disciples of his Holiness the Dalai Lama and his Serenity the Tashi Lama and profess the Buddhist religion. The Dalai Lama when visiting Mongolia founded the bank and appointed the persons above-named.[132]

At the same time, however, Charles Alfred Bell wrote to the Government of India:

Mr. Macdonald thinks that the Dalai Lama has not authorised the so-called plenipotentiaries on behalf of Thibet to sign the agreement. However, this may be, there can be no doubt that such an agreement would be welcome to the Dalai Lama in the present position of affairs.[133]

Certainly, at the Foreign Office, however, the treaty not only could not be ignored, but was considered a fact, the concrete document that openly linked – via Mongolia – Lhasa and Saint Petersburg:

Recent information from Peking and India has tended to confirm the impression that a large increase of Russian influence in Thibet is to be apprehended in the near future, while the course of events since 1907, culminating in the practical acquisition of independence by the Thibetans, and in the conclusion of treaties by Mongolia with Russia and Thibet respectively, would seem to have distinctly altered the *status quo* in Thibet, and both Russian and British relations towards that country.[134]

As Alex McKay rightly writes: 'The Tibet-Mongol treaty was one of many contemporary factors which indicated that the changes in Tibet required new international agreements'.[135] In Morrison's aforementioned letter to Dudley D. Braham of February 1913, Yüan Shih-k'ai's adviser wrote about the positions of Saint Petersburg and London with respect to the treaty between Urga and Lhasa:

> Russian action in Mongolia does not, I imagine, directly concern Great Britain, but indirectly it is of very great consequence indeed, for you must remember that Mongols who live on the Mongolian border which borders on the province of Chihli and on the border of Manchuria have made it known, no doubt from interested motives, that Great Britain and Russia are acting in accord in protecting Mongolia and Tibet and that these two great Nations are privy to the Mongolian Tibetan agreement. Statements made at rare intervals in the House of Commons denying these suggestions can do little to counteract the evidence furnished by the Mongols themselves.[136]

The Russians took two paths to extend their influence over Tibet. Firstly, Russian weapons had been supplied to the Tibetans to help repel the Chinese invasion in the last period of the Ch'ing dynasty.[137] According to Charles Alfred Bell:

> It is also indubitable that the agreement, if acted on, may prove a source of considerable embarrassment to us, for Mongolian assistance under article 4 brings appreciably nearer the danger of Russian intervention in Thibet.[138]

Secondly, the role of the Tibetan-Mongol religious bond was fundamental. This connection was materially realized in the monasteries, the focal points of the political, legal, and economic system of Tibet. Indeed, according to Sir Walter Langley:

> The monastic influence is being exerted even more energetically, the similarity of religious language and the solidarity and unity existing between the monastic establishments in both countries enabling the Mongolian monks, who are apparently migrating in large numbers at the present time into Thibetan monasteries, to act with considerable effect as the apostles of Russian ideas and influence.[139]

With no Chinese authority able to manage Tibetan issues formally (however completely inefficient – as seen – on a practical level), even the section relating to Tibet of the Anglo-Russian agreement of 1907 was put into crisis. The collapse of the Ch'ing dynasty and the full independence of Tibet and Mongolia crumbled, in the Far East, the political substratum of what was established in 1907. As already seen in the previous pages, the agreement had recognized Peking's suzerainty over Lhasa, while the British and Russians had to refrain from any interference in the internal administration of Tibet, in addition to the prohibition to send their representatives to the capital or to aspire to any concessions. Considering what has been explained so far, however, were these impediments still working for Russia? It was necessary for London to re-discuss the matter. The problem, however, was that – as we have seen – the 1907 agreement was articulated through a series of mutual exchanges and delicate balances which also affected Persia and Afghanistan. Some provisions of the agreement had not yet been implemented and furthermore the Afghan emir ☐abīballāh Khān had not recognized the Anglo-Russian Agreement.[140] Therefore it was necessary to proceed with extreme caution with respect to a new negotiation on Tibet to avoid a Russian counterproposal on Afghanistan.[141] Indeed, despite visiting India in early 1907, the emir of Afghanistan was not informed of the 1907 agreement until after the signing and this discourtesy – which the Viceroy of India, the Earl of Minto, had sought to avoid – had led the emir to reject it.[142] The Russians, however, in 1908, had confirmed, through foreign minister Izvolskiy, the validity of the agreement, regardless of the position of the emir.[143]

One way to go could be to link the acceptance of the Russo-Mongol agreement of 1912 by the British Government to a redefinition of the agreements on Tibet, without the Russian side asking for a '*quid pro quo*':

> Sir E. Grey would suggest, therefore, that in replying to the Russian Government's request for a favourable reception of the recent Russo-Mongolian Treaty, the whole situation should be frankly laid before them, and a discussion invited of the bearing of this treaty upon the position of Thibet, but that in doing this His Majesty's Government should not at first ask directly for a revision of the convention, but should merely invite the Russian Government to a discussion of the situation in the hope that by so doing a request for a *quid pro quo* might be avoided.[144]

Another important piece in the construction of these new geopolitical balances in Asia was also the arrival in Saint Petersburg, in February 1913, shortly after the arrival of the Mongolian mission, of a Tibetan delegation, with gifts for the tsar from the dalai lama.¹⁴⁵ Fifteen Tibetan boys who were to study in Russian schools also came with the delegation.¹⁴⁶ Dorzhiyev's goal, who arrived in the Russian capital before the arrival of the rest of the delegation, was to push Russia to act as mediator between Lhasa and London, 'the Thibetans being much incensed with England at the proposal made by her to China in regard to Thibet and the possibility of a Chinese protectorate'.¹⁴⁷ Dorzhiyev, however, was officially considered a subject of the tsar and, therefore, could not, according to the Russians, represent the dalai lama.¹⁴⁸ Furthermore, the letter from the ruler of Tibet to the tsar, asking for the establishment of an Anglo-Russian protectorate on the Land of the Snows, could not be taken into consideration either by London or by Saint Petersburg as formally in contrast with the Anglo-Russian Agreement of 1907.¹⁴⁹

Anyway, the earthquake triggered by the Hsin-hai Revolution had opened new scenarios that authorized the British to move diplomatically to try to redefine the order and balance of power in High Asia.

Urga to the Russians, Lhasa to the British

In September 1912 G. E. Morrison wrote to the editor of *The Morning Post*, Howell Arthur Gwynne:

> Look also at the way the Government are acting in connection with Tibet. Major W. F. O'Connor, who was with Younghusband in the Tibetan Expedition, desires the post of Consul General in Lhasa. I think it would be an excellent thing if we were to have a Consul General in Lhasa. I have always thought so. Presumably Russia will also have a Consul General, each Consulate having an official guard of its own Nationals. It would be a great advantage to our prestige in Nepal and on the frontier of India to know that there is a powerful British escort stationed in Lhasa. Russia is at present working for the autonomy of Mongolia. Japan is working for the recognition of her special rights in Manchuria. It has been an immense advantage to both Russia and Japan that England should seize this opportunity to interfere in the international administration of Tibet. [...] We have informed the Chinese that we will not recognise the Republic unless they have first signed with us an agreement regarding Tibet. We have thus convinced every Chinese that the policy of Japan in Manchuria, and of Russia in Mongolia is the guide of British

policy in Tibet. We are to do in Tibet as those two friendly powers are doing in Manchuria and in Mongolia.[150]

The real British fear, however, remained that of a Tibet under Russian control and the fate of Mongolia alone was of little interest to London as far as this did not interfere with the defense of the northern border of the Raj. Grey himself had confided to the German ambassador in London, Paul Metternich, at the beginning of 1912, in the still poorly defined moments of the birth of the Republic of China, that if the Russians wanted to transform Mongolia into a buffer state between them and China, the British wished the same for Tibet, although maintaining Chinese suzerainty:

> I said that the Russians had long wished Mongolia to be at least semi-autonomous, and a sort of buffer State between their territory and China proper. I did not think that they had departed from this policy. As for Thibet, we were not interfering with it, though our desire was similar to the Russian wish, as we should like to have Thibet as a buffer State under the suzerainty of China.[151]

But this fear of Mongolia as a springboard to Tibet existed: 'The situation is, in fact, very similar to that of 1903' explained the India Office in March 1913, with the notable difference, however, of the new attitude, certainly more favorable to Britain, of the dalai lama, 'now friendly, or, at all events, not yet openly hostile'.[152] Independence, however, left Tibet at the mercy of another power and if the country, as they wrote from the India Office to the Foreign Office, 'must be subject to some influence', the only conceivable influence then was British influence.[153] Two different options to achieve that goal in relation to Mongolia were outlined. On the one hand, there was the idea of Lord Crewe, secretary of state for India, who felt it necessary to meet the Mongolian delegation in Saint Petersburg, 'obtaining a footing in Mongolia which might prove of great value in future dealings with the Russian Government':

> The Marquess of Crewe fully appreciates the general grounds of policy on which His Majesty's Ambassador was instructed in Sir E. Grey's telegram No. 96 of the 4th February last not to receive the Mission. But he would submit for the consideration of the Secretary of State for Foreign Affairs that, by holding entirely aloof at the present juncture, His Majesty's Government may lose an opportunity, which is probably unlikely to recur, of obtaining a footing in Mongolia which might prove of great value in future dealings with the Russian Government. Stress was laid by Sir J. Jordan in his telegram

No. 64 of the 6th March, 1913, on the close connection of Mongolia with Thibet, and Lord Crewe cannot but fear that, if Russia and its subjects come to enjoy by treaty or practice a predominating influence in Mongolia as compared with other foreign States and their subjects, a revival of Russian influence in Thibet, which it has been the policy of His Majesty's Government for the last ten years to counteract, must inevitably follow.[154]

The position of Grey was different. Not that there were no clear openings on the Mongolian side to His British Majesty's Government. The Mongolian prince Haysan Bayantömöriyn, according to a letter sent to Morrison and written by T. A. Rustad – a Norwegian in Mongolia on behalf of the British and American Tobacco Company – saw in the British the possibility of limiting Russian interests.[155] According to Rustad:

Hai-Shun-Gung is the only man of the new Mongol government that realy [sic] does anything. The rest of them just drink and let things go as they best can, and leaves everything to Hai-Shun-Gung. He takes no salary and spends his own money. He wants the Mongols to be treated like human beings that is all he works for he says.[156]

In 1912, as explained by Rustad, Haysan Bayantömöriyn had decided to lease his gold-rich territories to any company that had the backing of the British government, in exchange for only 10% of the profits.[157] Mongolia was – and is – particularly rich from a mining point of view: the last amban had looked for gold mines, but his experts had been regularly placed on the wrong paths by the local guides.[158]

More realistically, however, the Foreign Office realized that it was not possible to undermine the Russians from that position that they were slowly building in Urga and, above all, the possibility of competing for a commercial primacy seemed distinctly impracticable – despite the possibility of an 'equal commercial treatment' – with Russia in the country and thus try to limit Russian influence on Tibet.[159] Therefore, the strategy had to use the Russian role in Mongolia as a pretext 'to justify any British action that it may be desirable to take in Thibet'.[160] Already on November 16, 1912, therefore a few days after the Russo-Mongol agreement, Jordan had written to Grey from Peking:

An opportunity of negotiating a revision of our Thibetan arrangement with Russia would seem to be presented by the conclusion of the recent Russo-Mongolian Agreement, which has caused much perturbation in China.[161]

The most adequate means, according to the Foreign Office, to gain influence over Tibet was to deal with the Chinese and Tibetans in India, perhaps through Nepal, and not get lost in a vain race with Saint Petersburg in the Mongolian grassland.[162]

This explains the true dimension of the importance that Mongolia held for the fate of the British Empire: a sort of exchange to peacefully redefine with the Russians what the 1907 Agreement had sanctioned so rigidly. Urga to the Russians and Lhasa to the British. Saint Petersburg was not to be confronted even on Mongolian territory, but a barter to be enforced on the diplomatic table was far more advantageous for both. For this reason it was of great importance to specify British lack of interest in Mongolia in the clearest way: in the first place by refusing to meet the Mongolian delegation in Saint Petersburg, a meeting that would have only fueled 'the suspicion of Russia and the hostility of China with very little compensating advantage'.[163] In short, a much cheaper and more reasonable political and diplomatic action that had convinced, without too many problems, even Lord Crewe, who thus renounced the meeting between Buchanan and the delegation, happy to know that also Grey understood the importance of continuing to exclude the Russians from the Land of Snows.[164]

The Simla conference, between 1913 and 1914, therefore, had to reshape the status of Tibet and at the same time undermine, with due caution, the results of the Anglo-Russian Agreement of 1907 regarding Lhasa. To do this it was therefore also necessary to obtain Russian consent. On May 23, 1913, Grey communicated to his ambassador in Saint Petersburg about the British decision to reach an agreement with the Chinese Tibetan governments on Tibet

> I HAVE to inform your Excellency that His Majesty's Government have decided to invite the Chinese and Thibetan Governments to a joint conference in India with a view to arriving at a settlement of the Thibetan question.[165]

The goal was to have Peking and Lhasa recognize Chinese suzerainty over Tibet and therefore the internal autonomy of the country.[166] The British and Chinese had to pledge to respect territorial integrity and Peking could not colonize Tibet or send soldiers to the Roof of the World, with the exception of no more than three hundred men as an escort for the Chinese representative in Lhasa.[167] Additionally, China was to be exempt from the Trade Regulations commitments of April 20, 1908, but responsibility passed directly to the Tibetans.[168] According to Grey and the British government, London was entitled to deal with the issue by the Anglo-Russian Convention of 1907 itself since the Saint Petersburg agreement did not concern the 1906 agreement made by China and Great Britain in 1906 and Article 1 committed the two countries to implement the Anglo-Tibetan Agreement of 1904:

> I am to state that His Majesty's Government base their action upon their rights under article 2 of the Anglo-Russian Convention of 1907, which excepts from the operation of the convention the engagements entered into by Great Britain and China in article 1 of the Anglo-Chinese Convention of 1906, among which is that "to take at all times such steps as may be necessary to secure the due fulfilment of the terms specified in the Anglo-Thibetan Agreement of 1904".[169]

The British government would inform the Russian government on the progress of the negotiations, but Grey preferred not to enter into negotiations with Saint Petersburg immediately.[170] The secretary of state for Foreign Affairs preferred to wait first for the progress of the negotiations with Tibet and China:

> If the negotiations in India result in the conclusion of a satisfactory tripartite agreement, it will probably be necessary to approach the Russian Government again with a view to securing sufficient freedom of action to enable His Majesty's Government to ensure that the agreement is carried out.[171]

Endnotes

1 Монгол Улсын Үндэсний статистикийн хороо (https://www.nso.mn).

2 On their history see O. LATTIMORE, *Pivot of Asia: Sinkiang and the Inner Asian Frontiers of China and Russia*, Boston 1950, pp. 134-137.

3 On the history of the region see K. N. MAKSIMOV, *Kalmykia in Russia's Past and Present National Policies and Administrative System*, translated by A. Yastrzhembska, Budapest – New York 2008.

4 Foreign Office, Historical Section, Peace Handbook, *Mongolia*, No. 68, London 1920, p. 13.

5 United Nations Department of Economic and Social Affairs/Population Division, *World Population Prospects: The 2010 Revision*, Vol. I: Comprehensive Tables, New York 2011, p. 88.

6 *The Correspondence of G. E. Morrison* 2013, n. 574, G. E. Morrison to D. D. Braham, February 18, 1913, p. 90.

7 A. BAUSANI, *Religion in Iran: From Zoroaster to Baha'u'llah*, translated by J. M. Marchesi, New York 2000, p. 248.

8 C. BELL, *Tibet Past and Present*, Oxford 1924, p. 106.

9 *British Documents on the Origins of the War: 1898–1914*, edited by G. P. Gooch and H. Temperley, Vol. IX: The Balkan Wars – Part I: The Prelude ; The Tripoli War, London 1933, p. 804.

10 TNA, FO 535/16, No. 137, Foreign Office to India Office, March 17, 1913, p. 98.

11 TNA, FO 535/16, No. 137, Foreign Office to India Office, March 17, 1913, p. 99.

12 TNA, FO 535/16, No. 137, Foreign Office to India Office, March 17, 1913, p. 99.

13 See the entries «'Hut'ukht'u» (No. 589) and «Cheptsundampa 'Hut'ukht'u» (No. 596) in: W. F. MAYERS, *The Chinese Government: a manual of Chinese*

titles, categorically arranged and explained with an appendix, second edition with additions by G. M. H. Playfair, Shanghai – Hongkong – Yokohama – London 1886; see also P. SCHWIEGER, *The Dalai Lama and the Emperor of China: A Political History of the Tibetan Institution of Reincarnation*, New York 2015, pp. 35-36.

14 See: K. SAGASTER, *The History of Buddhism among the Mongols*, in: *The Spread of Buddhism*, edited by A. Heirman and S. P. Bumbacher, Leiden – Boston 2007, p. 406; W. HEISSIG, *The Religions of Mongolia*, translated by G. Samuel, Berkeley – Los Angeles 1980, p. 31).

15 On this see: A. BAREJA-STARZYŃSKA, *The Mongolian Incarnation of Jo nang pa Tāranātha Kun dga' snying po: Öndör Gegeen Zanabazar Blo bzang bstan pa'i rgyal mtshan (1635-1723): A case study of the Tibeto-Mongolian Relationship*, in: The Tibet Journal, Vol. 34/35, No. 3/2, Special Issue: The Earth Ox Papers, Autumn 2009-Summer 2010, pp. 243-261; F. SANDERS, *The Life and Lineage of the Ninth Khalkha Jetsun Dampa Khutukhtu of Urga*, in: Central Asiatic Journal, Vol. 45, No. 2, 2001, pp. 278-286.

16 On this and for a history of the national symbols of independent Mongolia see J. BOLDBAATAR – C. HUMPHREY, *The Process of Creation of National Symbols and Their Adoption in the 1992 Constitution of Mongolia*, in: Inner Asia, Vol. 9, No. 1, 2007, pp. 3-22.

17 C. KAPLONSKI, *Truth, History and Politics in Mongolia: Memory of Heroes*, London 2004, p. 29. For a biography of Zanabazar see S. ICHINNOROV, *The biography of Öndör Gegeen*, translated by Baasanjav, in: *The History of Mongolia*, Vol. III, edited by D. Sneath and C. Kaplonski, Folkestone 2010, pp. 674-682.

18 A. ANDREYEV, *Soviet Russia and Tibet: the debacle of secret diplomacy, 1918-1930s*, Leiden 2003, p. 54. On the Mongol declaration of independence of 1911 see M. TACHIBANA, *The 1911 Revolution and "Mongolia": Independence, Constitutional Monarchy, or Republic*, in: Journal of Contemporary East Asia Studies, 3:1, 2014, pp. 69-90.

19 TACHIBANA 2014, p. 72.

20 TACHIBANA 2014, p. 73.

21 U. ONON – D. PRITCHATT, *Asia's First Modern Revolution: Mongolia proclaims its Independence in 1911*, Leiden 1989, p. 16. The translation of *Ih*

Mongol Uls provided by Urgunge Onon and Derrick Pritchatt in their book is 'great Mongolian nation'.

22 TNA, FO 405/208, No. 137, Sir J. Jordan to Sir Edward Grey, January 14, 1912, p. 165.

23 T. NAKAMI, *Mongolia from the Eighteenth Century to 1919*, in: *History of Civilizations of Central Asia*, pp. 348-349.

24 L. PETECH, *Asia Centrale*, in: *Le civiltà dell'Oriente. Storia, letteratura, religioni, filosofia, scienze e arte*, Vol. I: Storia, under the direction of G. Tucci, Firenze – Roma 1965, p. 948.

25 PETECH, *Asia Centrale* 1965, p. 948; P. C. PERDUE, *China Marches West: The Qing Conquest of Central Eurasia*, Cambridge – London 2005, pp. 175-176.

26 PETECH, *Asia Centrale* 1965, p. 956.

27 PETECH, *Asia Centrale* 1965, pp. 956-957; S. K. SONI, *Mongolia-China Relations: Modern and Contemporary Times*, New Delhi 2006, p. 30; M. LAN, China's "New Administration" in Mongolia, in: *Mongolia in the Twentieth Century: Landlocked Cosmopolitan*, edited by S. Kotkin and B. A. Elleman, Armonk – London 1999, p. 40.

28 T. E. EWING, *Between the Hammer and the Anvil? Chinese and Russian Policies in Outer Mongolia 1911-1921*, Uralic and Altaic Series, Vols 138-139, London – New York 2006, pp. 23-24.

29 S. K. SONI, *Mongolia-Russia Relations (Kiakhta to Vladivostok)*, New Delhi 2002, pp. 27-28.

30 TNA, FO 535/16, Enclosure in No. 184, Notes by Lieutenant Binsteed on the Mongolian Situation, March 20, 1913, p. 165. The Russian name of the city, Kyakhta, was adopted in this work. Hiagt is the Mongolian name, the Buryat one is Kyaagta and in Chinese is known as Ch'ia-k'o-t'u 恰克圖. In English it is often transcribed as Kyakhta or Klakhta. Kyakhta is today in Russia, in the Republic of Buryatia. In this work the Russian name of the city was adopted: Kyakhta.

31 TNA, FO 535/16, Enclosure in No. 184, Notes by Lieutenant Binsteed on the Mongolian Situation, March 20, 1913, p. 165.

32 ONON – PRITCHATT 1989, p. 5.

33 LAN 1999, p. 47.

34 *The Correspondence of G. E. Morrison* 2013, n. 554, T. A. Rustad to G. E. Morrison, November 5, 1912, pp. 48-49.

35 *The Correspondence of G. E. Morrison* 2013, n. 574, G. E. Morrison to D. D. Braham, February 18, 1913, pp. 90-91.

36 *The Correspondence of G. E. Morrison* 2013, n. 550, G. E. Morrison to C. W. Campbell, October 24, 1912, p. 41.

37 PETECH, *Asia Centrale* 1965, p. 956.

38 TNA, FO 535/16, Enclosure in No. 184, Notes by Lieutenant Binsteed on the Mongolian Situation, March 20, 1913, p. 165.

39 TNA, FO 535/16, Enclosure in No. 184, Notes by Lieutenant Binsteed on the Mongolian Situation, March 20, 1913, p. 165.

40 TNA, FO 405/208, No. 137, Sir J. Jordan to Sir Edward Grey, January 14, 1912, p. 165.

41 TNA, FO 405/208, No. 137, Sir J. Jordan to Sir Edward Grey, January 14, 1912, p. 165.

42 TNA, FO 535/16, Enclosure in No. 184, Notes by Lieutenant Binsteed on the Mongolian Situation, March 20, 1913, p. 165.

43 TNA, FO 535/16, Enclosure in No. 184, Notes by Lieutenant Binsteed on the Mongolian Situation, March 20, 1913, p. 167.

44 TNA, FO 535/13, No. 48 A, Government of India to Viscount Morley. – (Communicated by India Office, March 21.), March 19, 1910, p. 44*; TNA, FO 535/13, No. 48 C, Government of India to Viscount Morley. – (Communicated by India Office, March 22.), March 22, 1910, p. 44*.

45 YA HAN-CHANG 牙含章 1984, p. 231. Ya's source for the transcript of the plan of Wen Tsung-yao 溫宗堯 is: CHU CHIN-P'ING 朱錦屏, *Hsi tsang liu shih nien ta shih chi* 西藏六十年大事記.

46 EWING 2006, p. 18.

47 I. V. NAUMOV, *The History of Siberia*, edited by D. N. Collins, London – New York 2006, p. 123.

48 C. R. BAWDEN, *The Modern History of Mongolia*, London – New York 2009, p. 50; EWING 2006, pp. 16-17.

49 EWING 2006, p. 17.

50 M. KHODARKOVSKY, *Non-Russian subjects*, in: *The Cambridge History of Russia*, Vol. I: From Early Rus' to 1689, edited by M. Perrie, Cambridge 2006, p. 528. The complete text of the treaty (in French) is in J. B. DU HALDE, *Description géographique, historique, chronologique, politique, et physique de l'empire de la Chine et de la Tartarie chinoise, enrichie des Cartes générales et particulieres de ces Pays, de la Carte générale et des Cartes particulieres du Thibet, & de la Corée ; & ornée d'un grand nombre de Figures & de Vignettes gravées en tailledouce*, Tome Quatrième, La Haye 1736, pp. 242-245.

51 EWING 2006, p. 18.

52 EWING 2006, p. 18.

53 EWING 2006, p. 18.

54 EWING 2006, p. 18-19.

55 EWING 2006, p. 18.

56 TNA, FO 405/208, No. 48, Sir G. Buchanan to Sir Edward Grey, January 11, 1912, p. 52. English translation of the communiqué: TNA, FO 405/208, Enclosure in No. 66, Official Communiqué from the Ministry of Foreign Affairs, published in the "Official Messenger" dated December 29, 1911 (January 11), 1912, pp. 99-100.

57 TNA, FO 405/208, No. 56, Sir G. Buchanan to Sir Edward Grey, January 14, 1912, p. 57.

58 TNA, FO 405/208, No. 48, Sir G. Buchanan to Sir Edward Grey, January 11, 1912, p. 52; TNA, FO 405/208, Enclosure in No. 66, Official Communiqué from the Ministry of Foreign Affairs, published in the "Official Messenger" dated December 29, 1911 (January 11), 1912, p. 100.

59 TNA, FO 405/208, No. 56, Sir G. Buchanan to Sir Edward Grey, January 14, 1912, p. 57.

60 TNA, FO 405/208, No. 56, Sir G. Buchanan to Sir Edward Grey, January 14, 1912, p. 57.

61 TNA, FO 405/208, No. 137, Sir J. Jordan to Sir Edward Grey, January 14, 1912, p. 165.

62 TNA, FO 405/208, No. 137, Sir J. Jordan to Sir Edward Grey, January 14, 1912, p. 166.

63 TNA, FO 405/208, No. 215, Sir J. Jordan to Sir Edward Grey, January 29, 1912, p. 235. The source of the British ambassador is Mr. Sly, the British consul in Harbin. Man-chou-li is known in English as Manchuria Station and in Mongolian as Manjuur.

64 TNA, FO 405/208, No. 356, Sir J. Jordan to Sir Edward Grey, February 20, 1912, p. 330.

65 TNA, FO 405/208, No. 356, Sir J. Jordan to Sir Edward Grey, February 20, 1912, p. 330.

66 TNA, FO 405/208, No. 356, Sir J. Jordan to Sir Edward Grey, February 20, 1912, p. 331.

67 Current capital of the Hei-lung-chiang province (Chinese: *Ha-êrh-pin* 哈爾濱).

68 TNA, FO 405/208, No. 356, Sir J. Jordan to Sir Edward Grey, February 20, 1912, p. 331.

69 TNA, FO 405/208, Enclosure in No. 434, Acting Consul Sly to Sir J. Jordan, February 28, 1912, p. 388. Consul Sly's source was the American consul who had heard from a doctor, Dr. Jee, about Man-chou-li's (TNA, FO 405/208, No. 215, Sir J. Jordan to Sir Edward Grey, January 29, 1912, p. 235).

70 TNA, FO 405/208, No. 356, Sir J. Jordan to Sir Edward Grey, February 20, 1912, p. 331.

71 TNA, FO 405/208, Enclosure in No. 434, Acting Consul Sly to Sir J. Jordan, February 28, 1912, p. 388.

72 TNA, FO 405/208, Enclosure in No. 434, Acting Consul Sly to Sir J. Jordan, February 28, 1912, p. 388.

73 TNA, FO 405/208, Enclosure in No. 460, Acting Consul Sly to Sir J. Jordan, March 5, 1912, pp. 438-439.

74 TNA, FO 405/208, Enclosure in No. 539, Acting Consul Sly to Sir J. Jordan, March 31, 1912, p. 529.

75 TNA, FO 405/208, No. 539, Sir J. Jordan to Sir Edward Grey, April 5, 1912, pp. 528-529.

76 The text of the secret Convention of June 21, 1910 (July 4, 1910, according to the Gregorian calendar) in French (original text) and English translation is in PRICE 1933, pp. 113-116.

77 TNA, FO 535/16, No. 165, Sir J. Jordan to Sir Edward Grey, March 14, 1913, p. 133; full text of the memorandum: TNA, FO 535/16, Enclosure 2 in No. 165, Memorandum on Military Situation in Mongolia, pp. 135-137.

78 The province of Chih-li no longer exists and Ch'ih-feng is located in the Inner Mongolia Autonomous Region.

79 TNA, FO 535/16, Enclosure 2 in No. 165, Memorandum on Military Situation in Mongolia, pp. 135-136.

80 The source in this case is George Ernest Morrison, TNA, FO 535/16, Enclosure 2 in No. 165, Memorandum on Military Situation in Mongolia, p. 136.

81 The source in this case is George Ernest Morrison, TNA, FO 535/16, Enclosure 2 in No. 165, Memorandum on Military Situation in Mongolia, p. 136.

82 The source in this case is George Ernest Morrison, TNA, FO 535/16, Enclosure 2 in No. 165, Memorandum on Military Situation in Mongolia, p. 136.

83 The source in this case is George Ernest Morrison, TNA, FO 535/16, Enclosure 2 in No. 165, Memorandum on Military Situation in Mongolia, p. 136.

84 Jehol (Je-ho 熱河), today known as Ch'eng-te 承德, in the current province of Ho-pei.

85 The source in this case is George Ernest Morrison, TNA, FO 535/16, Enclosure 2 in No. 165, Memorandum on Military Situation in Mongolia, p. 136.

86 In Chinese: Chang-chia-k'ou 张家口. It is in historical Inner Mongolia, today in the province of Ho-pei. In English it is normally transcribed as Kalgan.

87 Ta-t'ung is in Shan-hsi.

88 TNA, FO 535/16, Enclosure 2 in No. 165, Memorandum on Military Situation in Mongolia, p. 136.

89 TNA, FO 535/16, Enclosure 2 in No. 165, Memorandum on Military Situation in Mongolia, p. 136.

90 TNA, FO 535/16, Enclosure 2 in No. 165, Memorandum on Military Situation in Mongolia, p. 136.

91 The source in this case is Frans August Larson, TNA, FO 535/16, Enclosure 2 in No. 165, Memorandum on Military Situation in Mongolia, pp. 136-137.

92 The source in this case is Lieutenant Binsteed, TNA, FO 535/16, Enclosure 2 in No. 165, Memorandum on Military Situation in Mongolia, p. 137.

93 The source in this case is George Ernest Morrison, TNA, FO 535/16, Enclosure 2 in No. 165, Memorandum on Military Situation in Mongolia, p. 137.

94 Full text (German translation of the Russian text and French translation of the Chinese version): H. TRIEPEL, *Nouveau Recueil Général de Traités et autres actes relatifs aux rapports de droit international*, Troisiéme Série, Tome VII, Leipzig 1913, pp. 11-17. Since I could not find the original texts, I had to rely on the translations.

95 TNA, Sir G. Buchanan to Sir Edward Grey, January 13, 1913, FO 535/16, No. 23, p. 13.

96 TNA, FO 535/16, Sir G. Buchanan to Sir Edward Grey, January 13, 1913, No. 23, p. 13; BAWDEN 2009, p. 194.

97 TNA, FO 535/16, Sir G. Buchanan to Sir Edward Grey, January 13, 1913, No. 23, p. 13.

98 TACHIBANA 2014, p. 73.

99 BAWDEN 2009, p. 194.

100 TNA, FO 535/16, No. 50, Sir G. Buchanan to Sir Edward Grey, January 26, 1913, p. 44. In this regard, the tsar himself had already expressed his agreement, TNA, FO 535/16, No. 50, Sir G. Buchanan to Sir Edward Grey, January 26, 1913, p. 44.

101 TNA, FO 535/16, No. 61, Sir G. Buchanan to Sir Edward Grey, January 31, 1913, p. 50.

102 TNA, FO 535/16, No. 61, Sir G. Buchanan to Sir Edward Grey, January 31, 1913, p. 50.

103 TNA, FO 535/16, No. 82, Sir G. Buchanan to Sir Edward Grey, February 5, 1913, p. 61.

104 TNA, FO 535/16, No. 82, Sir G. Buchanan to Sir Edward Grey, February 5, 1913, p. 61; TNA, FO 535/16, No. 136, Sir G. Buchanan to Sir Edward Grey, March 13, 1913, p. 98.

105 TNA, FO 535/16, No. 82, Sir G. Buchanan to Sir Edward Grey, February 5, 1913, p. 61.

106 TNA, FO 535/16, No. 82, Sir G. Buchanan to Sir Edward Grey, February 5, 1913, p. 61.

107 TNA, FO 405/211, Enclosure in No. 28, Mongolian Foreign Board to the British Foreign Office, p. 25.

108 TNA, FO 405/211, Enclosure in No. 28, Mongolian Foreign Board to the British Foreign Office, p. 25.

109 TNA, FO 405/211, No. 52, Sir Edward Grey to Sir G. Buchanan, January 16, 1913, p. 60.

110 *The Correspondence of G. E. Morrison* 2013, n. 574, G. E. Morrison to D. D. Braham, February 18, 1913, p. 91.

111 TNA, FO 535/16, No. 41, Board of Trade to Foreign Office, January 22, 1913, p. 28.

112 TNA, FO 535/16, No. 41, Board of Trade to Foreign Office, January 22, 1913, p. 28.

113 TNA, FO 535/16, No. 168, Foreign Office to India Office, March 29, 1913, p. 141.

114 TNA, FO 535/16, No. 136, Sir G. Buchanan to Sir Edward Grey, March 13, 1913, p. 98.

115 TNA, FO 535/16, No. 30, Sir G. Buchanan to Sir Edward Grey, January 17, 1913, p. 20.

116 TNA, FO 535/16, No. 88, Sir G. Buchanan to Sir Edward Grey, February 11, 1913, p. 66; TNA, FO 535/16, No. 88, Mongol-Thibetan Treaty, concluded at Urga December 29, 1912 (January 11, 1913), 1913, pp. 66-67; TNA, FO 535/16, Enclosure 2 in No. 88, Despatch from Actual State Councillor Korostovets, dated Urga, January 6 (19), 1913, pp. 67-68.

117 English translation of the treaty: TNA, FO 535/16, Enclosure 1 in No. 88, Mongol-Thibetan Treaty, concluded at Urga December 29, 1912 (January 11, 1913), 1913, pp. 66-67.

118 TNA, FO 535/16, Enclosure 2 in No. 88, Despatch from Actual State Councillor Korostovets, dated Urga, January 6 (19), 1913, p. 67. In the English translation of the dispatch in the Confidential Print there is an error in the dating, according to the Gregorian calendar, of the Russo-Mongol treaty: the treaty dates back to October 21, 1912, that is November 3, 1912, and not September 3, as indicated in the Confidential Print's document.

119 TNA, FO 535/16, No. 44, Foreign Office to India Office, January 24, 1913, p. 30.

120 TNA, FO 535/16, No. 80, Sir G. Buchanan to Sir Edward Grey, February 8, 1913, p. 60.

121 TNA, FO 535/16, Enclosure 2 in No. 88, Despatch from Actual State Councillor Korostovets, dated Urga, January 6 (19), 1913, pp. 67-68.

122 ZHWA SGAB PA DBANG PHYUG BDE LDAN, Vol. II 1976, pp. 135-136.

123 TNA, FO 535/12, Inclosure 1 in No. 7, Memorandum respecting an Interview between the Dalai Lama and the Maharaj Kumar of Sikkim, held at the Yellow Temple, Peking, on November 25, 1908, p. 9.

124 Full text of the report: TNA, FO 535/16, Enclosure in No. 164, Notes by Mr. Rose on Mongolian Affairs, pp. 131-133.

125 TNA, FO 535/16, No. 164, Sir J. Jordan to Sir Edward Grey, March 10, 1913, pp. 130-131.

126 TNA, FO 535/16, No. 130, Sir Edward Grey to Sir G. Buchanan, March 11, 1913, p. 94.

127 TNA, FO 535/16, Enclosure 2 in No. 88, Despatch from Actual State Councillor Korostovets, dated Urga, January 6 (19), 1913, p. 67.

128 TNA, FO 535/16, No. 112, Sir J. Jordan to Sir Edward Grey, February 10, 1913, p. 80.

129 TNA, FO 535/16, Enclosure in No. 129, Government of India to the Marquess of Crewe, March 9, 1913, p. 94.

130 His mother was a Lepcha, while his father was a Scottish planter. See MCKAY 1997, p. 44.

131 TNA, FO 535/16, Enclosure 2 in No. 255, British Trade Agent, Yatung, to the Political Officer, Sikkim, May 3, 1913, p. 255.

132 TNA, FO 535/16, Enclosure 2 in No. 255, British Trade Agent, Yatung, to the Political Officer, Sikkim, May 3, 1913, p. 255.

133 TNA, FO 535/16, Enclosure 1 in No. 255, Political Officer, Sikkim, to the Government of India, May 9, 1913, p. 255.

134 TNA, FO 535/16, No. 137, Foreign Office to India Office, March 17, 1913, p. 98.

135 MCKAY 1997, p. 56.

136 *The Correspondence of G. E. Morrison* 2013, n. 574, G. E. Morrison to D. D. Braham, February 18, 1913, p. 90.

137 TNA, FO 535/16, No. 137, Foreign Office to India Office, March 17, 1913, p. 99.

138 TNA, FO 535/16, Enclosure 1 in No. 255, Political Officer, Sikkim, to the Government of India, May 9, 1913, p. 255.

139 TNA, FO 535/16, No. 137, Foreign Office to India Office, March 17, 1913, p. 99.

140 TNA, FO 535/16, No. 137, Foreign Office to India Office, March 17, 1913, p. 98.

141 TNA, FO 535/16, No. 137, Foreign Office to India Office, March 17, 1913, p. 98.

142 SYKES 1940, pp. 226-229 and pp. 235-236.

143 SYKES 1940, p. 236.

144 TNA, FO 535/16, No. 137, Foreign Office to India Office, March 17, 1913, p. 99.

145 TNA, FO 535/16, No. 92, Sir G. Buchanan to Sir Edward Grey, February 13, 1913, p. 69.

146 TNA, FO 535/16, No. 92, Sir G. Buchanan to Sir Edward Grey, February 13, 1913, p. 69.

147 TNA, FO 535/16, No. 92, Sir G. Buchanan to Sir Edward Grey, February 13, 1913, p. 69.

148 TNA, FO 535/16, No. 89, Sir G. Buchanan to Sir Edward Grey, February 14, 1913, p. 68.

149 TNA, FO 535/16, No. 89, Sir G. Buchanan to Sir Edward Grey, February 14, 1913, p. 68.

150 *The Correspondence of G. E. Morrison* 2013, n. 541, G. E. Morrison to H. A. Gwynne, September 1912, pp. 27-28.

151 TNA, FO 405/208, No. 165, Sir Edward Grey to Sir E. Goschen, February 7, 1912, p. 190.

152 TNA, FO 535/16, No. 151, India Office to Foreign Office, March 25, 1913, p. 110.

153 TNA, FO 535/16, No. 151, India Office to Foreign Office, March 25, 1913, pp. 110-111.

154 TNA, FO 535/16, No. 152, India Office to Foreign Office, March 25, 1913, p. 111.

155 *The Correspondence of G. E. Morrison* 2013, n. 554, T. A. Rustad to G. E. Morrison, November 5, 1912, p. 51. Full text of the letter: *The Correspondence of G. E. Morrison* 2013, n. 554, T. A. Rustad to G. E. Morrison, November 5, 1912, pp. 47-53.

156 *The Correspondence of G. E. Morrison* 2013, n. 554, T. A. Rustad to G. E. Morrison, November 5, 1912, p. 52.

157 *The Correspondence of G. E. Morrison* 2013, n. 554, T. A. Rustad to G. E. Morrison, November 5, 1912, p. 51.

158 *The Correspondence of G. E. Morrison* 2013, n. 554, T. A. Rustad to G. E. Morrison, November 5, 1912, p. 51.

159 TNA, FO 535/16, No. 168, Foreign Office to India Office, March 29, 1913, p. 140. The full text of the document is in the Annexes.

160 TNA, FO 535/16, No. 168, Foreign Office to India Office, March 29, 1913, p. 141.

161 TNA, FO 535/15, No. 285, Sir J. Jordan to Sir Edward Grey, November 16, 1912, p. 223.

162 TNA, FO 535/16, No. 168, Foreign Office to India Office, March 29, 1913, p. 141.

163 TNA, FO 535/16, No. 168, Foreign Office to India Office, March 29, 1913, p. 141.

164 TNA, FO 535, No. 176, India Office to Foreign Office, April 2, 1913, p. 154.

165 TNA, FO 535/16, No. 231, Sir Edward Grey to Sir G. Buchanan, May 23, 1913, p. 237.

166 TNA, FO 535/16, Enclosure in No. 231, Revised Draft of Treaty with China respecting Thibet, p. 238.

167 TNA, FO 535/16, Enclosure in No. 231, Revised Draft of Treaty with China respecting Thibet, p. 238.

168 TNA, FO 535/16, Enclosure in No. 231, Revised Draft of Treaty with China respecting Thibet, p. 238.

169 TNA, FO 535/16, No. 231, Sir Edward Grey to Sir G. Buchanan, May 23, 1913, p. 237.

170 TNA, FO 535/16, No. 231, Sir Edward Grey to Sir G. Buchanan, May 23, 1913, pp. 237-238.

171 TNA, FO 535/16, No. 231, Sir Edward Grey to Sir G. Buchanan, May 23, 1913, p. 238.

4

The Chinese Backdown

The Russo-Chinese Agreement of 1913

A year after the Russo-Mongol Agreement, in a declaration signed in Peking on November 5, 1913 (October 23 of the Russian calendar), '[/]a Russie reconnaît que la Mongolie Extérieure se trouve sous la suzeraineté de la Chine', while the Chinese accepted Mongolian autonomy ('La Chine reconnaît l'autonomie de la Mongolie Extérieure').[1] The Russians had come to that agreement after having faced several difficulties. Indeed, in April 1913, while preparing to leave Urga, Korostovets had confessed to Morrison the complexity of dealing with the Mongols and also of enforcing the 1912 treaty:

> My position here is a trying one in every respect and the Mongols very difficult people to deal with. I have made my best to satisfy both sides that is my own people and the Government of Urga but have hardly succeeded. The treaty has been signed nearly six months ago and according to my opinion is not enforced yet and perhaps will not be. The new Consul General Miller must arrive in a fortnight and will continue my work, but on what lines and in what direction I do not venture to say.[2]

According to the agreement, Peking still had to grant Outer Mongolia 'le droit exclusif' in internal administration, in commercial and industrial matters and the newborn Republic of China could not send soldiers, civilian or military officials and obviously not even settlers. Likewise, the Russians also undertook not to colonize the country, nor to send soldiers, except for the consular guards, nor to intervene in the country's internal affairs. In an exchange of separate notes between Vasiliy Krupenskiy, Russian minister in Peking,[3] and Sun Pao-ch'i, the foreign minister in the Chinese government of Hsiung Hsi-ling,[4] the two countries agreed on the extension of the territory of Outer Mongolia, that is, those territories that had been under the jurisdiction of the amban of Urga, the 'Général tartare' of Uliastay and the Chinese amban of Hovd. Actually, as there were no detailed maps of the country and due to the vagueness of the administrative divisions, the Russians and Chinese agreed for a new meeting (already scheduled in point V of the agreement) to define the country's borders. That point in fact provided for 'pourparlers ultérieurs' on questions relating to the interests of Russia and China in Outer Mongolia, but the exchange of notes required Mongolian involvement in these future negotiations. Furthermore, according to the exchange of notes between the foreign minister of the Republic of China and the Russian minister in Peking:

> En ce qui concerne les questions d'ordre politique et territorial, le Gouvernement Chinois se mettra d'accord avec le Gouvernement Russe par des négociations auxquelles les autorités de la Mongolie Extérieure prendront part.

Not having obtained a copy of the agreement from the Russians, the Japanese minister in Peking had confidentially handed over to Beilby Alston, of the British embassy in China, the text of the document that the British diplomat had taken care to send to Grey.[5] However, the Russian minister in Peking pointed out to Alston the approximate borders of Outer Mongolia:

> On the China Inland Mission atlas, published 1908, map 22, the Russian Minister pointed out to me that the frontier of Outer Mongolia, comprising the four Aimaks[6] of Tsetsen, Sassaktu, Sainoin, Tuchetu, follows closely their boundaries as therein indicated. The exact definition will not be settled until the meeting of the conference which is proposed to hold. The western frontier is roughly the Altai range ; the southern follows the dotted line across the Gobi desert.[7]

Not yet informed of the signature the day before, Sir Edward Grey had therefore written to Alston on November 6, explaining that he had suggested to the India Office and the Board of Trade to get in touch with the Mongolian government 'with a view to recognising their autonomy and securing fair terms for British commerce'.[8] Furthermore, Grey also proposed to inform Russia of the favorable acceptance by the British of the Sino-Russian Agreement and the Russo-Mongol Treaty of 1912 'provided that a satisfactory commercial arrangement can be arrived at with the autonomous Mongolian Government, who were being approached in the matter'.[9] For the head of the Foreign Office it was necessary for 'the maintenance of the " open door " for British commerce'.[10] More important than the commercial conditions was the case of Tibet and the possibility of exploiting for British advantage, as mentioned previously, the changed conditions in Mongolia. However according to Grey – who had spoken to Sazonov – this was not the most suitable time to open the question with Saint Petersburg:

> Sir E. Grey has taken into consideration the possibility of making terms with Russia with regard to the Thibetan question in connection with the Russo-Chinese Agreement, but is of the opinion that it would be unwise to do so at present in view of the declared attitude of the Russian Government and the views expressed by M. Sazonof in his interviews with Sir E. Grey and Lord Crewe.[11]

However, the Sino-Russian Agreement was to become the model for an Anglo-Chinese agreement on Tibet and the Russian motivations for arriving at that document on Mongolia were the same as the British on Tibet:

> This would not, however, preclude His Majesty's Government from pointing out to the Russian Government should the necessity arise, that the same reason which has forced the Russian Government to stipulate with China for an autonomous Mongolia forces His Majesty's Government to make the same stipulation with regard to Thibet, in doing which they are not, as long as they do not ask for anything in Thibet beyond the scope of the pre-existing convention, taking any action contrary to the terms of the Anglo-Russian Agreement.[12]

The problem was linked to the broader question of industrial and railway loans which had been defined in September at the Paris Conference by France, Great Britain, Germany, Japan and precisely Russia, thus opening up the possibility of aid from these states to their respective private companies in China.[13] Grey wrote about the agreement:

> At meeting of groups yesterday industrial and railway loans were eliminated from the scope of the Sextuple Agreement, and at the same time the Triple and Quadruple Agreements were formally terminated. His Majesty's Government are therefore at liberty forthwith to support independent firms and groups in obtaining concessions or making industrial loans to China, since they will henceforth interpret article 17 of the Reorganisation Loan Agreement as precluding the issue but not the negotiation of loans before 5th February next.[14]

The Russian government did not like the terms of the new agreement, and authorized the signing only to avoid isolation from the other powers.[15] Indeed,

Russia feared a danger to its interests in Manchuria, Mongolia and Chinese Turkestan.[16] Therefore, following his line of not entering into conflict with Saint Petersburg on Mongolia, Grey wrote on November 13 to Hugh O'Beirne, an official of the British embassy in Russia, to reassure the tsar's government that British intentions did not aim at prejudicing Russian interests in Manchuria and Mongolia.[17] While recognizing the special interests of Saint Petersburg in Chinese Turkestan, British interest in that region was much higher than in Mongolia, considering the proximity to India, as well as the presence of many British subjects in the territory.[18] So on November 19, O'Beirne communicated to the Russian government a memorandum with Grey's indications.[19] Probably, according to Jordan, it was precisely on Chinese Turkestan that the Russians could ask for 'some form of compensation', in exchange for consent to a redefinition of the 1907 agreement on Tibet.[20] The basis of this consideration was a dispatch by Buchanan from Saint Petersburg addressed to Grey, dated July 22, 1913, where this type of exchange had already been envisaged:

> Russia had not, as he [*Sazonov*] expressed it, a policy in Kashgar as she had in Ili, Mongolia, or Manchuria. She would confine her attention to the protection of her subjects ; and I might give you the positive assurance that she would take no action of a political nature in Kashgar, except in agreement with His Majesty's Government, as he quite understood the interest which its proximity to British India caused them to take in this question.
>
> M. Sazanof spoke to me in such frank and categorical terms that I see no reason to doubt the sincerity of his assurances. His use, however, of the words " except in agreement with His Majesty's Government " confirm the impression which I have more than once expressed, that, in the event of our proposing to revise the Anglo-Russian Agreement to our advantage with regard to Thibet, he will ask for some counter concessions in Kashgaria.[21]

There was indeed a significant disproportion between Mongolia and Tibet; the status of Tibet had been regulated by the 1907 Convention, while this was not the case for Mongolia. Therefore, any British claim in the new order of High Asia that emerged from the end of the Ch'ing Empire, however logical in geopolitical terms, had to challenge the agreement that had put an end to the Great Game. British requests had to interfere with the delicate balance that had assigned the respective roles in Persia, Afghanistan, and Tibet. The Russian interventions in Mongolia, on the other hand, did not formally touch the agreement, even if those actions could mean – without too much imagination – a possible reopening of the issues on the Roof of the World, given the strong link between Urga and Lhasa. Therefore, it was not even possible for Saint Petersburg to pass any alteration of things in Mongolia as unrelated to a broader redefinition of balances and influences in High Asia. Formally, however, the British had to revise a treaty that had been signed in very different geopolitical and institutional conditions, when Tibet and Mongolia were still both within the Manchu imperial system, and not two territories that claimed their independence from a newborn Republic of China.

Therefore, in the event of a modification of the agreement, the British ambassador in Peking advised Grey to also take into consideration China, whose authorities for months had already suspected an Anglo-Russian negotiation on Tibet.[22] A possible loss of territory, without any involvement of Peking, could – according to Jordan – damage the British image in China to such an extent as to put British interests in severe crisis:

> any agreement made independently with a third Power, which affected a portion of Chinese territory, would cause deep resentment throughout the country, impair our prestige as traditional upholders of Chinese integrity, and inflict serious damage upon British interests in China, for which any concession in Thibet would be a poor compensation.[23]

Grey found Robert Crewe-Milnes in favor of the position of not communicating to the Russians – for the moment – London's position on the Tibetan question.[24] The head of the India Office, however, suggested that he wait to inform Saint Petersburg of British views on Mongolia until the Russian attitude towards Tibet was clarified.[25] Crewe-Milnes, knowing the imminent disclosure of the matter, wanted to ascertain in advance the possible Russian reaction:

> The Marquess of Crewe agrees with the Secretary of State for Foreign Affairs that it is not desirable to couple the Thibetan question with that of Mongolia at the present stage. But as it seems likely that the former question will shortly have to be taken up with the Russian Government, there might be advantage in deferring any communication to them on the subject of Mongolia until their attitude in regard to Thibet has been ascertained. His Lordship would therefore suggest for Sir E. Grey's consideration that this matter should be held in abeyance for the time being.[26]

In managing relations with Mongolia, prudence was necessary. British interests in the country were extremely limited, but any connection between Urga and London could turn, as a counterpoint, into a pretext for contact between Lhasa and Saint Petersburg:

> Lord Crewe is scarcely in a position to estimate the importance of British commercial interests in Mongolia. He agrees, however, as to the desirability of maintaining the " open door " for British trade ; and he sees no objection to the course of action proposed, provided Sir E. Grey is satisfied that direct negotiation with the Mongolian Government will not, in the event of our citing the analogy of Russian proceedings in Mongolia in support of our proposals regarding Thibet, lead to a demand by Russia for similar direct negotiation with the authorities at Lhasa.[27]

Furthermore, for Crewe-Milnes it was necessary, in the aftermath of the Sino-Russian Agreement on Mongolia and during the negotiations on Tibet in Simla, to clarify the legitimacy of the treaty between the Tibetans and the Mongols, and therefore to know whether that text had been actually authorized or not by the political leader of Tibet.[28] According to Crewe-Milnes and Grey, therefore, it was necessary to ask the Tibetan minister (*blon-chen*) Bshad-sgra[29] for clarification on the matter.[30] We have the reply of the blon-chen Bshad-sgra which is explained in a telegram from the Government of India to the Marquis of Crewe:

> He pretends to know nothing of conclusion of agreement in question, but does not deny that Thibet and Mongolia have all along had an alliance of mutual support and assistance, and that, irrespective of any new agreement, this is still in force. He adds that Dorjief was given two letters by Dalai Lamai [*sic*], the first of which laid down that the two countries should give each other help for benefit of Buddhism, while the second authorised Dorjief to work to this end. This second letter confers powers as wide as, if not wider than, those which Lonchen himself now holds ; it was given to Dorjief when Dalai Lama was in Urga, despondent about help from China or His Majesty's Government, and in close relations with Russia. To judge by phraseology of third article agreement of November 1912 between Russia and Mongolia, and by chain of thought which runs consecutively through series of Mongolian agreements which runs consecutively through series of Mongolian agreements, it appears quite probable that Russia inspired the Thibet-Mongolia agreement ; and whether or not existence of new agreement is admitted by Dalai Lama, we see no reason why its existence should be considered uncertain, or why we should doubt that its terms are as Korostovetz reported. Further, in absence of any provision in it for ratification, Dalai Lama may find difficulty in repudiating it

> even if he wants to do so, and would, in any case, have difficulty in refusing to Mongolia privileges for which it makes provision.
>
> We think that, in these circumstances, it is safer to reckon on the agreement as really existing, and to get it produced openly.[31]

So, there was a letter from the dalai lama authorizing Dorzhiyev to negotiate with Urga and, according to the Government of India, the Russians were likely at the bottom of the agreement between Lhasa and Urga. It was therefore necessary for the British to act taking into account, without any doubt, the existence of that document.

The Board of Trade was also in favor of Grey's position:

> The Board concur with Sir E. Grey in thinking that, in the interest of British trade, it would be desirable for His Majesty's Chargé d'Affaires to be instructed to get into touch with the Mongolian Government with a view to concluding an arrangement for securing fair terms and the maintenance of the " open door " for British trade, and that the Russian Government should also be informed that His Majesty's Government are prepared to receive favourably the Russo-Chinese Agreement and Russo-Mongolian Treaty and Protocol, provided that reasonable conditions can be secured for British subjects and their commerce.[32]

According to the Board the Russians were guaranteed the right to import 'goods of any origin free of duty'.[33] For the Board of Trade equal rights had to be guaranteed to the British and also

> that no import, transit, or other duties shall be imposed on the produce or manufactures of any part of His Majesty's territories which are not equally imposed on those of any other foreign countries.[34]

A draft agreement with the Mongolian authorities was also proposed by the Board; according to that, Britain was to be granted the status of most favored nation.[35] Naturally, the Board was more interested in the economic-commercial aspects, than in the broader function, in the Asian context, of the Mongolian question and therefore no political analysis was required.

Sayn noyon han Namnansüren's letter to the British ambassador

In December 1913, Sayn noyon han Namnansüren,[36] president of the Mongolian Council of Ministers and chargé of the extraordinary mission, wrote a letter to the British ambassador in Saint Petersburg, George Buchanan.[37] In the document, the Mongolian politician 'PAR la volonté de [...] le Souverain de Mongolie, et de son Gouvernement' communicated the transition to independence of Mongolia,

> [a]u moment de la chute en Chine de la dynastie mandchoue, à laquelle elle était liée par un pacte spécial [...] à l'effet de sauvegarder son unité et son indépendance nationales et l'intégrité de son territoire.

The text is particularly important: it clearly expresses the position of the Mongolian government on the issues at the center of the Sino-Russian dialogue on Urga and it was a further implicit brick of the political-diplomatic pillar that lay at the basis of the Simla agreement. The Mongols told the British that their link with the Empire was to be considered a link with the Manchu dynasty and not with the new Republic. Regarding the Mongol-Russian agreement of 1912, but also that of November (October, according to the Russian calendar) of 1913, Namnansüren expressed enthusiastic terms, considering the documents as proof of the recognition of Mongol independence not only by the Russians, but even by the newly formed Republic of China:

> Le Gouvernement mongol a pu constater avec la plus vive satisfaction que lesdits documents comportaient la sanction de la part de l'Empire de Russie et de la République chinoise de l'indépendance de l'État mongol, auquel était garantie pleine liberté dans toutes les affaires touchant à l'administration intérieure, au commerce, à l'industrie, aux lignes de chemin de fer et de télégraphe, et dans toutes les questions financières et économiques, avec toutes les conséquences résultant de cet état de choses, ainsi qu'une parfaite liberté de traiter amicalement avec d'autres États souverains.

The Mongols were evidently not satisfied with the Chinese recognition of internal autonomy. The letter to the British clarified Urga's interpretation of the agreements of 1912 and 1913, namely that of full Mongol sovereignty, also in terms of foreign affairs. The break with the Republic of China was total and therefore no suzerainty was recognized and the Mongolian government also claimed the right to annex territories inhabited by Mongols, beyond the limits set by the 1913 convention, which although still not defined with absolute certainty, excluded, without any doubt, Inner Mongolia:

> Néanmoins, le Gouvernement de Mongolie a cru de son devoir de rappeler aux Gouvernements de l'Empire de Russie et de la République chinoise qu'il a toujours maintenu, et maintient encore, que la Mongolie a rompu définitivement tous liens avec la Chine et qu'aucun droit de suzeraineté ne peut être reconnu à personne sur la Mongolie sans son approbation. En conséquence, le Gouvernement mongol se réserve une parfaite liberté d'appréciation touchant certains points de la déclaration et des notes diplomatiques ayant trait aux relations entre la Caine [sic, 'Chine' recte] et la Mongolie. En particulier, la Mongolie affirme son droit d'annexer les territoires qui ont toujours fait corps avec elle et à une telle délimitation de ses frontières qui comprendrait toutes les peuplades de race mongol qui ont déjà adhéré à l'État mongol. Sous ces réserves le Gouvernement de Mongolie se déclare prêt à prendre part aux pourparlers entre la Russie, la Chine et la Mongolie, prévus par la déclaration et les notes susindiquées.

In order to reach a peaceful condition between Mongolia and its neighbors, Namnansüren nevertheless communicated that his government had issued an order to suspend military activities against the Chinese:

> De plus, le Gouvernement de Mongolie, désireux de rétablir le plus tôt possible la bonne entente entre la Mongolie et les États limitrophes, a donné ordre à ses troupes de suspendre les opérations militaires contre les troupes chinoises et d'évacuer les positions avancées qu'elles occupaient, et il a adressé en même temps, par l'intermédiaire du Ministre des Affaires Étrangères de Russie et du Ministre de Chine à Saint-Pétersbourg, l'invitation au Gouvernement chinois d'avoir à retirer les troupes qui ont envahi le territoire de la Mongolie intérieure dont la population est intimement liée avec nous par affinités de race.

Naturally Ivan Korostovets, the architect – for the Russian side – of the 1912 agreement, had denied to Buchanan that kind of interpretation of the 1913 treaty: there had been no recognition of sovereignty to the Mongols as regards the railways, the telegraphs and foreign policy, nor, of course, was granted the right to annex parts of Inner Mongolia.[38] Korostovets recognized the fact that in the 1912 agreement, by Mongolian will, the name of the country was simply *Mongolia*, without the adjective *Outer*, but according to Korostovets it was Russia that had the right to define the borders of the territory covered by the convention.[39] Russian foreign minister Sazonov had also confirmed Korostovets' statements to Buchanan and had also communicated to the British diplomat that a meeting of Russians, Mongols and Chinese had soon be held to define the borders of Outer Mongolia.[40] Russia, of course, did not want to surrender on the Inner Mongolian issue, because, as seen above, it had already committed to a secret agreement with Japan and could not therefore allow that region to end up inside independent Mongolia:

> Their task would not be an easy one, and he need not remind me that Russia was precluded by her secret convention with Japan from allowing any portion of Inner to be incorporated in Outer Mongolia.[41]

Endnotes

1 Full text of the Déclaration in French and Russian (with exchange of notes between the foreign minister of the Republic of China and the Russian minister in Peking): *Извѣстія Министерства иностранныхъ дѣлъ*, Третій годъ нзданія, 1914, К. I, С.-Петербургъ 1914, Ст. 2801. Высочайшее повелѣніе, предложенное Правительствующему Сенату Министромъ Юстицій. Объ утвержденіи Декларацiи о признаніи автономія Внѣшней Монголіи и двухъ нотъ, дополняющихъ означенную Декларацію, N. 270, 6 Декабря 1913 г., Отдѣлъ первый, pp. 14-20.

2 *The Correspondence of G. E. Morrison* 2013, n. 588, Korostovets to G. E. Morrison, April 19, 1913, p. 134.

3 ONON – PRITCHATT 1989, p. 66.

4 KUNG SHU-TO 龚书铎 ET AL., *Chung kuo chin tai shih kang* 中国近代史纲, ti erh pan 第二版, Pei-ching 北京 1993, p. 367.

5 TNA, FO 535/16, No. 421, Mr. Alston to Sir Edward Grey, November 8, 1913, p. 397*.

6 Ajmag, in Chinese: 艾馬克 (*ai-ma-k'o*).

7 TNA, FO 535/16, No. 421, Mr. Alston to Sir Edward Grey, November 8, 1913, p. 397*; the atlas cited by Alston is: E. STANFORD, *Atlas of the Chinese Empire*, London 1908.

8 TNA, FO 535/16, No. 417, Sir Edward Grey to Mr. Alston, November 6, 1913, p. 394. The text of the letter from the Foreign Office to Board of Trade is in TNA, FO 535/16, No. 420, Foreign Office to Board of Trade, November 7, 1913, p. 396; the text of the letter from the Foreign Office to the India Office is in TNA, FO 535/16, No. 421, Foreign Office to India Office, November 7, 1913, pp. 396-397.

9 TNA, FO 535/16, No. 417, Sir Edward Grey to Mr. Alston, November 6, 1913, p. 394.

10 TNA, FO 535/16, No. 420, Foreign Office to Board of Trade, November 7, 1913, p. 396.

11 TNA, FO 535/16, No. 421, Foreign Office to India Office, November 7, 1913, p. 397.

12 TNA, FO 535/16, No. 421, Foreign Office to India Office, November 7, 1913, p. 397.

13 TNA, FO 405/212, No. 168, Hong Kong and Shanghai Banking Corporation to Foreign Office, September 26, 1913, pp. 111-112.

14 TNA, FO 405/212, No. 171, Sir Edward Grey to Mr. Alston, September 27, 1913, p. 112. The notes of the agreements are in the annexes of TNA, FO 405/212, No. 178, Mr. Addis to Foreign Office, September 29, 1912, pp. 112-116A.

15 TNA, FO 405/212, No. 183, Mr. O'Beirne to Sir Edward Grey, October 5, 1913, p. 118.

16 TNA, FO 405/212, No. 183, Mr. O'Beirne to Sir Edward Grey, October 5, 1913, p. 118.

17 TNA, FO 535/16, No. 425, Sir Edward Grey to Mr. O'Beirne, November 13, 1913, p. 401.

18 TNA, FO 535/16, No. 425, Sir Edward Grey to Mr. O'Beirne, November 13, 1913, pp. 401-402.

19 TNA, FO 535/16, No. 438, Mr. O'Beirne to Sir Edward Grey, November 19, 1913, p. 417; TNA, FO 535/16, Enclosure in No. 438, Memorandum, pp. 417-418.

20 TNA, FO 535/16, No. 443, Sir J. Jordan to Sir Edward Grey, November 27, 1913, p. 427.

21 TNA, FO 535/16, No. 327, Sir G. Buchanan to Sir Edward Grey, July 22, 1913, p. 328.

22 TNA, FO 535/16, No. 443, Sir J. Jordan to Sir Edward Grey, November 27, 1913, p. 427.

23 TNA, FO 535/16, No. 443, Sir J. Jordan to Sir Edward Grey, November 27, 1913, p. 427.

24 TNA, FO 535/16, No. 437, India Office to Foreign Office, November 19, 1913, p. 417.

25 TNA, FO 535/16, No. 437, India Office to Foreign Office, November 19, 1913, p. 417.

26 TNA, FO 535/16, No. 437, India Office to Foreign Office, November 19, 1913, p. 417.

27 TNA, FO 535/16, No. 437, India Office to Foreign Office, November 19, 1913, p. 417.

28 TNA, India Office to Foreign Office, November 17, 1913, FO 535/16, No. 432, p. 412.

29 Blon chen Bshad sgra dpal 'byor rdo rje. Transcribed as Lonchen Shatra in the British documents.

30 TNA, FO 535/16, No. 432, India Office to Foreign Office, November 17, 1913, p. 412.

31 TNA, FO 535/16, Enclosure in No. 459, Government of India to the Marquess of Crewe, December 9, 1913, p. 442.

32 TNA, FO 535/16, No. 444, Board of Trade to Foreign Office, November 27, 1913, p. 427.

33 TNA, FO 535/16, No. 444, Board of Trade to Foreign Office, November 27, 1913, p. 427.

34 TNA, FO 535/16, No. 444, Board of Trade to Foreign Office, November 27, 1913, p. 427.

35 TNA, FO 535/16, Enclosure in No. 444, Board of Trade's proposal for an agreement with Mongolia, p. 428.

36 Sayn noyon han Tögs-Ochirïn Namnansüren.

37 Full text of the letter: TNA, FO 535/16, Enclosure in No. 471, Letter left at British Embassy in St. Petersburgh by Member of Mongolian Mission (Traduc-

tion), le [missing] jour du mois moyen d'hiver de la IIIa année de l'ère "Olana ergougdeksn", December 1913, pp. 461-462.

38 TNA, FO 535/16, No. 471, Sir G. Buchanan to Sir Edward Grey, December 24, 1913, p. 460.

39 TNA, FO 535/16, No. 471, Sir G. Buchanan to Sir Edward Grey, December 24, 1913, p. 460.

40 TNA, FO 535/16, No. 471, Sir G. Buchanan to Sir Edward Grey, December 24, 1913, p. 461.

41 TNA, FO 535/16, No. 471, Sir G. Buchanan to Sir Edward Grey, December 24, 1913, p. 461.

5

The Parallel Negotiation

On July 3, 1914, the British and Tibetans signed the Simla Convention.[1] Much has been written about this document, which is so important for East and South Asia.[2] The agreement recognized Chinese suzerainty over Outer Tibet, but also the full autonomy for internal matters – including the choice of the dalai lama – of the Tibetan government in Lhasa. Peking could not transform Outer Tibet into a province of the Republic and at the same time the British undertook not to annex the country to their dominions. The Chinese, as is known, refused to sign the Convention.

Previous pages have discussed the weight of Mongol independence on the British approach to the Tibetan question. At this point, Russian interventions in Mongolia had authorized the idea of a British action in Tibet. Furthermore, having secured a solid bond with Nepal, Sikkim and Bhutan strengthened a very long stretch of the northern border of the Raj. Further west, Ladakh, another important Himalayan region, had lost its independence in 1842 and had come under the control of Golab Sīng who, in 1846, with the protection of the British, ascended the throne of Kashmir.[3]

Alongside the talks in Simla, the Foreign Office was carrying out another negotiation. To reach any lasting solution on Tibet, it was even more important for the British to persuade Russia to modify what had been established seven years earlier in Saint Petersburg. This result, however, had to be achieved without losing the positions acquired in other areas of Asia. In the preceding pages, I have introduced the guideline for the political and diplomatic action of the Foreign Office in this parallel negotiation between Edward Grey, represented by Buchanan, and Sazonov. In essence, it was necessary to try to convince the Russian foreign minister of British legitimacy to ask for a revision of the pacts on the basis of the changed condition in Outer Mongolia after independence and the end of the Manchu dynasty. This chapter will therefore be divided into reconstructing and analyzing this negotiation.

The first months of 1914

At the beginning of 1914 it was now time to clarify the matter with the Russians. The definition of the status of Tibet in Simla was now taking shape – albeit without the Chinese signature at the end – and it was necessary for the British to expressly define the changes that occurred in High Asia after the Chinese Revolution. It was to be communicated to the Russians that the British, in Simla, were about to propose to their counterparts the creation of two regions: Outer Tibet and Inner Tibet.[4]

Not being able to submit to the Russian government a definitive proposal on the Mongolian question yet – because he was engaged, as seen, in defining the topic first with the India Office – Edward Grey was, however, interested in anticipating the new structure of interests and balances to his counterpart Sazonov through Buchanan:

> the alteration in the status of Mongolia which has resulted from the recent action of the Russian Government has had an indirect but important effect on the position of Thibet.[5]

In addition to this, Article 3 of the Sino-Russian Agreement of 1913, which guaranteed Mongolia self-government on internal matters, also by regulating commercial and industrial matters, directly touched British commercial interests.[6]

As explained above, however, the British were in the most uncomfortable position in terms of negotiations with Russia regarding Tibet, since the 1907 Convention did not mention Mongolia. For the Russian foreign minister, Saint Petersburg's aid to Urga was not in violation of any agreement.[7] Ambassador Buchanan wrote to Grey about his conversation with Sazonov on January 31, 1914:

> I spoke yesterday as instructed, and in course of friendly conversation Minister for Foreign Affairs virtually admitted our right to ask for open door, but contended that in helping Mongolians Russia had acted within her rights, and had done nothing to change situation as regards Thibet.[8]

Buchanan, in conversation with Sazonov, had explained to the minister that the Russian 'veiled protectorate' over Mongolia had changed the balance in Asia 'and, as above changes might react on Thibet, it was natural we should wish to safeguard our interests there'.[9] For Sazonov, however, Russia did not have any protectorate over Mongolia, but he would still analyze Grey's proposal 'in friendly spirit', despite fearing the negative judgment of Russian public opinion 'were he gratuitously to renounce all rights' deriving from the 1907 agreement.[10] The Russian minister was therefore willing to negotiate for a redefinition of the status of Tibet, but the changed condition in Mongolia could not be sufficient to undermine the decisions of seven years earlier:

> [*Sazonov*] trusted that Mongolia would not be quoted as a reason for asking for concessions in Thibet, as the two questions had nothing to do with each other, and ought not to be mentioned in the same breath.[11]

For the Russian minister, the situation in Mongolia was comparable to the extent of British influence in South Africa:

> M. Sazonof interposed by protesting against my use of the term " protectorate " and by remarking that Russia might as well ask for compensation in the event of our extending our sphere of influence in South Africa.[12]

It was obviously an ineffective example to defend the Russian position and the terms of the 1907 agreement. Buchanan rightly reminded Sazonov of the religious ties between the two High Asian countries and furthermore the Tibetan-Mongol treaty of 1913 was clear proof of a future collaboration:

> I replied that such a contention was very far-fetched. The Thibetans and Mongols were connected by spiritual ties; and though the treaty signed by M. Dorjief might be of no political importance for the moment, it was symptomatic of a tendency towards closer relations in the future.[13]

As for economic issues, according to Sazonov commercial interest in Mongolia was not an issue for the British: the country was too poor to establish serious trade.[14] Buchanan replied 'that this did not tally with the information which we had received from one or two British firms, who were already doing a considerable business with the Mongols'.[15] Faced with Sazonov's firmness, however, the British ambassador supported the position of the Foreign Office, which had to be pursued in order to obtain, through the Mongolian case, a revision of the Anglo-Russian agreement:

> I said that I could not share this view, and reminded him that Russia herself had recognised special interests which we had for geographical reasons in Thibet.

> It will be difficult to induce Minister for Foreign Affairs to admit connection between the two questions, but I propose to continue to argue that our recognition of Russia's privileged position in Mongolia entitles us to expect consideration in Thibet.[16]

It is reasonable to think that commercial interests in Mongolia were just another pretext for the British. In this context, they did not have to appeal to the Tibetan-Mongol historical and religious ties and try to translate them not only in geopolitical terms, but also in legal and diplomatic language. Did the new status of Outer Mongolia change the British trade rights and privileges? Although extremely limited, the Mongolian market could be another card in British hands. For this reason, Sazonov tried to underestimate the economic potential of the country, while Buchanan evidently had to exalt it. Even not having a British consul in Urga certainly had a certain weight in the articulation of the primitive commercial relationship between British and Mongolian companies, as demonstrated by a letter from Urga written by Mamen, a Norwegian,[17] head of British-American Tobacco Company in the Mongolian capital.[18] In February 1913, he complained to the director of his company about the 10% tax on the sale price of wine and cigarettes, instead of the 5%, as for other goods.[19] Russian goods coming from Russia – but not from China – were not subject to any tax by the Mongolian authorities: '[t]his is of course much better than it was formerly, when Russians could import all the goods they wanted from China without any kind of duty'.[20] However, it was not easy for Mamen to negotiate alone without even the presence of a British or American consul:

> Many times I have been asked if it was possible to get a British or American consul to Urga. They [the Mongols] have asked me if I would write to the British Legation and invite a consul ; they have promised that Britishers and Americans should get better conditions than anybody else if they sent their consuls or agents here ; they have even gone so far as to ask if a consul would come here when they brought me into trouble. To all this I hardly answer at all, and from me this news does not go further than this letter ; but personally I wish that somebody would come and talk over matters with the Mongols. I learn that a German consul is coming here soon and, so far as I know, there are no German firms in Mongolia, and I cannot see why nothing should be done for us after we have been here more than two years.[21]

It was true – even the Germans were thinking of sending a career consul to Urga, but ignoring the autonomy of Outer Mongolia, which Berlin still considered part of China.[22]

It was important to Grey to have formal recognition of Sazonov's acknowledgment of British commercial reasons before negotiating a trade deal directly with the Mongolian authorities.[23] In the event that the Russian minister had again discussed the Tibetan issue with Buchanan, the ambassador should report that London was not demanding any compensation in Tibet for what Russia had obtained in Mongolia.[24] At the same time, however, it was not possible to ignore the changes that had resulted from the new situation:

> the changes which have recently taken place in regard to the status of Outer Mongolia have materially altered the general situation in those regions, and have affected, in a measure, the relations between Thibet and her neighbours.[25]

The main commercial problem facing the British was that, to get to Mongolia, British goods had to pass through China – while the Russians could enter from the northern border – and therefore were already charged with a 7.5% tax from the Chinese authorities; in case of further taxes required by the Mongolian government, the final price of the British products would have lost any chance of competing with the Russian ones.[26] To overcome this problem, the Board of Trade had proposed, in addition to the trade agreement with Mongolia to guarantee the British the status of most favored nation,[27] another agreement with the Chinese authorities, already suggested by Alston, for the refund of taxes on the import of goods sent to Mongolia and which were transiting through China.[28] On March 3, however, the Russian foreign minister explained to Buchanan that his country's goods enjoyed a 'prescriptive right to free entry into Mongolia' and therefore no taxes could be imposed on Russian products.[29] They could enter Mongolia without customs duties, but this did not mean, however, according to the British ambassador, that they were exempt from taxes on foreign products within the country.[30] Buchanan told Sazonov openly that Russia, in Mongolia, had broken 'the principle of Chinese integrity of which she had been a guaranteeing Power'.[31] Sazonov replied, however, fully recognizing the founding principle of Mongol independence, namely the previous link with the dynasty and not with China itself:

> M. Sazanof, in reply, argued that Mongolia had never been an integral part of China but a vassal State of the Manchu dynasty ; and the fall of that dynasty had released it from the ties that bound it to China.[32]

The tsar's foreign minister also reiterated the issue of Mongolian poverty and the resulting commercial inconsistency.[33] So, Buchanan asked about the attempt to exclude the British from such a poor trade.[34] The Foreign Office, through Buchanan, was linking the commercial issue to the political aspects of the affair. If the country was so poor, it was logical to think that Russia was interested in political control over the region and, therefore, in a change in the equilibrium in High Asia, although Sazonov continued to deny the connection between the Tibetan and the Mongolian questions, if not limited to the fact that both Lhasa and Urga had to defend themselves from China.[35] In any case, Sazonov was ready to recognize British interests, but he necessarily had to ask, to avoid internal criticism, for compensation, which he was not yet able to define.[36] In exchange, the British had to obtain two things from the Russians: first, the cancellation of Article 4 of the 1907 agreement, which prevented the possibility of asking for concessions in Tibet.[37] So formally, according to the India Office, Russia could also benefit from the new arrangement.[38] Then it was important for London to have the recognition of the right of the British trade agent in Rgyal-rtse to go to Lhasa.[39] This was probably the hardest point for Sazonov to accept. Buchanan had proposed to Grey to raise the level of British requests, leaving more space to deal with the Russian minister.[40] As a result, the India Office foreshadowed Grey the possibility of not simply asking for recognition of the agent's right in Rgyal-rtse to visit Lhasa, but even asking for a permanent British representative in the Tibetan capital.[41] However, not yet able to predict the Russian counter-offer, according to the India Office there was a certain risk that the Russians would ask for exactly the same thing, namely their own permanent representative in Lhasa, and therefore

> a somewhat delicate situation would arise, and it might be difficult to produce an alternative proposal, on the lines of the actual requirements of His Majesty's Government, without appearing unduly suspicious of Russian intentions.[42]

For Crewe-Milnes, another option was to present to the Russians the draft of Article 5 of the agreement under discussion in Simla:

> The Governments of China and Thibet engage that they will not enter into any negotiations or agreements regarding Thibet with one another, or with any other Power, excepting such negotiations and agreements between Great Britain and Thibet as are provided for by the convention of the 17th September, 1904, between Great Britain and Thibet and the Convention of the 27th April, 1906 between Great Britain and China.[43]

The conversations between Buchanan and Sazonov in the spring of 1914: 'a matter of hard bargaining'

The negotiations in Simla were about to end and therefore it became necessary to reach an agreement with Russia as soon as possible. Before the end of April an agreement with the Tibetans and Chinese seemed to have been found and Henry McMahon,[44] from Simla, suggested signing the text anyway and then waiting for the Russian consent in the space of time before ratification.[45] Negotiations with the Chinese representative had been complex, but in the end McMahon was able to obtain his consent to sign the agreement:

> The final stages of negotiation have been marked throughout by most vigorous resistance maintained by Chinese delegate to any final settlement : it was only with utmost difficulty that his consent to initial the convention was secured to-day.[46]

Knowing the results today, the British representative must be recognized for particular political wisdom in proposing to anticipate the signature: '[t]herefore it may be well to advance the date of signature in order to avoid possible further obstruction by Chinese'.[47] Moreover, the blon-chen Bshad-sgra, the Tibetan delegate, had no desire to wait for the Indian summer to cross the border and return to his country.[48] Another issue to push McMahon to ask to get to the signing immediately was to maintain secrecy, which was put at risk by further delays.[49] However, on April 29, the Government of India sent a communication to the India Office in London: in the text McMahon explained that the Chinese Government had no intention of authorizing its delegate to sign the agreement, disavowing the commitment that Chen had given the British and Tibetan representatives, while allowing the negotiations to continue.[50] For the secretary of state for India, Crewe-Milnes, however, it was more important to reach an agreement with Russia before signing in Simla:

> The Marquess of Crewe would suggest [*to the Foreign Office*] that steps should now be taken, with as little delay as possible, to obtain the assent of the Russian Government to the convention in its final form. Until that assent has been obtained, his Lordship understands that it is not considered desirable that the actual signature of the convention should take place.[51]

On May 4, therefore, Grey asked Buchanan to deliver to Sazonov a copy of the draft of the tripartite convention, together with its accompanying maps, and also copies of the Trade Regulations and of an Indo-Thibet Boundary Agreement which have been separately negotiated and initialled by the British and Thibetan plenipotentiaries.[52]

According to Grey, the Simla Convention interfered 'as little as possible' with the other previous agreements 'and above all with the Anglo-Russian Convention of 1907', but was 'a reasonable compromise between the extravagant claims put forward by the Chinese and Thibetan Governments, provide adequate guarantees of a permanent settlement'.[53]

According to the secretary of state for Foreign Affairs, the problems with Russia were only those relating to financial and industrial concessions to Great Britain (guaranteed by the cancellation, in Article 6 of the Tripartite Agreement, of Article 3 of the Anglo-Chinese Convention 1906) and the visits to Lhasa by the British trade agent.[54] At the same time, however, Grey decided to explain in detail the other points of the agreement to Buchanan in order to respond to any Russian criticism.[55] Under the agreements of 1906 and 1907, only China possessed the monopoly of concessions in Tibet, 'a monopoly which has hitherto been little, if at all, exercised'.[56] However, given the recent political developments, it was now necessary to break that monopoly, opening the economy of Tibet to other countries, while still guaranteeing the possibility for China to obtain concessions.[57] If the Simla Convention had not been accompanied by the cancellation of Article 4 of the Anglo-Russian Agreement of 1907, only Great Britain and Russia would have been excluded, paradoxically, from the possibility of obtaining concessions from the Tibetan government.[58] As for the British trade agent, Buchanan had to explain to Sazonov that visits to Lhasa would only occur,

> when absolutely necessary, and that permission for him to do so is only sought on grounds of convenience, as it has been found in practice that the right of direct communication on commercial matters with the Thibetan authorities given to His Majesty's Government by article 2 of the Anglo-Russian Convention can only be carried out successfully if matters are from time to time discussed in person with higher officials than those at Gyantse.[59]

The difficulty in communicating with Tibetans, Grey recalled, was 'one of the principal causes of the events' that had led the British to organize the Younghusband Expedition ten years earlier.[60] Furthermore, given the enormous divergences between Chinese and Tibetan claims, the only possible solution, according to Grey, was the division of Tibet, basically according to a scheme that followed the division of Mongolia: Outer Tibet, controlled by the Tibetans, and Inner Tibet, controlled by the Chinese.[61]

Among other critical points was the recognition, in Article 10 of the draft Convention, of British mediation in the event of future differences between Chinese and Tibetans. Indeed, this took the form of a sort of British pre-eminence because Sino-Tibetan relations, from then on, would have to be established on the basis of the Simla Agreement.[62] It was a difficult issue: on the one hand, the agreement recognized Chinese suzerainty over Tibet, but still placed the British above it, as guarantors and interpreters of the agreement. Understanding the risk of Russian opposition, Grey was ready to replace that privilege with a more acceptable recognition of the English version of the agreement as the authoritative source in case of disputes.[63]

The Russians could also object to the definition of the border between India and Tibet.[64] By 1914, in fact, the British, through the McMahon Line, assigned to the Raj a large region north of Assam and east of Bhutan which largely corresponds to the current Indian state of Arunachal Pradesh and which the Chinese still claim today as part of the Tibet Autonomous Region.[65] The British, however, based the border line separating the area inhabited by Tibetans (to the north and therefore within Outer Tibet) from the region inhabited by various semi-independent tribal groups ('the Miris, Abors, Daphlas, and the other tribes') that fell within the sphere of influence of the United Kingdom.[66] Buchanan had to explain, in the remote case of Russian requests for clarification, that the British had had to wait for a long 'survey work' that had only recently occurred.[67]

Finally, the last point on which to prepare a possible answer concerned the new Trade Regulations between Tibet and Great Britain.[68] For the British government, the new regulations did not affect Russia, but in case of objections, the British ambassador should explain to Sazonov that it was only 'a necessary adjustment' of the Trade Regulations of 1908 (authorized by Article 2 of the section relating to Tibet of the Anglo-Russian Agreement of 1907) due to the changed conditions resulting from the new agreements.[69] Furthermore, Grey wrote in his letter to Buchanan:

> it is of the greatest importance that the assent of the Russian Government to these proposals should be received as soon as possible, as it will be necessary that the Chinese and Thibetan delegates should remain in India until signature can take place, and, apart from the injury to his health which is feared by the Thibetan plenipotentiary as a result of a prolonged sojourn in India during the hot weather, it is most desirable to

avoid a long delay between initialling and signature which will enable the Chinese Government to raise objections and difficulties which may prove fatal to the successful conclusion of these lengthy negotiations.[70]

However, in those days, Sazonov was in Crimea, in Livadiya, to meet the Ottoman representatives and he was not expected to return for several days.[71] Meanwhile Buchanan had outlined the content of Grey's explanations in a note he had read to Anatoliy Neratov, assistant minister for foreign affairs, on May 8, also summarizing his previous meetings with the minister.[72] Buchanan had explained to Neratov – who obviously had to wait for the minister to return to Saint Petersburg to give an answer to the ambassador – that the definition of the Indo-Tibetan border, the division of Tibet into two areas and the new Trade Regulations had no effect on Russia and furthermore that the British had reduced their demands to a minimum, and consequently the demand for Russian counter-concessions was not necessary, trusting 'that the Imperial Government would give an unconditional consent to our proposals, which in no way affected any Russian interest'.[73] Then, Buchanan told Neratov that his government needed a British agent in Lhasa precisely to avoid a new expedition.[74] 'Chinese intrigues' had to be prevented and also the Japanese were showing some interest on the Land of Snows.[75]

Back in the capital on May 16, Sazonov met with Buchanan the same day.[76] According to the Russian minister, Article 8 of the agreement – concerning the British agent in Lhasa – and in particular the formulation of Article 10 – which, as we have seen, had to place the British as mediators between Chinese and Tibetans in the event of disputes over the agreement – essentially meant the abolition of what was established on Tibet in 1907 and the establishment of the British protectorate over Lhasa.[77] Sazonov reiterated what he had already explained to Buchanan previously, thus not changing the position: the tsar's minister was not interested in Tibet ('He said that he personally did not care what we did with Thibet'), but at the same time he could not renounce a compensation for Russia, 'a *quid pro quo* that would satisfy public opinion'.[78] Otherwise Sazonov feared being accused by the Nationalists 'of being the dupe of England, just as he had been accused of having been duped by Germany at Potsdam',[79] where, in 1910, an agreement was reached between the Russians and the Germans about their respective interests in Persia.[80]

According to Sazonov, Article 10 of the Simla Convention made the British 'the arbiter of Thibet's destinies' and also Russia could have asked for the same right provided for the British agent in Article 8 'though she would not use it'.[81] In reply Buchanan explained that the British had always acted as mediators between Peking and Lhasa and that therefore 'the rôle of arbitrator naturally devolved on' London.[82] After all, as we have seen, the Russians too had become mediators between the Chinese and the Mongols. Furthermore, according to Buchanan, unlike the United Kingdom, Russia had no special interests in Tibet to send an agent to Lhasa.[83] Knowing that Grey had considered the option of changing the Article 10, Buchanan had opened up the possibility of looking for 'another formula', without, however, explaining immediately the alternative that had been envisioned by the secretary of state for Foreign Affairs.[84]

Sazonov explained to Buchanan that Russia's economic interests in Afghanistan were greater than the British interests in Tibet and therefore, in order to obtain his consent, he requested the sending of Russian agents to the emirate, if not to Kabul:

> Minister for Foreign Affairs then said that Russia had economic interests of a far more important kind in Afghanistan than we had in Thibet, and that if he consented to our proposals we must allow her to send agents into Afghanistan, though not to Cabul, to discuss with the authorities questions which concerned her closely, such as irrigation, &c. He had repeatedly appealed to our good offices in the hope of getting these questions settled, but without success.[85]

As mentioned above, a demand on Afghanistan was the Foreign Office's first fear that had slowed down the dialogue with Russia on the redefinition of the 1907 Agreement.[86] As the Foreign Office had written to the India Office on March 17, 1913:

> It must be remembered, however, that any proposal made to the Russian Government to alter the Anglo-Russian Convention of 1907 as regards any one of the subjects dealt with by it may precipitate a proposal from the Russian Government to revise the convention about Afghanistan, on the ground that the Ameer has never recognised it and that some of its provisions are not operating.[87]

A year and two months later, Buchanan was confronted with Sazonov's claims on Afghanistan. Obviously the ambassador explained to the minister that such a request, would have involved a long negotiation, 'indefinitely' postponing the signing of the tripartite agreement in Simla.[88] Sazonov replied that, having waited weeks for the details of the requests, the British could not expect to get an answer within a day.[89] However, he was ready to receive suggestions about other counter-concessions.⁹⁰ Buchanan therefore reiterated the basic line: British actions sprang from what had happened in Mongolia in the past years.⁹¹ According to Buchanan, it was Russia who had established a protectorate on Urga, not the British on Lhasa.⁹² In Mongolia, Russia,

> controlled the administration, and without her consent Mongolia could not conclude treaties with foreign countries nor even accord us commercial [? privilege]⁹³ we were entitled to by our treaty with China.⁹⁴

According to the diplomat, the first consequence of the new political order of Mongolia was precisely the Tibetan-Mongol treaty: 'The closest relations had been established between them, and Russian rifles were being imported into Thibet through Mongolia'.⁹⁵

Sazonov, evidently concerned about the reaction of the Nationalists in the event of a blatant failure to deny British demands, was willing to accept all the proposals, but this was not to be made public and advised not to mention them in the convention.⁹⁶ Russia would secretly assure the British while the latter should allow the occasional dispatch of a native agent to Herāt.⁹⁷ Buchanan was 'greatly disappointed': he reminded Sazonov that he had repeatedly given his support to the Russian 'views when I considered them well founded'.⁹⁸ Buchanan realized that Sazonov was turning the issue into 'a matter of hard bargaining'.⁹⁹ At that point, the diplomat was forced to put on the table the case of Persia, the first pillar of the 1907 Agreement, denouncing the presence of twelve thousand Russian soldiers in the country and the buying of land in Āẕerbāījān to transform the region 'into a Russian possession'.¹⁰⁰ Sazonov replied that the soldiers were only half as many as the ambassador said and that Saint Petersburg was not intervening in the central administration of the country.¹⁰¹ For Buchanan, however, those soldiers in Persia meant 'indefinite military occupation'.¹⁰² In that way, the Russian Empire 'violated the principle of Persian integrity, which was the basis of our understanding', but for these 'slight modifications' to the 1907 agreement, the British had to face Russian 'counter-proposals that would cause us the greatest embarrassment'.¹⁰³ The British ambassador, however, understood Sazonov's concerns and the latter's need to achieve something politically relevant.

> Minister for Foreign Affairs is evidently so afraid of the criticisms of his colleagues that he wants to save his face by getting something which he can represent as a counter-concession. I am not aware whether there is anything which

we can offer that will convey the impression desired without costing us too much.[104]

At that point, according to Buchanan, asking about a permanent British representative to Lhasa, instead of simple occasional visits, was perhaps better: the Russian foreign minister 'seems to draw no distinction between our maximum and minimum demands'.[105] According to Buchanan, '[w]e can get over his [*Sazonov's*] objections to article 10 by substituting proposed alternative article'.[106] Furthermore, London would not veto Russian requests for concessions in Tibet.[107] Regarding Article 8, according to the ambassador, the British government had to be committed not to let it enter into force before an agreement with Russia.[108]

Two days later, on May 18, Buchanan met Sazonov again.[109] The ambassador wrote to Grey that he had found the Russian minister 'in a more friendly spirit'.[110] Sazonov had explained to him once more that he was in difficulty, asking once more for the secrecy of the agreement and again proposing the question of sending a Russian agent to Herāt, because contacts between the border authorities were not sufficient.[111] Saint Petersburg wanted to deal directly with the Afghan authorities on issues related to economic interests, and water supplies, and also avoid the possibility of railways in the north of the country without the consent of Russia.[112] Buchanan, however, reiterated the British refusal.[113] Given the demonstrated lack of propensity of the Afghans to negotiate, the British feared the killing of the Russian agent, with a consequent punitive expedition.[114] Buchanan had explained to Sazonov that Britain had tried to secure Russian interests in water supplies, but under the 1907 Agreement, peaceful diplomacy was the only way to exert influence over Afghanistan:

> We had done all that we could to help Russia in the question of the water supply, but his Excellency must remember that, by the terms of the Anglo-Russian Agreement, we could only exercise our influence in Afghanistan in a pacific sense.[115]

However, the ambassador knew very well the importance that that Central Asian country continued to play for Russia:

> Though his Excellency dropped the question of Afghanistan for the moment, it is one which His Majesty's Government must be prepared to see reopened at any moment. Russia's standpoint with regard to it is very similar to that of the European Powers as regards the application of the Monroe doctrine. If they may not themselves take measures to

safeguard their threatened interests, they expect the United States to do so for them ; and if we are not able to procure satisfaction for Russia with regard to the irrigation and other kindred questions, she will one day insist on taking the matter into her own hands.[116]

As for the articles of the treaty, Sazonov again challenged Article 10, considering it as London's protectorate over Lhasa, which Buchanan again tried to deny.[117] Moreover, Sazonov also demanded the definition, within the tripartite convention, of greater guarantees for Russia: he wanted the same rights that the British were obtaining with Articles 6 and 8, including a Russian representative to Lhasa, as well as concessions in Tibet.[118] The ambassador, therefore, explained that the British were not willing to veto Russia and were also willing to prepare an exchange of notes on the matter, despite Russia being able, at that time, to legally exclude Britain's trade from Outer Mongolia.[119] For Sazonov, on the contrary, Russia had no veto power to exclude the British from Mongolia, but the ambassador recalled that London had to appeal to Russia to ask for the recognition of the open door principle even in Outer Mongolia.[120] In any case, having Sazonov denied any right of veto, that statement could be enough, for the British, to open a channel of communication with the Mongols.[121] Furthermore, according to the Russian foreign minister, the British could get their products to Mongolia through the Russo-Mongolian border, as the Germans already did, and not necessarily from China, but Saint Petersburg could not prevent the Mongols from taxing the products from other countries.[122]

Buchanan admitted the historical hostility towards the Russians of the officials of the Raj, but because of the 'intrigues of Russian agents in the past, which had been one of the direct causes of the troubles which led to our intervention in 1903'.[123] If now Russia, with no interest in Tibet, had demanded an agent in Lhasa, 'her motives might be misinterpreted in India and suspicions which it was so important to allay might be revived'.[124] At that point in the conversation, Buchanan was obviously forced to propose the modification of Article 10 as Grey had proposed, to save Articles 6 and 8, finding, at least, Sazonov's consent.

> I then said that if he would consent to articles 6 and 8 I would suggest that article 10 should be replaced by an article declaring English text of convention authoritative. Minister for Foreign Affairs at once said that such a substitution would be very agreeable to him.[125]

Another problem was obviously the absence of Tibetans and Chinese in those discussions. Sazonov promised that the right of the Russian agent was merely symbolic: 'he made suggestion that if Russia's right to send an agent to Lhasa were inserted in article 8 he would give us secret assurance that he would never send one there'.[126] Buchanan, however, explained to him that it was not easy to get the Chinese and Tibetans to accept that possibility.[127] Another option suggested by Sazonov was an exchange of notes on Article 8:

> Finally, he said that he might consent to leave article 8 as it stood were we to undertake, by an exchange of notes which could be published, not to put this article into force without a previous agreement with Russia. He might then give us a secret assurance that he would not withhold his consent from visits of our agent to Lhassa when the time came for his giving it.[128]

For the Russians, however, it was also necessary that the British agent be a mere trade agent, without a political role.[129] As for concessions, even there, for Sazonov, the question could be resolved with an exchange of notes: Great Britain and Russia had to undertake not to ask for concessions for their subjects, except with mutual consent.[130] According to Buchanan, Sazonov was also ready to guarantee, always secretly, that he would not support or otherwise encourage Russian requests for concessions and that he would not oppose the British ones.[131]

The next day, May 18, Buchanan telegraphed Sazonov's requests to Grey about the new shape of Articles 10, 6 and 8.[132] Furthermore, the Russian foreign minister also asked the British Government to write a note to the Russian Government in which London pledged not to support the requests of British subjects for irrigation works, railways or preferential rights for commercial or industrial enterprises in Northern Afghanistan:

> " His Majesty's Government engage not to support any demand on the part of British subjects for irrigation works, railways, or any preferential rights for commercial or industrial enterprises in Northern Afghanistan."[133]

For Sazonov, the British were 'tearing up' the 1907 Agreement on Tibet, without any compensation for the Russians 'and the above proposals were his last word'.[134] Buchanan confessed to Grey that he did not believe he could get anything better ('I fear that it is impossible for me to obtain better terms').[135] If the Russian requests were not acceptable, then the British government should, according to Buchanan, find 'some counter-concession to offer to Russia outside Thibet', but it was necessary to hurry, because Sazonov had to leave the Russian capital for several weeks 'and he cannot telegraph proposed arrangement to the Emperor until he knows whether His

Majesty's Government will accept it'.¹³⁶ Buchanan knew that Neratov could sign the notes to be exchanged, but there was no point trying to discuss the issues with the assistant minister.¹³⁷ Sazonov also said that he should have asked, with a note, 'to recognise more fully Russia's predominant interests' in northern Persia to avoid British protests over the activity of the Russian consuls in the country.¹³⁸ Buchanan replied that the British had always recognized the Russian 'predominant interests' in the region, but London had to defend the principle of independence and integrity of Persia.¹³⁹ However, Sazonov had no intention of including this point in the list of counter-concessions, but he would still prepare a note – which could, however, remain secret and did not require a response – to ask that the British agents in Persia conformed to the recognition of the predominance of Saint Petersburg's interests in the area of Russian influence.¹⁴⁰ According to Sazonov, the British sometimes created problems for the Russians, as had happened recently over a concession for water plants near the city of Eşfahān.¹⁴¹

Furthermore, on May 21, the Russian Foreign Ministry wrote an *aide-mémoire*, delivered to Buchanan, on the issue of the continuation of the open door policy in Mongolia.¹⁴² The text argued that the right of the Russians to import products, 'sans distinction de provenance, en franchise de droits' – a right that the British also claimed on the basis of the principle of the most favored nation – was actually derived from older Russo-Chinese treaties, and that, therefore, the Russo-Mongol protocol of October 21, 1912 had simply guaranteed the continuation of the previous situation.¹⁴³ The text of the memorandum expressly mentions the treaties of 1862 and 1881

> Or, les sujets russes jouissent du droit susmentionné depuis le commencement des relations commerciales russes avec la Mongolie par voie de terre. Des stipulations à cet effet ont été introduites dans les traités russo-chinois de 1862 et de 1881, et le protocole conclu à Urga avec le Gouvernement mongol n'avait pour but que de confirmer l'état de choses déjà existant.¹⁴⁴

According to the memorandum, Britain already recognized a similar right along the border between British Burma and China:¹⁴⁵

> Ces différents régimes établis pour le commerce des pays qui ont avec la Chine des frontières communes n'ont jamais été considérés contraires aux principes de la nation la plus favorisée qui régissent le commerce avec la Chine par voie de mer.¹⁴⁶

Products arriving by sea were taxed for both import and transit and had to pay local taxes to offices in the eighteen provinces of 'Chine intérierure'.[147] The Chinese government, in 1911, before the proclamation of Mongolian independence (the text of the memorandum naturally talks about 'autonomie'), had also established an office in Urga, without any protest from the foreign powers and the new Mongolian government only adopted 'pour le commerce le régime pratiqué en Chine et introduit en Mongolie par le Gouvernement chinois' and also the Russians, for products imported by sea and not from the Russo-Mongolian border, had to comply with the same rules as for other countries.[148] For Saint Petersburg, therefore, the British claims were not conceivable:

> Par contre, le Gouvernement anglais semblerait prétendre à une situation sans précédent pour le commerce avec la Mongolie. Il réclame notamment une franchise de droits d'entrée, de transit et autres non pas pour les marchandises importées par ses sujets, mais pour toutes les marchandises de provenance anglaise, ce qui est absolument contraire aux principes qui ont fait jusqu'ici la base des traités de commerce de la Chine. Il réclame pour son commerce par voie de mer un régime de faveur dont aucune Puissance, sans excepter la Russie, ne jouit ni dans la Chine propre, ni dans les régions soumises à la suzeraineté chinoise.[149]

However, the point on which the Russians and the British diverged was that, for the latter, the agreements – in particular Article 12 of the Russo-Chinese Treaty of 1881 – did not exempt Russian products, which entered Mongolia through the border with Russia, from internal taxes imposed by the Mongolian government on foreign goods.[150]

The *aide-mémoire* was communicated by the Foreign Office to the India Office and the Board of Trade on June 18, 1914.[151] According to Grey it had to be explained to the Russians that the British were not aiming for any privileged position, but only to maintain the same treatment for their products – on which customs and transit taxes were paid upon entry into China and therefore provided with transit permits – which were purchased by Chinese or other merchants in Chinese territory and then perhaps sent to Mongolia without any other tax to pay.[152] In such a case, therefore, an agreement aimed at guaranteeing exemption from Mongolian taxes only for British subjects would be of no use.[153] The only valid option for the secretary of state for Foreign Affairs was to extend the freedom of trade to this type of goods of British origin, 'as would be entitled to most-favoured-nation treatment in China proper'.[154] Grey also suggested that the India Office and the Board of Trade support Buchanan's position on Article 12 of the Sino-Russian Treaty of 1881 which, according to the ambassador, did not guarantee Russian goods exemption from any internal taxes on foreign products in Mongolia.[155] Given that for Saint Petersburg the privileges granted to Russian trade were due only to a border trade agreement – comparable to the Anglo-Chinese agreement on the trade across the border between British Burma and China – according to Sir Edward Grey it was necessary to remind the tsar's government that products crossing the Sino-Burmese border only got a thirty percent reduction in ordinary customs duties.[156] Furthermore, not all products enjoyed this reduction, but only goods that crossed the Sino-Burmese border by two defined roads, while there was no such limit for products arriving in Mongolia from Russia.[157] To be precise, on January 26, 1915, the India Office clarified to the Foreign Office that there were currently three roads and that on the basis of the Convention of Peking of February 4, 1897, it was possible for border commissioners to expand the number of roads.[158]

The summer of 1914

A few days later, on June 23, 1914, the Foreign Office received a communication from Peking, dated June 5.[159] The British ambassador had received a letter from the Mongolian government – written in April – which he was now forwarding to London.[160] Urga claimed its independence from the Republic of China, in addition to communicating the position of the bogd haan, sovereign of Mongolia and head of Buddhism in the country:

> The Imperial Mongolian Government beg to notify your Excellency that Mongolia, having declared herself an independent State, is no longer under the Government of China.
>
> The ruler of Mongolia is Djibson Dampa Llama, the Bogda or Hituktoo, residing in Urga, and being at the same time the head of the Buddhistic religion of this country.[161]

In the letter, the Mongolian government asked Jordan to send an authorized consul or other representative in order to sign a treaty of trade and friendship, just as they had already reached a commercial treaty with Saint Petersburg.[162] The Mongolian government would have liked to send its own delegates to foreign powers, but it did not have officials able to speak languages other than Mongolian and Chinese and for this reason it asked the British government to send representatives to the capital.[163] The Mongols said they were ready to grant the British the same privileges accorded to the Russians:

According to the treaty between the Russian and Mongolian Governments, we still retain the power to give to your Excellency's Government the same terms as we have extended to Russia.[164]

Twice already the government of the bogd haan had sent communications to the other world powers, without obtaining answers, therefore the Mongols were not able to know if the British had received their proposals or not.[165] The letter had been delivered to Jordan by Frans August Larson, the Republic of China's adviser for Mongolian affairs.[166] According to Jordan, the other powers to which the Mongols had sent the same letter were the United States, Germany and France.[167] According to the Russian chargé d'affaires, Vladimir Grave,[168] heard by Jordan, the basis of the attempt to sign treaties with other countries was the disappointment of the Mongols for their own situation; in fact, after the signing of the 1913 Agreement, China was trying to reassert its role at the expense of the Russians with counter-offers that were actually impracticable.[169] The Mongolian government, on the other hand, had tried, without results, to obtain loans from Russian adventurers or from other European countries.[170] Jordan wrote to Grey:

> The result now is that the Mongols refuse to take part in the tripartite conference which was to have been held at Kiakta, and which was expected to regulate, amongst other things, the commercial situation in Mongolia.[171]

The British ambassador recognized the weakness of British trade in Mongolia, 'but such as it is it has been placed at a distinct disadvantage by the Russian agreements'.[172] British goods could arrive in Mongolia by paying a tax of 7 and a half percent to China, but then they were burdened with another tax, which ranged from 5 to 10%, to be paid to the Mongols, and the latter would hardly renounce it.[173] New terms could not be negotiated with the Chinese – as the Board of Trade proposed to obtain reimbursement, as we have already seen above, of the import taxes on British goods sent to Mongolia but transiting through China[174] – in the first place because Peking could not be brought to sign a treaty involving the idea of an Outer Mongolia outside of China, and then because technically and practically it was impossible:

> The Chinese taxation is fixed by treaty, and though it might be argued that goods destined for Outer Mongolia are merely passing through China in transit, the Chinese Government are most unlikely to agree to any modification of the treaty which would affect the principle that Mongolia is Chinese territory. In

practice, too, it would be quite impossible with the existing means of communication to devise any arrangement for sending goods in bond through China to Outer Mongolia.[175]

So Jordan at this point – probably also considering the failure of the original line of the Foreign Office, that was to exchange Russian influence in Mongolia with the new British position in Tibet – realized the need, in case of failure of the negotiations with Saint Petersburg, of direct British action in Mongolia, sending a consul to the capital, as they had already done in Kashgar seven years earlier with George Macartney:

> If our negotiations with Russia fail to produce a solution, the best course, in my opinion, would be to do as we did in 1907 at Kashgar. We should appoint a consul to reside in Urga and trust to his influence to work out a solution, as Sir George Macartney has done in the New Dominion [*English translation of the Chinese name of Hsin-chiang*], where our trade now enjoys in practice all the privileges accorded to Russia by treaty. Neither Russia nor China could offer any reasonable objection to such a step.[176]

Indeed, according to Jordan, the British had the right to protect their interests in Outer Mongolia, which were put in difficulty by Russia.[177] Moreover, China could favorably consider the presence of British and German consuls to Urga, to counterbalance Russian influence in the country.[178] Furthermore, the British consul had to be subject to the British Embassy in Peking and this meant full recognition of the suzerainty of the Republic of China over Mongolia.[179] On the contrary, the Russian consul was not under the authority of the Russian legation in the Chinese capital.[180]

In theory, Jordan's views could have some effectiveness, but it was clear that sending a consul to Urga, following a formal request from the Mongolian government, could not fail to create a certain Chinese resentment. A few days later, in fact, on June 16, 1914, the Chinese minister in London communicated to the British a telegram from the Wai-chiao Pu,[181] addressed to him, in which he was asked to inform the Foreign Office, reaffirming the suzerainty of Peking on Outer Mongolia and therefore the impossibility for Urga to deal directly with other countries:

> FOREIGN legations in Peking have received a communication from Outer Mongolia styling herself as an independent country, and requesting them to send representatives to negotiate treaties with her. We hear that the Ministers in Peking have already communicated this Mongolian request to their respective Governments. You are hereby requested to draw the attention of the

> British Foreign Office to the various documents passed between the Chinese and Russian Governments declaring and acknowledging the suzerainty of China over Outer Mongolia. Outer Mongolia being a part of the dominion of China has certainly no right to receive and send representatives to negotiate treaties directly with foreign Governments.[182]

Meanwhile, on July 17, 1914, the Foreign Office, by forwarding to the Board of Trade Jordan's letter on the consul in Mongolia and the telegram from the Wai-chiao Pu, opened the possibility of a consul to Urga with exclusively consular and commercial functions:

> Sir E. Grey would propose, subject to the concurrence of the Board of Trade, to adopt the following course:–
>
> 1. To inform the Russian Government that His Majesty's Government have received a request from the Mongolian Government that they should send a consul to Urga to negotiate a commercial treaty, and that His Majesty's Government intend to comply with this request and to inform the Chinese accordingly.
>
> 2. On receipt of a reply from the Russian Government to inform the Chinese Government of the action contemplated assuring them at the same time that the duties of this official will be of a purely consular and commercial character.[183]

Ten days earlier, on July 7, the Board of Trade had responded to Grey's previous communication of June 18, substantially agreeing with him on the reply to be made to the tsar's government regarding Russian commercial privileges and British disadvantages in Mongolia.[184] The only difference concerned the reason for the British claims: the position proposed by His Majesty's government, according to which British trade enjoyed the same rights as it had had when Mongolia was within the Chinese Empire, allowed for a fiscal exemption on imports to Mongolia in all circumstances.[185] The draft agreement prepared by the Board in November 1913, on the other hand, provided for the recognition of the status of most favored nation and, therefore, British goods were to benefit from the exemption, but only in coincidence with the exemption granted to Russian or other countries' products.[186] According to the Board this distinction had to be highlighted in communications with the Russians.[187] However, the Board of Trade had not given up on the idea of agreeing with the Chinese the reimbursement of import taxes paid on goods destined for Mongolia.[188] For the Board, the question had to be presented to the Russians in this way: if Outer Mongolia was still part of Chinese territory, then Russia was entitled to enjoy the privileges previously granted on goods arriving in Mongolia through the formal Russo-Chinese border (i.e. Russo-Mongolian), but at the same time customs barriers could not be imposed between China and Mongolia.[189] If, on the other hand, Outer Mongolia was considered as an autonomous state, no longer part of the Chinese territory, then the rights of Russian goods that arrived in Mongolia by land ceased.[190] The privileges provided to goods crossing the border could not apply, because that agreement concerned the land border between China and Russia, but in the case of an autonomous Mongolian state, products directed to Mongolia only passed the Russo-Mongolian border and not the Russo-Chinese one.[191] Finally, the Board agreed with Grey in supporting Buchanan's position regarding Article 12 of the Russo-Chinese Treaty of 1881, which did not guarantee Russian goods exemption from internal taxes levied in Mongolia on foreign goods.[192]

The Foreign Office's reply to the Board of Trade came on July 17, underlining the problem of the mere status of most favoured nation:

> If His Majesty's Government confine themselves to claiming most-favourered-nation [sic] treatment in autonomous Mongolia, freedom from dues will only be secured as is pointed out by the Russian note, for goods actually imported by British subjects, since by the Urga Protocol this privilege is only extended to Russian subjects and not to all goods of Russian origin. Consequently, any attempt based upon the right of His Majesty's Government to claim most-favoured-nation treatment in Mongolia alone will only benefit such British goods as are actually imported by British subjects, and will leave the larger class of goods which is imported by British subjects into China, and there purchased by Chinese merchants, for importation into Manchuria [sic, Mongolia recte] without redress.
>
> Sir E. Grey would, therefore, be glad to have the opinion of the Board as to the necessity for claiming not merely most-favoured-nation treatment, but the right to negotiate with the Mongolian Government for the freedom from duty of all British goods which would have been entitled to most-favoured-nation treatment under the commercial treaties with China if the duties now imposed by the Mongolian Government had been imposed by the Chinese Government before the status of Mongolia was altered by the intervention of Russia.[193]

Furthermore, a tax exemption on British products in Mongolia did not exclude Chinese customs duties and transit taxes and, therefore, an advantage still existed with respect to the competitiveness of the price that the Russians could offer for their products that entered in Mongolia directly.[194] Any reduction in Chinese taxes would not give a 'privileged position' to British products:

> Sir E. Grey desires to point out that, even if complete freedom from dues levied in Mongolia is obtained for British goods, they will still be subject to the Chinese customs and transit dues, and will, to this extent, be handicapped in competing with Russian goods which are imported directly from their country of origin, and any reduction of the Chinese duties which may eventually be obtained will only tend to place them more nearly on an equality with Russian goods and would not in any sense give them a privileged position.[195]

For this reason, according to Grey, the Russian government should have no objection to British action aimed at reducing Chinese tariffs for British products in transit to Mongolia.[196]

From Simla and from London

According to a letter dated May 21, 1914 from the Government of India to the Marquess of Crewe, McMahon was less favorable to the change of Article 10 of the Simla Agreement; the British delegate feared that the modification of the document could offer the Chinese the possibility of reopening discussions, after Chen had already initialled the text, perhaps not even signing the agreement.[197] On that point, however, according to Buchanan, it was really impossible to go back:

> Minister for Foreign Affairs' objections to article 10 are, I fear, insuperable, and we have now, by communication which I made to him yesterday respecting provisional arrangement, virtually agreed to delete it.[198]

The Government of India was in favor only of the other two conditions concerning Articles 6 and 8: the two articles were not modified, but their effects had to be regulated by exchanges of notes between London and Saint Petersburg.[199] Furthermore, the British agent could also be officially appointed as a trade agent, but nevertheless, for Delhi, he needed the necessary powers to enforce Article 8.[200] On this point, however, there was no opposition from Sazonov; for the minister – evidently always interested in safeguarding his position in the eyes of the Russian public opinion – officially the British agent was to be considered a trade agent, but not denying the real political role.[201]

As for the note on northern Afghanistan that Sazonov had asked of the British government, the Government of India reported to the India Office that they had no particular problems in this regard, but it was preferable to keep it secret to avoid misunderstandings by the Afghan emir.[202] If not, Delhi asked for the necessary time to notify the emir in advance 'and to explain it to him in suitable manner'.[203] Sazonov's problem, however, was precisely the need to make that note public to demonstrate that he had obtained compensation from the British.[204] Buchanan therefore suggested writing the text in such a way as to avoid misunderstandings on the part of the emir.[205] The British ambassador proposed to Grey, hoping for Sazonov's approval, to start with the recognition of Russian interests in 'such questions as that of irrigation' and with the fact that the 1907 Convention put Afghanistan out of Saint Petersburg's influence, and only then specify the commitment made by the British government.[206] The Government of India, on the other hand, considered the note on northern Persia – that Sazonov had said he wanted to prepare – 'entirely unconnected' with the agreement on Tibet.[207] Delhi was also opposed to any Russian strengthening in northern Persia aimed at dividing the country, except in exchange for an equal strengthening of the British position in the south.[208] Edward Grey, on the other hand, was not opposed to the modification of Article 10.[209] As we have seen previously, the one who had considered that option was the secretary of state for Foreign Affairs himself.[210] The Foreign Office, however, could not give a definitive answer to the question before Sazonov's departure, without having heard the position of the Government of India.[211] At the same time, no more weeks could be waited for the final signing of the Simla Convention.[212] Grey therefore proposed, to his Russian counterpart, the replacement of Article 10 with the simple recognition of the English text as authoritative, as well as the guarantee of an official note to the Russian Government to clarify that Articles 6 and 8 could not be implemented by the British without an agreement with Saint Petersburg.[213] In case of publication of the Simla Convention, Grey was ready to make the note public as well.[214] Furthermore, in the meantime, the secretary of state for Foreign Affairs did not ask for any secret commitment prior to the official note, as had instead been proposed by Sazonov, while the 1907 Convention continued to be considered in force.[215] On the basis of these conditions, for Grey, the Simla Convention could therefore be signed:

> The position, in fact, is this : His Majesty's Government would, by the Tripartite Convention, obtain the consent of Thibet and China to seek concessions in Thibet and to send the British trade agent from Gyantse to Lhassa, but they recognise that, owing to the Anglo-Russian agreement of 1907, the consent of Russia also is required for these things, and they would undertake not to do them till that consent has been obtained.[216]

Sazonov, actually, as explained by Buchanan to Grey in a letter dated May 24, preferred the signing of the Simla Convention only after the British definitive acceptance of the conditions he had set.[217] However, in the face of Buchanan's explanations, he lowered his demand: the signing did not have to be made public before a definitive agreement between London and Saint Petersburg and perhaps also secrecy should be imposed on the Chinese and Tibetans.[218] In case of leaks, however, Sazonov would make the note public.[219]

Time was undoubtedly now very short. On May 25 Sazonov had to leave the Russian capital, to return only on June 7, for just two nights.[220] Then he would leave again for Constantza (Constanța), where the tsar was to meet with Charles I of Romania.[221] According to the British ambassador, it was therefore 'advisable' to give Sazonov an answer by June 7.[222] The foreign minister would then submit the matter to Nicholas II.[223] Buchanan, however, explained to Sazonov that, according to him, if the British government accepted the conditions, 'words " without previous agreement with Imperial Government " ought, in my opinion, to be added to the engagement which we were asked to give about Afghanistan' on the note relating to Afghanistan.[224] Sazonov replied that he was not against it, but Russia could never approve British concessions in the areas envisaged by the note, in northern Afghanistan.[225] For Sazonov 'it was matter of vital moment to Russia that no irrigation works should be undertaken in Afghanistan that might in any way prove prejudicial to her'.[226]

Two days later, therefore, Grey wrote to Buchanan communicating the modification of Article 10 of the Simla Convention, which thus became:

> " The English, Chinese, and Thibetan texts of the present convention have been carefully compared and found to correspond, but in the event of there being any difference of meaning between them the English text shall be authoritative. "[227]

In addition, the secretary asked the ambassador to Russia to show Sazonov a draft of a note recognizing the need for an agreement with Saint Petersburg before making effective Articles 6 and 8 which amended the terms on which, seven years earlier, the two countries had agreed:

> " His Majesty's Government have the honour to communicate to the Imperial Russian Government a copy of a convention which has been signed between Great Britain, China and Thibet. His Majesty's Government recognise that articles 6 and 8 of this convention confer certain powers on Great Britain, the exercise of which, in a measure, conflict with the provisions of the Anglo-Russian Convention regarding Thibet of 1907. His Majesty's Government therefore engage that they will not exercise the powers conferred by the above-mentioned articles until they have come to an understanding with the Imperial Russian Government on the subject. "[228]

The note had to be signed and officially presented as soon as the Simla Convention was signed.[229] In this way, even if a definitive agreement on northern Afghanistan had not been reached, that note would still formally guarantee Russian interests from the changes defined by the two articles.[230] Furthermore, in the event that the Chinese used the amendment to Article 10 as a pretext for making other changes to the Convention, they could also continue negotiations on concessions in northern Afghanistan.[231]

Meanwhile, on May 31, from Peking, Jordan communicated to Grey that the Chinese were essentially opposed to the agreements concerning the border, asking for a redefinition in order to be able to sign the Convention.[232] According to the Chinese government, Chen had initialled the agreement, clarifying, however, that he would not put his signature without Peking's authorization.[233] Jordan was, however, confident in a Chinese signature at the end, 'but they will do so with a bad grace', weakening the Convention anyway and with negative consequences also on the negotiations regarding 'our railway and mining negotiations'.[234] As for Article 10, according to Jordan the Chinese were probably already aware of its changes 'and will in any case know that it emanates from Russia'.[235]

On June 5, 1914, the Foreign Office wrote a memorandum to the Chinese in which the latter were informed of the proposal to change Article 10 of the Convention, but that at the same time it was not possible to make other changes to the text or to the geographical maps.[236] Furthermore, according to the memorandum:

> Should China persist in her dissentient attitude and decline to sign a document concluding the conference, she will naturally be debarred from the privileges contemplated by the tripartite convention.[237]

The agreement on Afghanistan

Regarding the agreement on Afghanistan, the borders of «Northern Afghanistan» had to be precisely defined. For the India Office, in fact, it was necessary to delimit that area, making it coincide with the territory north of the Hindū Kush chain that extends from the Sino-Afghan border up to the border with Persia, including the mountain massif of Band-e-Bābā.[238] Crewe-Milnes also preferred to avoid including Harī Rūd, the ancient Arius (*rūd* in Persian means «river»), 'though he recognises that, if the point is insisted on by Russia, it may be necessary to extend the second part of the declaration so as to cover irrigation rights on that river'.[239]

In that case, however, Crewe-Milnes had to ask the Government of India for another opinion.[240] In the meantime, for Delhi and for the India Office, it was still necessary to ask Russia to officially recognize Afghanistan outside the sphere of influence of Saint Petersburg.[241] With such an official statement, it was even easier to explain the situation to the emir.[242] For the Government of India, however, defining the extent of Northern Afghanistan, as Crewe had proposed,[243] would entail the idea of having transformed Afghanistan into another Persia.[244] Furthermore, reference to the entire Harī Rūd and not to a particular point was 'somewhat vague'.[245]

The Government of India continued to attach importance to having to inform the Afghan emir prior to the publication of the note on the country.[246] Delhi was certainly the most dissatisfied with the agreement reached with the Russians. The changes in the situation in Mongolia prompted the British to re-discuss their role in Tibet and Sazonov's assurances to Buchanan about his assent to make Articles 6 and 8 effective did not reassure the viceroy of India, Charles Hardinge:

> It is Russia's action in Mongolia and the consequential definite change to our disadvantage of the *status quo* in Thibet since the convention of 1907 was concluded, that has forced this new convention on us. Against that change we secure no other direct advantage for Great Britain than the concession which article 8 contemplates and the undertaking which Russia is to give us in a secret note [...]. We attach the highest importance to the securing of both these concessions.[247]

Grey therefore asked Buchanan to communicate to the Russian government the willingness of the British government to sign a joint declaration in which Saint Petersburg had to recognize Afghanistan outside its sphere of influence, while London undertook not to support the requests of British subjects for irrigation works, railways and even for privileged rights for commercial or industrial activities in northern Afghanistan.[248] As for the definition of the area, this was to include the territory north of a line that started from Eshkāshem, a few miles outside the Wakhan (*Vākhān*) Corridor, and continued westwards, up to Z⁻ū ol-Faqār, where the Harī Rūd entered the territories of the Russian Empire:

> " Ishkasham [*Eshkāshem*] on Abipanja [*Āb-e Panjah*] to Zebak [*Zībāk*], thence to Munjan Pass [*Monjān Kūtal*], thence to Nawak [*Nāvak*] Pass, thence to Murgh Pass [*Morgh Kūtal*], thence to Doshi [*Dūshī*], from there viâ Sinjitak [*Senjetak*] and Badkak [*Bādqāq*] Passes to Doab-i-Shah Pasand [*Dūāb-e Shāh Pasand*], thence to Tarkuch [*Tarkūch*] on Bandiamir [*Band-e Amir*], thence to Daulat Yar [*Daūlat Yār*]. From this point line would follow crests of following ranges : Bandibaba [*Band-e Bābā*] and Siyah Bubak [*Sīyah Būbak*] and thence to point where Hari Rud enters Russian territory at Zulfikar [*Zū ol-Faqār*]."[249]

In this way, the Afghan side of the Harī Rūd was excluded, even if the British government was ready to bring back the exclusion of official support also for irrigation from the Harī Rūd 'whether within or without the area defined above'.[250]

But in that case, Grey explained to Buchanan,

> [n]o mention, however, should be made of the willingness of His Majesty's Government to give this further concession unless the Russian Government are dissatisfied with the definition of Northern Afghanistan as given above or themselves raise the question of the Hari Rud.[251]

More important, for His Majesty's Government, was not to include in the definition neither Herāt and its surroundings, nor the peaks of the Hindū Kush from Nawak to the west: '[i]t is undesirable that Russia should have even a shadowy claim in either case'.[252]

Indeed, the Russian foreign minister himself informed Buchanan, in a meeting on June 10 – a few hours before leaving again for another ten days – that Saint Petersburg could not accept the exclusion of the Harī Rūd, since it was very important for the irrigation of the Transcaspian province.[253] For Sazonov, the line had to pass south of the Harī Rūd:

> Line of demarcation, he said, must follow mountain chain of Sefid and Kouh to the south of Hari Rud to point where that river commences to form frontier between Afghanistan and Persia.[254]

This line would include not only the entire Afghan Harī Rūd, but also the city of Herāt, which is located a few miles north of Harī Rūd. Sazonov reiterated to Buchanan – who had not yet been authorized to extend the boundaries of the territory – that he wanted something in return for allowing the British to cancel the 1907 Agreement on Tibet.[255] Buchanan then recalled that, according to what had been said up to then, Sazonov's goal was only to convince the Russian public opinion of his work and that the notes would not define the territory and therefore not even the question of Harī Rūd.[256] When Sazonov told him 'that term " Northern Afghanistan " was too vague' and subject to different interpretations 'by the "Times" and "Novoe Vremya." ', Buchanan replied that it was 'his Excellency himself' who had chosen that definition.[257] The British, while not wanting to divert the rivers of northern Afghanistan, could not define an agreement that risked being considered a renunciation of their interests in Herāt.[258] The ambassador explained to the minister that one option that could be considered was to leave the definition of northern Afghanistan unchanged, and to add the British commitment not to support requests for irrigation works from the Harī Rūd.[259] In this way, official support was guaranteed for concessions of another nature in the area, but at the same time the flow of water of the river was safeguarded. Sazonov was initially reluctant to accept that proposal, but '[s]ubsequently he said that if we [the British] gave such an undertaking it would have to be published'.[260] Another central point in the discussion concerned the railway network: Sazonov in fact thought that not publishing the exact area of northern Afghanistan would create controversy in parliament in London and Saint Petersburg, as well as in the press.[261] Sazonov again explained his position on northern Afghanistan in a letter that he delivered to Buchanan at the end of the meeting.[262] The text also asked for a clause to be added to the agreement that guaranteed the Russian Buddhists the right to travel to Lhasa, as they had done several times, via India, given the difficulty in reaching the capital of Tibet from the north.[263] In fact, in April 1914, there had been a Russian protest because the Government of India had prevented Russian pilgrims from entering Tibet.[264]

Before leaving, Sazonov instructed Kimon Argiropulo and the head of the Eastern Department, to try to find a solution to the matter and Buchanan would continue to negotiate with them.[265] However, as he wrote to Grey, the British ambassador was aware of the difficulty in keeping the definition of the area of northern Afghanistan secret.[266] The next day, June 11, Buchanan again sent Grey two more communications on the matter,[267] suggesting to separate the problem of irrigation works from the question of the railways.[268] The British Government could propose to the Russian minister that it would undertake not to support the requests of British subjects for irrigation works with water from the Harī Rūd, the Morghāb[269] or any other river indicated by Sazonov.[270] Furthermore, the British Government would not support its subjects' 'applications for railways, &c.' in the area of northern Afghanistan, as defined by London.[271] The ambassador also explained to Grey that the Russian foreign minister had no objection to continuing to recognize Afghanistan outside of Saint Petersburg's sphere of political influence, but still wanted to include Herāt and both sides of the Harī Rūd in the definition of northern Afghanistan.[272] Furthermore:

> From my conversation with his Excellency I carried away the impression that, whether or not we come to an arrangement with Russia with regard to Northern Afghanistan, the Russian Government will before long take the law into their own hands if the Afghans persist in diverting the waters of the Heri-Rud, and other rivers to the prejudice of Transcaspia.[273]

Evidently, however, these terms of the negotiations were not so pleasing to the India Office, as demonstrated by a communication to the Foreign Office:

> For reasons which it is unnecessary to elaborate, Lord Crewe has felt the utmost reluctance in assenting to the proposed declaration in regard to Afghanistan in any form, and he is strongly opposed to making further concessions on this point if it can by any means be avoided.[274]

At this point Sazonov, for Crewe-Milnes, seemed to be the real winner of the negotiations and the Russian foreign minister's old concerns could vanish:

> The new convention, as qualified by the notes to the Russian Government which are to be published simultaneously with it, will present anything but the appearance of a British diplomatic triumph at Russia's expense. On the contrary, the position acquired by Russia under the Agreement of 1907 will be found to have been jealously safeguarded.[275]

It could be said that the question of political reputation was now being reversed, because what was to be published was clearly in favor of the Russians, who formally, in the eyes of public opinion, became the real holders of the power to implement or not the Simla Convention, being able to decide the fate of Articles 6 and 8.[276] There was certainly Sazonov's assurance not to pose obstacles, and therefore to allow the British to ask for concessions in Tibet and to send their agent to Lhasa, however, Saint Petersburg was bound only by a secret note, while the notes that sanctioned the Russian diplomatic strength, the results obtained by Sazonov at the expense of the United Kingdom, would be public, therefore ready to be brought to the attention of Westminster and the country.[277] Crewe-Milnes therefore asked Grey, in the event that Sazonov had continued to demand the publication of the definition of northern Afghanistan, to demand the same thing also for the Russian commitment not to oppose Articles 6 and 8.[278] To make the matter easier, according to Crewe-Milnes, the public and secret notes could simply be replaced with a public acknowledgment of the convention by the Russian government.[279] So,

> [t]he published documents would then present to the world a fair diplomatic bargain, in which either party would have made concessions for a specified return, and which neither Government should find it difficult to defend against domestic criticism.[280]

Crewe-Milnes did not want to widen the definition of the area of northern Afghanistan, but was prepared to accept Buchanan's proposal to include the British commitment not to support the demands for exploitation of the rivers chosen by Sazonov, as well as to separate the question of irrigation works from the railway one.[281] He recalled, however, the need expressed by the Government of India to give explanations to the Afghan emir, before the publication of any agreement.[282] There were no problems even regarding the possibility of Russian Buddhist pilgrims to continue to go to Lhasa via the Indian border, but knowing more details (for example the number of pilgrims), as well as the reason for such a long path.[283] In fact, until April 1914, Lord Crewe was not even aware of the existence of Russian requests to reach Tibet via India.[284]

Simla and Sarajevo

Meanwhile, on July 3, 1914, the Simla Convention had finally been signed, but not by the Chinese delegate, whose government, in the end, refused to accept the terms on the definitions of the line that was to divide Inner Tibet from Outer Tibet, demanding a different arrangement of the border and thus offering only a simple 'adhesion to the majority of articles of the convention'.[285] Grey then wrote to Buchanan to communicate the result of the agreement to the Russian government, underlining, however, the British commitment in reaching a signature also with the Chinese and that the latter had indeed rejected the agreement only because of the border issue, however accepting the rest of the convention 'and that His Majesty's Government still hope that they may, after reflection, agree to signature'.[286] Furthermore, Buchanan had to make it clear to the Russians that the British would not implement the provisions of the Convention contrary to the Anglo-Russian Convention of 1907 without consulting with Saint Petersburg.[287] Confidently Grey had also revealed to the ambassador that McMahon and the blon-chen Bshad-sgra had recognized the validity and binding character of the agreement for London and Lhasa, while China would be excluded from the privileges provided by the document 'as long as she withheld signature'.[288] Furthermore, the British government had guaranteed the Tibetan delegate British support, with weapons and ammunition from India, in the event of a Chinese invasion.[289]

As for the Russian protests over the bans imposed on Russian Buddhist pilgrims who wanted to travel to Tibet from India, the Government of India had decided, given the situation, to also prevent British subjects from reaching Lhasa for any reason.[290] But as soon as the conditions allowed it, there would be no objection on the part of the British government to allowing Russian pilgrims to travel there, naturally under the control of the Indian authorities and on the basis of the Frontier Crossing Regulations.[291] However, Buchanan should point out to Sazonov that although London did not want to prevent Russian Buddhists from traveling to Tibet for religious reasons, the British Government was not bound by the Anglo-Russian Convention to open the Indo-Tibetan border to Russian pilgrims.[292]

In the meantime, however, on the same day that Grey gave these further instructions to Buchanan, on July 28, 1914, exactly one month after the assassination of Archduke Franz Ferdinand and his wife Sofia under the fire of Gavrilo Princip in Sarajevo, the Austro-Hungarian Empire opened the conflict with the Kingdom of Serbia. On August 1 Germany, an ally of Vienna, declared war on Russia and on August 3 on France. The next day British troops were preparing to leave for the front against German soldiers. It was the beginning of the First World War. It is not difficult to imagine that in the precipice where Europe was ending, with Russia and Great Britain placed on the same front, the rivalries and misunderstandings in High Asia took on a completely different color. In such a delicate moment in the history of the Empire, as will be seen, Grey could not allow the risk of relations with the allies cracking due to differences on Asian issues.

Endnotes

1 Full text of the treaty: TNA, FO 535/17, Enclosure 8 in No. 231, Convention between Great Britain, China, and Thibet, pp. 262-265.

2 See, inter alia: BELL 1924, pp. 148-159; H. E. RICHARDSON, *Tibet and Its History*, Boulder – London 1984, pp. 107-120; MCKAY 1997, pp. 56-58. On the legitimacy of the agreement see N. C. SINHA, *The Simla Convention 1914: A Chinese Puzzle*, in: Bulletin of Tibetology, No. 1, 1977, pp. 35-39. For a comparison between the British sources and the Tibetan account of the conference see R. KOBAYASHI, *An Analytical Study of the Tibetan Record of the Simla Conference (1913-1914): Shing stag rgya gar 'phags pa'i yul du dbyin bod rgya gsum chings mol mdzad lugs kun gsal me long*, in: *Current Issues and Progress in Tibetan Studies, Proceedings of the Third International Seminar of Young Tibetologists, Kobe 2012*, edited by T. Takeuchi, K. Iwao, A. Nishida, S. Kumagai and M. Yamamoto, Kobe 2013, pp. 183-200.

3 L. PETECH, *The Kingdom of Ladakh: C. 950-1842 A.D.*, Roma 1977, p. 151. In addition to Petech's text, on the history of Ladakh see also J. RIZVI, *Ladakh: Crossroads of High Asia*, Delhi 1996.

4 TNA, FO 535/17, No. 11, Minutes by Sir W. Langley respecting the Tripartite Agreement, January 20, 1914, p. 12.

5 TNA, FO 535/17, No. 15, Sir Edward Grey to Sir G. Buchanan, January 24, 1914, p. 15.

6 TNA, FO 535/17, No. 15, Sir Edward Grey to Sir G. Buchanan, January 24, 1914, p. 15.

7 TNA, FO 535/17, No. 21, Sir G. Buchanan to Sir Edward Grey, February 1, 1914, p. 21.

8 TNA, FO 535/17, No. 21, Sir G. Buchanan to Sir Edward Grey, February 1, 1914, p. 21.

9 TNA, FO 535/17, No. 21, Sir C. Buchanan to Sir Edward Grey, February 1, 1914, p. 21.

10 TNA, FO 535/17, No. 21, Sir G. Buchanan to Sir Edward Grey, February 1, 1914, p. 21.

11 TNA, FO 535/17, No. 21, Sir G. Buchanan to Sir Edward Grey, February 1, 1914, p. 21.

12 TNA, FO 535/17, No. 26, Sir G. Buchanan to Sir Edward Grey, February 3, 1914, p. 24.

13 TNA, FO 535/17, No. 26, Sir G. Buchanan to Sir Edward Grey, February 3, 1914, p. 24.

14 TNA, FO 535/17, No. 26, Sir G. Buchanan to Sir Edward Grey, February 3, 1914, p. 24.

15 TNA, FO 535/17, No. 26, Sir G. Buchanan to Sir Edward Grey, February 3, 1914, p. 24.

16 TNA, FO 535/17, No. 21, Sir G. Buchanan to Sir Edward Grey, February 1, 1914, p. 21.

17 B. BULSTRODE, *A Tour in Mongolia*, London 1920, p. 147. Mamen was Rustad's cousin (*The Correspondence of G. E. Morrison* 2013, n. 554, T. A. Rustad to G. E. Morrison, November 5, 1912, p. 53).

18 Full text of the letter: TNA, FO 535/17, Enclosure 2 in No. 118, Mr. Mamen to Mr. Thomas (British American Tobacco Company), February 13, 1914, pp. 135-136.

19 TNA, FO 535/17, Enclosure 2 in No. 118, Mr. Mamen to Mr. Thomas (British American Tobacco Company), February 13, 1914, p. 135.

20 TNA, FO 535/17, Enclosure 2 in No. 118, Mr. Mamen to Mr. Thomas (British American Tobacco Company), February 13, 1914, p. 135.

21 TNA, FO 535/17, Enclosure 2 in No. 118, Mr. Mamen to Mr. Thomas (British American Tobacco Company), February 13, 1914, p. 135.

22 TNA, FO 535/17, No. 118, Sir J. Jordan to Sir Edward Grey, April 27, 1914, p. 134.

23 TNA, FO 535/17, No. 38, Sir Edward Grey to Sir G. Buchanan, February 27, 1914, p. 60.

24 TNA, FO 535/17, No. 38, Sir Edward Grey to Sir G. Buchanan, February 27, 1914, pp. 60-61.

25 TNA, FO 535/17, No. 38, Sir Edward Grey to Sir G. Buchanan, February 27, 1914, p. 61.

26 TNA, FO 535/17, No. 4, Board of Trade to Foreign Office, January 7, 1914, p. 2; TNA, FO 535/17, No. 45, Sir G. Buchanan to Sir Edward Grey, March 4, 1914, p. 67.

27 TNA, FO 535/16, Enclosure in No. 444, Board of Trade's proposal for an agreement with Mongolia, p. 428.

28 TNA, FO 535/17, No. 4, Board of Trade to Foreign Office, January 7, 1914, p. 2.

29 TNA, FO 535/17, No. 45, Sir G. Buchanan to Sir Edward Grey, March 4, 1914, p. 67.

30 TNA, FO 535/17, No. 45, Sir G. Buchanan to Sir Edward Grey, March 4, 1914, p. 67.

31 TNA, FO 535/17, No. 45, Sir G. Buchanan to Sir Edward Grey, March 4, 1914, p. 67.

32 TNA, FO 535/17, No. 45, Sir G. Buchanan to Sir Edward Grey, March 4, 1914, p. 67.

33 TNA, FO 535/17, No. 45, Sir G. Buchanan to Sir Edward Grey, March 4, 1914, p. 67.

34 TNA, FO 535/17, No. 45, Sir G. Buchanan to Sir Edward Grey, March 4, 1914, p. 67.

35 TNA, FO 535/17, No. 45, Sir G. Buchanan to Sir Edward Grey, March 4, 1914, p. 68.

36 TNA, FO 535/17, No. 45, Sir G. Buchanan to Sir Edward Grey, March 4, 1914, p. 68.

37 TNA, FO 535/17, No. 60, India Office to Foreign Office, March 26, 1914, p. 77.

38 TNA, FO 535/17, No. 60, India Office to Foreign Office, March 26, 1914, p. 77.

39 TNA, FO 535/17, No. 60, India Office to Foreign Office, March 26, 1914, p. 77.

40 TNA, FO 535/17, No. 45, Sir G. Buchanan to Sir Edward Grey, March 4, 1914, p. 68.

41 TNA, FO 535/17, No. 60, India Office to Foreign Office, March 26, 1914, p. 77.

42 TNA, FO 535/17, No. 60, India Office to Foreign Office, March 26, 1914, p. 77.

43 The complete text of the draft, updated to February 20, 1914, is in TNA, FO 535/17, Enclosure in No. 35, Proposed Tripartite Convention, pp. 57-58.

44 Sir Arthur Henry McMahon (1862-1949).

45 TNA, FO 535/17, Enclosure 1 in No. 102, Government of India to the Marquess of Crewe, April 27, 1914, p. 121.

46 TNA, FO 535/17, Enclosure 1 in No. 102, Government of India to the Marquess of Crewe, April 27, 1914, p. 121.

47 TNA, FO 535/17, Enclosure 1 in No. 102, Government of India to the Marquess of Crewe, April 27, 1914, p. 121.

48 TNA, FO 535/17, Enclosure 1 in No. 102, Government of India to the Marquess of Crewe, April 27, 1914, p. 121.

49 TNA, FO 535/17, Enclosure 1 in No. 102, Government of India to the Marquess of Crewe, April 27, 1914, p. 121.

50 TNA, FO 535/17, No. 104, Government of India to the Marquess of Crewe, April 29, 1914, p. 123.

51 TNA, FO 535/17, No. 105, India Office to Foreign Office, April 30, 1914, p. 124.

52 TNA, FO 535/17, No. 112, Sir Edward Grey to Sir G. Buchanan, May 4, 1914, p. 128.

53 TNA, FO 535/17, No. 112, Sir Edward Grey to Sir G. Buchanan, May 4, 1914, p. 129.

54 TNA, FO 535/17, No. 112, Sir Edward Grey to Sir G. Buchanan, May 4, 1914, p. 129.

55 TNA, FO 535/17, No. 112, Sir Edward Grey to Sir G. Buchanan, May 4, 1914, p. 129.

56 TNA, FO 535/17, No. 112, Sir Edward Grey to Sir G. Buchanan, May 4, 1914, p. 129.

57 TNA, FO 535/17, No. 112, Sir Edward Grey to Sir G. Buchanan, May 4, 1914, p. 129.

58 TNA, FO 535/17, No. 112, Sir Edward Grey to Sir G. Buchanan, May 4, 1914, p. 129.

59 TNA, FO 535/17, No. 112, Sir Edward Grey to Sir G. Buchanan, May 4, 1914, pp. 129-130.

60 TNA, FO 535/17, No. 112, Sir Edward Grey to Sir G. Buchanan, May 4, 1914, p. 130.

61 TNA, FO 535/17, No. 112, Sir Edward Grey to Sir G. Buchanan, May 4, 1914, p. 130.

62 TNA, FO 535/17, No. 112, Sir Edward Grey to Sir G. Buchanan, May 4, 1914, p. 130.

63 TNA, FO 535/17, No. 112, Sir Edward Grey to Sir G. Buchanan, May 4, 1914, p. 130.

64 TNA, FO 535/17, No. 112, Sir Edward Grey to Sir G. Buchanan, May 4, 1914, p. 130.

65 On the question and the history of Arunachal Pradesh see, inter alia: M. L. BOSE, *History of Arunachal Pradesh*, New Delhi 1997; L. TENPA, *An Early History of the Mon Region (India) and its Relationship with Tibet and Bhutan*, Dharamshala 2018. Lobsang Tenpa's text concerns the western area of the current state of Arunachal Pradesh and where Rta-dbang (Tawang), the birthplace of the sixth dalai lama, is located.

66 TNA, FO 535/17, No. 112, Sir Edward Grey to Sir G. Buchanan, May 4, 1914, p. 130.

67 TNA, FO 535/17, No. 112, Sir Edward Grey to Sir G. Buchanan, May 4, 1914, p. 130.

68 TNA, FO 535/17, No. 112, Sir Edward Grey to Sir G. Buchanan, May 4, 1914, p. 130.

69 TNA, FO 535/17, No. 112, Sir Edward Grey to Sir G. Buchanan, May 4, 1914, p. 130.

70 TNA, FO 535/17, No. 112, Sir Edward Grey to Sir G. Buchanan, May 4, 1914, p. 131.

71 Buchanan communicated this to Grey on May 8, 1914, a Friday, explaining that Sazonov would not return until the end of the following week. In fact, Sazonov returned on May 16 (TNA, FO 535/17, No. 116, Sir G. Buchanan to Sir Edward Grey, May 8, 1914, p. 132; TNA, FO 535/17, No. 123, Sir G. Buchanan to Sir Edward Grey, May 17, 1914, p. 138).

72 TNA, FO 535/17, No. 116, Sir G. Buchanan to Sir Edward Grey, May 8, 1914, p. 132; TNA, FO 535/17, No. 125, Sir G. Buchanan to Sir Edward Grey, May 9, 1914, p. 141. Full text of the note (in French): TNA, FO 535/17, Enclosure in No. 125, Sir G. Buchanan to M. Sazonof, le 25 avril (8 mai), 1914, pp. 142-144.

73 TNA, FO 535/17, No. 116, Sir G. Buchanan to Sir Edward Grey, May 8, 1914, p. 132.

74 TNA, FO 535/17, No. 125, Sir G. Buchanan to Sir Edward Grey, May 9, 1914, p. 141.

75 TNA, FO 535/17, No. 125, Sir G. Buchanan to Sir Edward Grey, May 9, 1914, p. 141.

76 TNA, FO 535/17, No. 123, Sir G. Buchanan to Sir Edward Grey, May 17, 1914, p. 138.

77 TNA, FO 535/17, No. 123, Sir G. Buchanan to Sir Edward Grey, May 17, 1914, p. 138.

78 TNA, FO 535/17, No. 123, Sir G. Buchanan to Sir Edward Grey, May 17, 1914, p. 138.

79 TNA, FO 535/17, No. 123, Sir G. Buchanan to Sir Edward Grey, May 17, 1914, p. 138.

80 On this agreement see *The Potsdam Accord*, in: *Handbook for the Diplomatic History of Europe, Asia, and Africa, 1870-1914*, by F. M. Anderson – A. S. Hershey (with the assistance of 50 contributors), prepared for the National Board for Historical Service, Government Printing Office, Washington 1918, pp. 407-409.

81 TNA, FO 535/17, No. 123, Sir G. Buchanan to Sir Edward Grey, May 17, 1914, p. 138.

82 TNA, FO 535/17, No. 123, Sir G. Buchanan to Sir Edward Grey, May 17, 1914, p. 138.

83 TNA, FO 535/17, No. 123, Sir G. Buchanan to Sir Edward Grey, May 17, 1914, p. 138.

84 TNA, FO 535/17, No. 123, Sir G. Buchanan to Sir Edward Grey, May 17, 1914, p. 138.

85 TNA, FO 535/17, No. 123, Sir G. Buchanan to Sir Edward Grey, May 17, 1914, p. 138.

86 TNA, FO 535/16, No. 137, Foreign Office to India Office, March 17, 1913, p. 98.

87 TNA, FO 535/16, No. 137, Foreign Office to India Office, March 17, 1913, p. 98.

88 TNA, FO 535/17, No. 123, Sir G. Buchanan to Sir Edward Grey, May 17, 1914, p. 138.

89 TNA, FO 535/17, No. 123, Sir G. Buchanan to Sir Edward Grey, May 17, 1914, p. 138.

90 TNA, FO 535/17, No. 123, Sir G. Buchanan to Sir Edward Grey, May 17, 1914, p. 138.

91 TNA, FO 535/17, No. 123, Sir G. Buchanan to Sir Edward Grey, May 17, 1914, p. 138.

92 TNA, FO 535/17, No. 123, Sir G. Buchanan to Sir Edward Grey, May 17, 1914, p. 138.

93 The text in square brackets, in this case, belongs to the person who transcribed the document for the Confidential Print.

94 TNA, FO 535/17, No. 123, Sir G. Buchanan to Sir Edward Grey, May 17, 1914, p. 138.

95 TNA, FO 535/17, No. 123, Sir G. Buchanan to Sir Edward Grey, May 17, 1914, p. 138.

96 TNA, FO 535/17, No. 123, Sir G. Buchanan to Sir Edward Grey, May 17, 1914, p. 138.

97 TNA, FO 535/17, No. 123, Sir G. Buchanan to Sir Edward Grey, May 17, 1914, p. 138.

98 TNA, FO 535/17, No. 123, Sir G. Buchanan to Sir Edward Grey, May 17, 1914, p. 139.

99 TNA, FO 535/17, No. 123, Sir G. Buchanan to Sir Edward Grey, May 17, 1914, p. 139.

100 TNA, FO 535/17, No. 123, Sir G. Buchanan to Sir Edward Grey, May 17, 1914, p. 139.

101 TNA, FO 535/17, No. 123, Sir G. Buchanan to Sir Edward Grey, May 17, 1914, p. 139.

102 TNA, FO 535/17, No. 123, Sir G. Buchanan to Sir Edward Grey, May 17, 1914, p. 139.

103 TNA, FO 535/17, No. 123, Sir G. Buchanan to Sir Edward Grey, May 17, 1914, p. 139.

104 TNA, FO 535/17, No. 123, Sir G. Buchanan to Sir Edward Grey, May 17, 1914, p. 139.

105 TNA, FO 535/17, No. 123, Sir G. Buchanan to Sir Edward Grey, May 17, 1914, p. 139.

106 TNA, FO 535/17, No. 123, Sir G. Buchanan to Sir Edward Grey, May 17, 1914, p. 139.

107 TNA, FO 535/17, No. 123, Sir G. Buchanan to Sir Edward Grey, May 17, 1914, p. 139.

108 TNA, FO 535/17, No. 123, Sir G. Buchanan to Sir Edward Grey, May 17, 1914, p. 139.

109 TNA, FO 535/17, No. 127, Sir G. Buchanan to Sir Edward Grey, May 18, 1914, p. 146.

110 TNA, FO 535/17, No. 127, Sir G. Buchanan to Sir Edward Grey, May 18, 1914, p. 146.

111 TNA, FO 535/17, No. 127, Sir G. Buchanan to Sir Edward Grey, May 18, 1914, p. 146.

112 TNA, FO 535/17, No. 132, Sir G. Buchanan to Sir Edward Grey, May 19, 1914, p. 151.

113 TNA, FO 535/17, No. 127, Sir G. Buchanan to Sir Edward Grey, May 18, 1914, p. 146.

114 TNA, FO 535/17, No. 132, Sir G. Buchanan to Sir Edward Grey, May 19, 1914, p. 150.

115 TNA, FO 535/17, No. 132, Sir G. Buchanan to Sir Edward Grey, May 19, 1914, p. 150.

116 TNA, FO 535/17, No. 132, Sir G. Buchanan to Sir Edward Grey, May 19, 1914, p. 150.

117 TNA, FO 535/17, No. 127, Sir G. Buchanan to Sir Edward Grey, May 18, 1914, p. 146.

118 TNA, FO 535/17, No. 127, Sir G. Buchanan to Sir Edward Grey, May 18, 1914, p. 146.

119 TNA, FO 535/17, No. 127, Sir G. Buchanan to Sir Edward Grey, May 18, 1914, p. 146; TNA, FO 535/17, No. 132, Sir G. Buchanan to Sir Edward Grey, May 19, 1914, p. 151.

120 TNA, FO 535/17, No. 132, Sir G. Buchanan to Sir Edward Grey, May 19, 1914, p. 151.

121 TNA, FO 535/17, No. 132, Sir G. Buchanan to Sir Edward Grey, May 19, 1914, p. 151.

122 TNA, FO 535/17, No. 132, Sir G. Buchanan to Sir Edward Grey, May 19, 1914, p. 151.

123 TNA, FO 535/17, No. 127, Sir G. Buchanan to Sir Edward Grey, May 18, 1914, p. 146.

124 TNA, FO 535/17, No. 127, Sir G. Buchanan to Sir Edward Grey, May 18, 1914, p. 146.

125 TNA, FO 535/17, No. 127, Sir G. Buchanan to Sir Edward Grey, May 18, 1914, p. 146.

126 TNA, FO 535/17, No. 127, Sir G. Buchanan to Sir Edward Grey, May 18, 1914, p. 146.

127 TNA, FO 535/17, No. 127, Sir G. Buchanan to Sir Edward Grey, May 18, 1914, p. 146.

128 TNA, FO 535/17, No. 127, Sir G. Buchanan to Sir Edward Grey, May 18, 1914, pp. 146-147.

129 TNA, FO 535/17, No. 130, Sir G. Buchanan to Sir Edward Grey, May 19, 1914, p. 148.

130 TNA, FO 535/17, No. 127, Sir G. Buchanan to Sir Edward Grey, May 18, 1914, p. 147.

131 TNA, FO 535/17, No. 127, Sir G. Buchanan to Sir Edward Grey, May 18, 1914, p. 147.

132 TNA, FO 535/17, No. 130, Sir G. Buchanan to Sir Edward Grey, May 19, 1914, p. 148.

133 TNA, FO 535/17, No. 130, Sir G. Buchanan to Sir Edward Grey, May 19, 1914, p. 148.

134 TNA, FO 535/17, No. 130, Sir G. Buchanan to Sir Edward Grey, May 19, 1914, p. 148.

135 TNA, FO 535/17, No. 130, Sir G. Buchanan to Sir Edward Grey, May 19, 1914, p. 148.

136 TNA, FO 535/17, No. 130, Sir G. Buchanan to Sir Edward Grey, May 19, 1914, p. 148.

137 TNA, FO 535/17, No. 130, Sir G. Buchanan to Sir Edward Grey, May 19, 1914, p. 148.

138 TNA, FO 535/17, No. 130, Sir G. Buchanan to Sir Edward Grey, May 19, 1914, p. 148.

139 TNA, FO 535/17, No. 130, Sir G. Buchanan to Sir Edward Grey, May 19, 1914, p. 148.

140 TNA, FO 535/17, No. 130, Sir G. Buchanan to Sir Edward Grey, May 19, 1914, p. 148.

141 TNA, FO 535/17, No. 130, Sir G. Buchanan to Sir Edward Grey, May 19, 1914, p. 148.

142 TNA, FO 535/17, No. 136, Sir G. Buchanan to Sir Edward Grey, May 22, 1914, p. 153; full text of the memorandum: TNA, FO 535/17, Enclosure in No. 136, Memorandum communicated to Sir G. Buchanan, pp. 153-154.

143 TNA, FO 535/17, Enclosure in No. 136, Memorandum communicated to Sir G. Buchanan, p. 153. The Chinese and Russian text of the Convention of Peking for the Land Trade between Russia and China of 1862 is published in *Treaties, Conventions, etc., between China and Foreign States* 1917, pp.

127-143. The French, Chinese and Russian text of the 1881 Treaty of Saint Petersburg is in *Treaties, Conventions, etc., between China and Foreign States 1917*, pp. 168-207.

144 TNA, FO 535/17, Enclosure in No. 136, Memorandum communicated to Sir G. Buchanan, p. 153.

145 TNA, FO 535/17, Enclosure in No. 136, Memorandum communicated to Sir G. Buchanan, pp. 153-154.

146 TNA, FO 535/17, Enclosure in No. 136, Memorandum communicated to Sir G. Buchanan, p. 154.

147 TNA, FO 535/17, Enclosure in No. 136, Memorandum communicated to Sir G. Buchanan, p. 154.

148 TNA, FO 535/17, Enclosure in No. 136, Memorandum communicated to Sir G. Buchanan, p. 154.

149 TNA, FO 535/17, Enclosure in No. 136, Memorandum communicated to Sir G. Buchanan, p. 154.

150 TNA, FO 535/17, No. 136, Sir G. Buchanan to Sir Edward Grey, May 22, 1914, p. 153.

151 TNA, FO 535/17, No. 178, Foreign Office to India Office (Also to Board of Trade, mutatis mutandis), June 18, 1914, p. 180.

152 TNA, FO 535/17, No. 178, Foreign Office to India Office (Also to Board of Trade, mutatis mutandis), June 18, 1914, p. 181.

153 TNA, FO 535/17, No. 178, Foreign Office to India Office (Also to Board of Trade, mutatis mutandis), June 18, 1914, p. 181.

154 TNA, FO 535/17, No. 178, Foreign Office to India Office (Also to Board of Trade, mutatis mutandis), June 18, 1914, p. 181.

155 TNA, FO 535/17, No. 178, Foreign Office to India Office (Also to Board of Trade, mutatis mutandis), June 18, 1914, p. 181.

156 TNA, FO 535/17, No. 178, Foreign Office to India Office (Also to Board of Trade, mutatis mutandis), June 18, 1914, p. 181.

157 TNA, FO 535/17, No. 178, Foreign Office to India Office (Also to Board of Trade, mutatis mutandis), June 18, 1914, p. 181.

158 TNA, FO 535/18, No. 4, India Office to Foreign Office, January 26, 1915, p. 2. For the text of the Convention see *Treaties and Agreements with and concerning China, 1894-1919*, Vol. I: Manchu Period (1894-1911), compiled and edited by J. V. A. MacMurray, New York 1921, pp. 94-98.

159 TNA, FO 535/17, No. 180*, Sir J. Jordan to Sir Edward Grey, June 5, 1914, p. 182 A.

160 TNA, FO 535/17, Enclosure in No. 180*, Mongol Government to Sir J. Jordan, April 1914, p. 182 B.

161 TNA, FO 535/17, Enclosure in No. 180*, Mongol Government to Sir J. Jordan, April 1914, p. 182 B.

162 TNA, FO 535/17, Enclosure in No. 180*, Mongol Government to Sir J. Jordan, April 1914, p. 182 B.

163 TNA, FO 535/17, Enclosure in No. 180*, Mongol Government to Sir J. Jordan, April 1914, p. 182 B.

164 TNA, FO 535/17, Enclosure in No. 180*, Mongol Government to Sir J. Jordan, April 1914, p. 182 B.

165 TNA, FO 535/17, Enclosure in No. 180*, Mongol Government to Sir J. Jordan, April 1914, p. 182 B.

166 TNA, FO 535/17, No. 180*, Sir J. Jordan to Sir Edward Grey, June 5, 1914, p. 182 A.

167 TNA, FO 535/17, No. 180*, Sir J. Jordan to Sir Edward Grey, June 5, 1914, p. 182 A.

168 Vladimir Vladimirovich Grave (1880-1930), first secretary of the Russian embassy in Peking between 1912 and 1920 (НИКОЛАЕВИЧ КРЫЛОВ-ТОЛСТИКОВИЧ, А., *Придворный календарь на 1915 год. Комментарии*, Москва 2015, p. 209).

169 TNA, FO 535/17, No. 180*, Sir J. Jordan to Sir Edward Grey, June 5, 1914, p. 182 A.

170 TNA, FO 535/17, No. 180*, Sir J. Jordan to Sir Edward Grey, June 5, 1914, p. 182 A.

171 TNA, FO 535/17, No. 180*, Sir J. Jordan to Sir Edward Grey, June 5, 1914, p. 182 A.

172 TNA, FO 535/17, No. 180*, Sir J. Jordan to Sir Edward Grey, June 5, 1914, p. 182 A.

173 TNA, FO 535/17, No. 180*, Sir J. Jordan to Sir Edward Grey, June 5, 1914, p. 182 A.

174 TNA, FO 535/17, No. 4, Board of Trade to Foreign Office, January 7, 1914, p. 2.

175 TNA, FO 535/17, No. 180*, Sir J. Jordan to Sir Edward Grey, June 5, 1914, p. 182 A.

176 TNA, FO 535/17, No. 180*, Sir J. Jordan to Sir Edward Grey, June 5, 1914, p. 182 A. On Macartney in Qeshqer see C. P. SKRINE – P. NIGHTINGALE, *Macartney at Kashgar: New Light on British, Chinese and Russian Activities in Sinkiang, 1890-1918*, London 1973.

177 TNA, FO 535/17, No. 180*, Sir J. Jordan to Sir Edward Grey, June 5, 1914, p. 182 A.

178 TNA, FO 535/17, No. 180*, Sir J. Jordan to Sir Edward Grey, June 5, 1914, p. 182 A.

179 TNA, FO 535/17, No. 180*, Sir J. Jordan to Sir Edward Grey, June 5, 1914, p. 182 A.

180 TNA, FO 535/17, No. 180*, Sir J. Jordan to Sir Edward Grey, June 5, 1914, p. 182 A.

181 The new name of the Ministry of Foreign Affairs of the Republic of China (外交部).

182 TNA, FO 535/17, No. 175, Translation of Telegram from the Wai-chiao Pu, dated June 12.–(Communicated by the Chinese Minister, June 16, 1914), p. 179.

183 TNA, FO 535/17, No. 217, Foreign Office to Board of Trade, July 17, 1914, pp. 217-218.

184 TNA, FO 535/17, No. 202, Board of Trade to Foreign Office, July 7, 1914, pp. 199-200.

185 TNA, FO 535/17, No. 202, Board of Trade to Foreign Office, July 7, 1914, p. 199.

186 TNA, FO 535/17, No. 202, Board of Trade to Foreign Office, July 7, 1914, p. 199. The draft agreement drawn up by the Board is in TNA, FO 535/16, Enclosure in No. 444, Board of Trade's proposal for an agreement with Mongolia, p. 428. The draft was sent to the Foreign Office by the Board of Trade on November 27, 1913 (TNA, FO 535/16, No. 444, Board of Trade to Foreign Office, November 27, 1913, p. 427).

187 TNA, FO 535/17, No. 202, Board of Trade to Foreign Office, July 7, 1914, p. 199.

188 TNA, FO 535/17, No. 202, Board of Trade to Foreign Office, July 7, 1914, p. 199.

189 TNA, FO 535/17, No. 202, Board of Trade to Foreign Office, July 7, 1914, p. 200.

190 TNA, FO 535/17, No. 202, Board of Trade to Foreign Office, July 7, 1914, p. 200.

191 TNA, FO 535/17, No. 202, Board of Trade to Foreign Office, July 7, 1914, p. 200.

192 TNA, FO 535/17, No. 202, Board of Trade to Foreign Office, July 7, 1914, p. 200.

193 TNA, FO 535/17, No. 218, Foreign Office to Board of Trade, July 17, 1914, p. 218.

194 TNA, FO 535/17, No. 218, Foreign Office to Board of Trade, July 17, 1914, p. 218.

195 TNA, FO 535/17, No. 218, Foreign Office to Board of Trade, July 17, 1914, p. 218.

196 TNA, FO 535/17, No. 218, Foreign Office to Board of Trade, July 17, 1914, p. 218.

197 TNA, FO 535/17, No. 133, Government of India to the Marquess of Crewe, May 21, 1914, p. 151.

198 TNA, FO 535/17, No. 138, Sir G. Buchanan to Sir Edward Grey, May 25, 1914, p. 155.

199 TNA, FO 535/17, No. 133, Government of India to the Marquess of Crewe, May 21, 1914, p. 151.

200 TNA, FO 535/17, No. 133, Government of India to the Marquess of Crewe, May 21, 1914, p. 151.

201 TNA, FO 535/17, No. 138, Sir G. Buchanan to Sir Edward Grey, May 25, 1914, p. 155.

202 TNA, FO 535/17, No. 133, Government of India to the Marquess of Crewe, May 21, 1914, p. 151.

203 TNA, FO 535/17, No. 133, Government of India to the Marquess of Crewe, May 21, 1914, p. 151.

204 TNA, FO 535/17, No. 138, Sir G. Buchanan to Sir Edward Grey, May 25, 1914, p. 155.

205 TNA, FO 535/17, No. 138, Sir G. Buchanan to Sir Edward Grey, May 25, 1914, p. 155.

206 TNA, FO 535/17, No. 138, Sir G. Buchanan to Sir Edward Grey, May 25, 1914, p. 155.

207 TNA, FO 535/17, No. 133, Government of India to the Marquess of Crewe, May 21, 1914, p. 151.

208 TNA, FO 535/17, No. 133, Government of India to the Marquess of Crewe, May 21, 1914, p. 151.

209 TNA, FO 535/17, No. 134, Sir Edward Grey to Sir G. Buchanan, May 22, 1914, p. 152.

210 TNA, FO 535/17, No. 112, Sir Edward Grey to Sir G. Buchanan, May 4, 1914, p. 130.

211 TNA, FO 535/17, No. 134, Sir Edward Grey to Sir G. Buchanan, May 22, 1914, p. 152.

212 TNA, FO 535/17, No. 134, Sir Edward Grey to Sir G. Buchanan, May 22, 1914, p. 152.

213 TNA, FO 535/17, No. 134, Sir Edward Grey to Sir G. Buchanan, May 22, 1914, p. 152.

214 TNA, FO 535/17, No. 134, Sir Edward Grey to Sir G. Buchanan, May 22, 1914, p. 152.

215 TNA, FO 535/17, No. 134, Sir Edward Grey to Sir G. Buchanan, May 22, 1914, p. 152.

216 TNA, FO 535/17, No. 134, Sir Edward Grey to Sir G. Buchanan, May 22, 1914, p. 152.

217 TNA, FO 535/17, No. 135, Sir G. Buchanan to Sir Edward Grey, May 24, 1914, p. 152.

218 TNA, FO 535/17, No. 135, Sir G. Buchanan to Sir Edward Grey, May 24, 1914, p. 152.

219 TNA, FO 535/17, No. 135, Sir G. Buchanan to Sir Edward Grey, May 24, 1914, p. 152.

220 TNA, FO 535/17, No. 135, Sir G. Buchanan to Sir Edward Grey, May 24, 1914, p. 152.

221 TNA, FO 535/17, No. 135, Sir G. Buchanan to Sir Edward Grey, May 24, 1914, p. 152.

222 TNA, FO 535/17, No. 135, Sir G. Buchanan to Sir Edward Grey, May 24, 1914, p. 153.

223 TNA, FO 535/17, No. 135, Sir G. Buchanan to Sir Edward Grey, May 24, 1914, p. 153.

224 TNA, FO 535/17, No. 135, Sir G. Buchanan to Sir Edward Grey, May 24, 1914, p. 153.

225 TNA, FO 535/17, No. 135, Sir G. Buchanan to Sir Edward Grey, May 24, 1914, p. 153.

226 TNA, FO 535/17, No. 135, Sir G. Buchanan to Sir Edward Grey, May 24, 1914, p. 153.

227 TNA, FO 535/17, No. 140, Sir Edward Grey to Sir G. Buchanan, May 26, 1914, p. 156.

228 TNA, FO 535/17, No. 140, Sir Edward Grey to Sir G. Buchanan, May 26, 1914, p. 156.

229 TNA, FO 535/17, No. 140, Sir Edward Grey to Sir G. Buchanan, May 26, 1914, p. 156.

230 TNA, FO 535/17, No. 140, Sir Edward Grey to Sir G. Buchanan, May 26, 1914, p. 157.

231 TNA, FO 535/17, No. 140, Sir Edward Grey to Sir G. Buchanan, May 26, 1914, p. 157.

232 TNA, FO 535/17, No. 146, Sir J. Jordan to Sir Edward Grey, May 31, 1914, p. 160.

233 TNA, FO 535/17, No. 146, Sir J. Jordan to Sir Edward Grey, May 31, 1914, p. 160.

234 TNA, FO 535/17, No. 146, Sir J. Jordan to Sir Edward Grey, May 31, 1914, p. 160.

235 TNA, FO 535/17, No. 146, Sir J. Jordan to Sir Edward Grey, May 31, 1914, p. 160.

236 TNA, FO 535/17, No. 156, Memorandum to the Chinese Minister, June 5, 1914, p. 166.

237 TNA, FO 535/17, No. 156, Memorandum to the Chinese Minister, June 5, 1914, p. 167.

238 TNA, FO 535/17, No. 148, India Office to Foreign Office, June 2, 1914, p. 161. The Band-e-Bābā, also known as Sīāh Būbak, corresponds to the ancient Παροπάμισος / Paropamisus (BL, IOR/L/MIL/17/14/4, *Military Report on Afghanistan*, 1906, compiled in the Division of the Chief of the Staff, Army Head Quarters, India, Simla 1906, p. 57; see also the entry «Band-i-Baba», in: L. W. ADAMEC, *Historical Dictionary of Afghanistan*, Lanham – Toronto – Plymouth 2012).

239 TNA, FO 535/17, No. 148, India Office to Foreign Office, June 2, 1914, p. 161.

240 TNA, FO 535/17, No. 148, India Office to Foreign Office, June 2, 1914, p. 161.

241 TNA, FO 535/17, No. 148, India Office to Foreign Office, June 2, 1914, p. 161.

242 TNA, FO 535/17, Enclosure 2 in No. 148, Government of India to the Marquess of Crewe, May 28, 1914, p. 162.

243 TNA, FO 535/17, Enclosure 1 in No. 148, The Marquess of Crewe to Government of India, May 26, 1914, p. 162.

244 TNA, FO 535/17, Enclosure 2 in No. 148, Government of India to the Marquess of Crewe, May 28, 1914, p. 162.

245 TNA, FO 535/17, Enclosure 2 in No. 148, Government of India to the Marquess of Crewe, May 28, 1914, p. 162.

246 TNA, FO 535/17, Enclosure 2 in No. 148, Government of India to the Marquess of Crewe, May 28, 1914, p. 162.

247 TNA, FO 535/17, Enclosure 2 in No. 148, Government of India to the Marquess of Crewe, May 28, 1914, p. 162.

248 TNA, FO 535/17, No. 160, Sir Edward Grey to Sir G. Buchanan, June 6, 1914, p. 169.

249 TNA, FO 535/17, No. 160, Sir Edward Grey to Sir G. Buchanan, June 6, 1914, p. 169. In order to identify the locations, I relied on *Historical and Political Gazetteer of Afghanistan*, Vols 1-6, edited by L.W. Adamec, Graz 1972-1985 and on the maps of the US Army Map Service (AMS): Series 1301 (GSGS 4646), edition 4-AMS, sheet NI 41, Herāt, scale: 1:1,000,000; Series 1301 (GSGS 2555), edition 5-AMS, sheet NI 42, Kābul, scale: 1:1,000,000.

250 TNA, FO 535/17, No. 160, Sir Edward Grey to Sir G. Buchanan, June 6, 1914, p. 169.

251 TNA, FO 535/17, No. 160, Sir Edward Grey to Sir G. Buchanan, June 6, 1914, p. 169.

252 TNA, FO 535/17, No. 160, Sir Edward Grey to Sir G. Buchanan, June 6, 1914, p. 169.

253 TNA, FO 535/17, No. 164, Sir G. Buchanan to Sir Edward Grey, June 10, 1914, pp. 170-171.

254 TNA, FO 535/17, No. 164, Sir G. Buchanan to Sir Edward Grey, June 10, 1914, p. 170.

255 TNA, FO 535/17, No. 164, Sir G. Buchanan to Sir Edward Grey, June 10, 1914, p. 171.

256 TNA, FO 535/17, No. 164, Sir G. Buchanan to Sir Edward Grey, June 10, 1914, p. 171.

257 TNA, FO 535/17, No. 164, Sir G. Buchanan to Sir Edward Grey, June 10, 1914, p. 171.

258 TNA, FO 535/17, No. 164, Sir G. Buchanan to Sir Edward Grey, June 10, 1914, p. 171.

259 TNA, FO 535/17, No. 164, Sir G. Buchanan to Sir Edward Grey, June 10, 1914, p. 171.

260 TNA, FO 535/17, No. 164, Sir G. Buchanan to Sir Edward Grey, June 10, 1914, p. 171.

261 TNA, FO 535/17, No. 164, Sir G. Buchanan to Sir Edward Grey, June 10, 1914, p. 171.

262 TNA, FO 535/17, No. 164, Sir G. Buchanan to Sir Edward Grey, June 10, 1914, p. 171; the French text of the letter is in TNA, FO 535/17, Enclosure 2 in No. 171, M. Sazanof to Sir G. Buchanan, le 28 mai (10 juin), 1914, pp. 175-176.

263 TNA, FO 535/17, No. 164, Sir G. Buchanan to Sir Edward Grey, June 10, 1914, p. 171.

264 TNA, FO 535/17, No. 224, Sir Edward Grey to Sir G. Buchanan, July 28, 1914, p. 222.

265 TNA, FO 535/17, No. 164, Sir G. Buchanan to Sir Edward Grey, June 10, 1914, p. 171; TNA, FO 535/17, No. 171, Sir G. Buchanan to Sir Edward Grey, June 11, 1914, p. 174.

266 TNA, FO 535/17, No. 164, Sir G. Buchanan to Sir Edward Grey, June 10, 1914, p. 171.

267 TNA, FO 535/17, No. 167, Sir G. Buchanan to Sir Edward Grey, June 11, 1914, p. 172; TNA, FO 535/17, No. 171, Sir G. Buchanan to Sir Edward Grey, June 11, 1914, pp. 173-174.

268 TNA, FO 535/17, No. 167, Sir G. Buchanan to Sir Edward Grey, June 11, 1914, p. 172.

269 'Murgab' in the document, the Margus in the ancient Margiana.

270 TNA, FO 535/17, No. 167, Sir G. Buchanan to Sir Edward Grey, June 11, 1914, p. 172.

271 TNA, FO 535/17, No. 167, Sir G. Buchanan to Sir Edward Grey, June 11, 1914, p. 172.

272 TNA, FO 535/17, No. 171, Sir G. Buchanan to Sir Edward Grey, June 11, 1914, p. 174.

273 TNA, FO 535/17, No. 171, Sir G. Buchanan to Sir Edward Grey, June 11, 1914, p. 174.

274 TNA, FO 535/17, No. 173, India Office to Foreign Office, June 16, 1914, p. 177.

275 TNA, FO 535/17, No. 173, India Office to Foreign Office, June 16, 1914, p. 177.

276 TNA, FO 535/17, No. 173, India Office to Foreign Office, June 16, 1914, pp. 177-178.

277 TNA, FO 535/17, No. 173, India Office to Foreign Office, June 16, 1914, pp. 177-178.

278 TNA, FO 535/17, No. 173, India Office to Foreign Office, June 16, 1914, p. 178.

279 TNA, FO 535/17, No. 173, India Office to Foreign Office, June 16, 1914, p. 178.

280 TNA, FO 535/17, No. 173, India Office to Foreign Office, June 16, 1914, p. 178.

281 TNA, FO 535/17, No. 173, India Office to Foreign Office, June 16, 1914, p. 178.

282 TNA, FO 535/17, No. 173, India Office to Foreign Office, June 16, 1914, p. 178.

283 TNA, FO 535/17, No. 173, India Office to Foreign Office, June 16, 1914, p. 178.

284 TNA, FO 535/17, No. 173, India Office to Foreign Office, June 16, 1914, p. 178.

285 TNA, FO 535/17, No. 208, Sir Edward Grey to Sir G. Buchanan, July 10, 1914, p. 203.

286 TNA, FO 535/17, No. 208, Sir Edward Grey to Sir G. Buchanan, July 10, 1914, p. 203.

287 TNA, FO 535/17, No. 208, Sir Edward Grey to Sir G. Buchanan, July 10, 1914, p. 203.

288 TNA, FO 535/17, No. 208, Sir Edward Grey to Sir G. Buchanan, July 10, 1914, p. 203.

289 TNA, FO 535/17, No. 208, Sir Edward Grey to Sir G. Buchanan, July 10, 1914, p. 203.

290 TNA, FO 535/17, No. 224, Sir Edward Grey to Sir G. Buchanan, July 28, 1914, p. 222.

291 TNA, FO 535/17, No. 224, Sir Edward Grey to Sir G. Buchanan, July 28, 1914, p. 222.

292 TNA, FO 535/17, No. 224, Sir Edward Grey to Sir G. Buchanan, July 28, 1914, p. 222.

6

The British and the Kyakhta Accords

The Russo-Mongol agreement of 1914

On September 30, 1914 (September 17 of the Russian calendar) the Russians and Mongols reached an agreement, signed in Kyakhta, on the Russo-Mongolian border, with which Petrograd,[1] while recognizing the right of the Mongols to build railways on their territory, would negotiate and decide together with Mongolia, the route of a railway with the explicit objective of connecting the Mongolian railway with the Siberian Railway.[2]

In addition to this, there was the concession given by the Mongolian government to the Central Administration of Posts and Telegraphs of the Russian Empire to build a telegraph line between the Russian settlement of Monda, in Irkut·sk, and the Mongolian center of Uliastay.[3] For the Russians, the Agreement of September 1914 did not come into conflict with the status of Outer Mongolia defined with the Chinese in 1913, because, as seen previously, Urga was autonomous in terms of internal administration and also in decisions on commercial and industrial matters.[4] In January 1915, Jordan therefore communicated to Grey the Russian intention to extend the Verkhneudinsk[5]-Kyakhta Railway project to Urga.[6] In November 1914, Ch'ing-tao 青島,[7] a German concession in China,[8] had fallen, opening new perspectives to Russian trade and industry in the Far East.[9] In fact, the creation of a Sino-Russo-Japanese society was sought.[10] Furthermore, the Russian government was also planning the introduction of a silver currency in Mongolia.[11] The war was favoring the Russian commercial dimension in Mongolia: according to an article published in the *Novosti Zhizni* of Harbin, in January 1915, due to the decrease in British and German products arriving from the south, about 80% of imports into the country were under Russian control.[12] Out of 12 million rubles (the total amount of imports into Outer Mongolia, according to the article), 9 million were Russian.[13] A steamship service was also put into operation on the Kos Gol' lake[14] by the Russians, thus facilitating the reach of Uliastay from Irkut·sk (in Russia).[15]

Meanwhile, the commercial question remained open for the British. In December 1914, the Board of Trade's response to the July 17 communication[16] reached the Foreign Office.[17] In the summer the Foreign Office, as previously seen, had objected to the Board that the mere recognition of Britain's most favored nation status (as proposed by the Board on July 7, 1914)[18] would only apply to imported British goods into Mongolia by British subjects, while Grey asked instead for the opinion of the Board on the right to negotiate with the Mongolian government to extend the exemption to all British goods, as recognized by trade treaties with China.[19] Also in the July communication, the Foreign Office had explained to the Board of Trade that, even in case of tax exemption for the British products in Mongolia, these goods would still carry a disadvantage compared to Russian products entering the Russo-Mongolian land border, due to customs duties and transit fees.[20]

In its response of December 11, the Board of Trade explained to the Foreign Office that the differences between the two departments were presumably due precisely to the uncertainty of the international status of Outer Mongolia, to be considered an integral part of China – and, therefore in that case it could be expected that British goods in Mongolia would be 'free from all duty', because customs duties and transit taxes had already been paid – or autonomous from Peking, and consequently demanded the exemption of all taxes 'not imposed equally on the goods of any other country (including Russia)'.[21] In any case,

> if Sir E. Grey is prepared to claim freedom from all duty for British goods in Mongolia instead of mere most-favoured-nation treatment the Board are not disposed to offer any objection to this course.[22]

A few days later, on December 19, the Foreign Office reiterated Grey's position to the India Office and, given the communication by the Board of Trade, they sought the approval of the secretary of state for India to communicate to Buchanan, in Petrograd, to inform the Russian Government of London's position to exempt products from further taxes in Mongolia, regardless of the seller's nationality.[23] Crewe-Milnes agreed with Grey, suggesting, however, to the secretary of state for Foreign Affairs, on January 26, 1915, in case of Russian resistance, that the Foreign Office negotiate the matter directly with the Chinese government which, having recognized, with the Sino-Russian Declaration of November 5, 1913, Mongolia's fiscal autonomy could not now claim to obtain 'the same benefit from the external trade of that country as when it still formed, for fiscal purposes, an integral part of the Chinese Empire'.[24] These instructions were sent to Buchanan on February 5.[25]

Meanwhile, however, in January, a communication from Buchanan to Grey informed the latter of the imminent birth of a National Bank of Mongolia.[26] The

Russian presence in Mongolia was further strengthened. The bank, whose creation had been approved by the tsar's finance minister, had a capital of one million rubles and was created 'by a financial group in which the Siberian-Commercial Bank is largely interested'.[27] The headquarters were in Petrograd, with branches in Urga, Uliastay and Hovd.[28] The Mongolian government was guaranteed 15 percent of the bank's annual net profits, as well as the possibility of buying the bank fifty years after its opening, i.e. starting from January 14, 1915 (January 1 of the Russian calendar).[29]

On February 20, Buchanan spoke with Sazonov again on the trade question, explaining the position of the British government, but without great results, if not the guarantee given by the Russian minister to examine the *aide-mémoire* that the ambassador had left him.[30] Again, Sazonov had simply suggested the possibility of bringing British products to Mongolia via Russia.[31]

The 1915 agreement

As explained above, in the pages dedicated to the Sino-Russian Declaration of November (October) 1913, the Russians and Chinese had however planned a new meeting that should further clarify the aspects of the agreement. Above all, however, the Mongols should also be involved in the new meeting. The agreement was reached on June 7, 1915, again in Kyakhta, where Russians, Mongols and Chinese signed a new treaty of twenty-two articles by which Outer Mongolia recognized the agreements of 1913 between the Russian Empire and the Republic of China, that is the Chinese suzerainty over Outer Mongolia, while Peking and Petrograd recognized Mongolian autonomy (Article 2).[32] Mongolia thus formally recognized the Sino-Russian Declaration of 1913 (Article 1):

> La Mongolie extérieure reconnaît la déclaration russo-chinoise et les notes échangées entre la Russie et la Chine le 23 octobre, 1913 (5☐ jour, 11☐ mois, de la 2☐ année de la République chinoise).

This was the extension of Outer Mongolia (according to Article 11):

> Conformément à l'article 4 des notes échangées entre la Russie et la Chine le 23 octobre, 1913 (le 5ᵉ jour du 11ᵉ mois de la 2ᵉ année de la République chinoise) le territoire de la Mongolie extérieure autonome comprend les régions qui ont été sous la juridiction de l'amban chinois d'Ourga, du général tartare d'Ouliassoutai et de l'amban chinois de Kobdo, et touche aux confins de la Chine par les limites des khochounes des quatre aimaks de Khalkha et du district de Kobdo, limitrophes du district de Houloun-bouir[33] à l'est, de la Mongolie intérieure au sud, de la province de Sinkiang au sud-ouest et du district de l'Altaï à l'ouest.

The same article then specified that the precise borders between Outer Mongolia and China had to be defined by a Sino-Russo-Mongolian commission:

> La délimitation formelle entre la Chine et la Mongolie extérieure autonome sera effectuée par une commission spéciale de délégués de la Russie, de la Chine et de la Mongolie extérieure autonome, qui se mettra aux travaux de délimitation dans un délai de deux ans du jour de la signature du présent accord.

The country could not conclude international treaties on political and territorial issues (Article 3), but it had total autonomy for commercial and industrial agreements with other countries, as well as, of course, in internal administration (Article 5), while the Republic of China had the right to confer '[/]e titre Bogdo Djembzoun Damba Khoutoukhtou Khan' (Article 4). The Chinese dignitary in Urga could have an escort of no more than two hundred men, while no more than fifty men would be assigned to each of his assistants in the other Mongolian cities, at the time Uliastay, Hovd and the Mongolian side of Kyakhta (Article 7). The Russian consular guard in Urga, on the other hand, was not to exceed one hundred and fifty men, while the limit was set at fifty for the men placed to defend the other consulates or vice-consulates of Petrograd in Mongolia (Article 8). The commercial aspects were regulated by Article 12 as follows:

> Il est entendu que des droits de douanes ne sont pas établis pour les marchandises de quelque provenance qu'elles soient importées par les marchands chinois dans la Mongolie extérieure autonome. Néanmoins, les marchands chinois payeront toutes les taxes de commerce intérieures qui sont établies dans la Mongolie extérieure autonome et qui pourront y être établies dans l'avenir, payables par les Mongols de la Mongolie extérieure autonome. De même, les marchands de la Mongolie extérieure autonome important toute espèce de marchandises de provenance locale dans la Chine intérieure payeront toutes les taxes de commerce qui sont établies dans la Chine intérieure et pourront y être établies dans l'avenir payables par les marchands chinois. Les marchandises de provenance étrangère importées du côté de la Mongolie extérieure autonome dans la Chine intérieure seront frappées des droits de douanes stipulés par le règlement pour le commerce par voie de terre de 1881 (de la septième année du règne Kuanghsui).

Two days after the signing of the agreement, on June 9 (May 27 according to the Russian calendar) Sazonov communicated to Buchanan in a verbal note that, precisely on the basis of Article 12 of the agreement, 'il n'y aura pas de douanes sur la frontière de la Mongolie autonome et de la Chine propre' and that, therefore, the Chinese merchants would only pay the internal Mongolian taxes.[34]

Furthermore, this was the interpretation of the Russian government:

> Le Gouvernement russe interprète cette stipulation dans les sens que les marchandises étrangères importées en Chine par voie de mer et ayant acquitté les tarifs de douane et de transit pourront comme auparavant pénétrer en Mongolie sans être frappées d'autres taxes, c'est-à-dire que ces marchandises seront traitées en Mongolie tout comme dans les autres provinces de la Chine.[35]

The Russian government thus hoped to have fulfilled British demands for trade in Outer Mongolia.[36] Indeed, for Sir Edward Grey, based on that interpretation of Article 12 of the Kyakhta Tripartite Agreement, London's claims on British goods imported into Mongolia by Chinese merchants were upheld.[37] However, for the secretary of state for Foreign Affairs, that was not necessarily the outcome of Article 12, because the Mongolian government retained the right to impose unfavorable taxation on goods imported by Chinese merchants.[38] For Grey, the approval of the Mongolian government was required with respect to the Russian interpretation of Article 12.[39] The Foreign Office also required that the status of most favored nation, implicitly recognized by the Russian government in two notes of May 1914, was also formally recognized by the Mongolian government.[40] On these two points Grey wished to reach the signing of an agreement between Urga and London.[41] The Board of Trade agreed with the line suggested by the secretary of state for Foreign Affairs, but also asked for clarification in communications with the Russian government that the exemption on customs duties should also cover goods produced in British factories in China and not just foreign goods imported into China by sea.[42] Even according to the ambassador to Peking, Jordan, in his letter addressed to Grey and dated November 8, 1915, the Sino-Russo-Mongolian Tripartite Agreement did not in itself guarantee British commercial interests in Outer Mongolia, but the diplomat suggested to Grey about being more detailed on the disadvantages of the Kyakhta agreement for British.[43] Jordan reiterated to the secretary of state for Foreign Affairs that, while it is true that, theoretically for many years, British subjects had enjoyed the treatment of most favored nation, in reality they were at a disadvantage compared to Russian goods which could, as reiterated several times, enter Mongolia by land and without duties.[44] Therefore, even not having had further taxes in Mongolia in the past still did not compensate for the entry and transit duties.[45] Jordan continued:

> It was of no use in the past to claim from China the privilege of the most favoured nation, because the answer would have been that, on the one hand, all that this privilege would effect would be to allow British merchants to import across the Russian frontier on the same terms as Russian merchants–a valueless conces-

sion—and that, on the other hand, Russian goods imported through China proper were already subject to the same taxation as British goods.[46]

For the ambassador it was not possible to overcome the initial fiscal disadvantage, 'which is due largely to geographical conditions', but it was necessary to aim to obtain, for British goods, the same treatment that the goods of the other countries received, or to preserve the situation prior to Urga's autonomy.[47] Jordan also gave a concrete example of the damage:

> Prior to 1912 a case of English-made cigarettes sent from Tientsin [*T'ien-chin* 天津] to Urga, after paying import duty (nominally 5 per cent.) at Tien-tsin, paid there an additional half-duty, and was given a certificate exempting it, whether in British or Chinese hands, from all inland charges whatsoever to its destination, including, it may be remarked, any charges that might otherwise have been levied by the taxing station referred to in the Russian Memorandum of the 21st May, 1914, as having been established at Urga in 1911. British goods were thus, in Mongolia, free, like Russian goods, from all internal taxation. After Mongolia became autonomous, the same procedure was followed, and is followed to this day, as regards the issue of transit pass, but the Mongol authorities, refusing to recognise the Chinese pass, now levy on the cigarettes, on arrival at Urga, a destination tax amounting to 10 per cent *ad valorem*.[48]

According to Jordan, the tripartite agreement of 1915 would continue to guarantee 'this extra levy' to the detriment of British products, often brought to Mongolia by Chinese merchants, with the simple condition of not exceeding the taxation on Mongolian merchants.[49] Jordan reasonably did not understand the basis of the Russian interpretation of the agreement.[50] Furthermore, the diplomat complained that he had no possibility of exerting diplomatic pressure on the Mongolian government, as could be done on Peking when illegal taxes were applied to British goods in some provinces (which in any case were also imposed on other foreign merchants).[51] For the British ambassador, the strangeness of the situation lay precisely in the tripartite agreement, with a Chinese government that issued 'transit passes' for Urga, formally part of the Chinese territory, but which at the same time did not control the internal administration of the country.[52] Jordan proposed two options: the British had to ask Peking to recognize Mongolia as a foreign country, and therefore ask for a refund of the import taxes on goods that entered and then left China, or they had to ask the Mongolian government to recognize the validity of Chinese transit permits in Outer Mongolia and therefore waive further taxes.[53] The problem with this negotiation, Jordan explained, was that, in return, London had nothing to offer Peking and Urga.[54] For the British diplomat, the cause of everything was Russia and 'it seems to me that we are entitled to look to Russia alone to readjust that position'.[55]

On May 29 of the following year, Grey therefore wrote to Buchanan to communicate to the Russian government precisely the objections to the agreement (and the practical example) made by Jordan.[56] It had to be explained to Sazonov that the Sino-Russo-Mongol agreement did not guarantee British trade in Mongolia at all:

> The agreement, moreover, contains no provision calculated to preserve the facilities, for many years enjoyed by British subjects, for themselves importing goods on the same terms as the most-favoured nation ; nor is it clear whether the exemption from customs duty in Mongolia will, under the terms of article 12, apply to goods manufactured in British factories in China, as well as to goods imported into China by sea.[57]

Sazonov's intervention with the Mongol authorities in favor of English trade was therefore requested.[58] As previously mentioned, however, Grey was well aware of the delicacy of the moment and of the impossibility, given the world conflict, to offend the sensibilities of the allies and left Buchanan to decide the best time to give these communications to the Russian foreign minister.

> In view of the somewhat controversial nature of this subject, I would leave it entirely to your Excellency's discretion to decide upon the favourable moment for presenting the above reply to the Minister for Foreign Affairs.[59]

1916

On December 12, 1915, Yüan Shih-k'ai had comically tried to restore the Empire, changing the name of the Republic to «Chinese Empire» (中華帝國 *Chung-hua ti-kuo*).[60] On January 24, 1916, another agreement was signed in Urga between the Chinese, Mongols and Russians, which transferred the Haalgan-Urga-Kyakhta telegraph line to the Mongolian government.[61] According to George Ernest Morrison it was a very bad agreement for the Chinese, but they had renounced everything in order to have the recognition, in the text, of the first year of Hung-hsien 洪憲 – that was the emperor's name of Yüan Shih-k'ai – considering the acceptance of that date by Russia equivalent to the approval of the Empire:

> China has signed many disastrous agreements since then [*since the Revolution*]. Her telegraph agreements seem to be specially injurious. On January 24th she signed a Telegraph Convention

at Urga, the only advantage of which, but a very great one in the opinion of the Ministry at the time, was the absurd one that the Convention was signed in the first year of Hung Hsien. In order to obtain the date inserted in this way, China was prepared to give away any advantage demanded of her. She thought that by having the Hung Hsien date inserted it meant the thin edge of the wedge, the tacit approval of Russia to the Empire, and the first step towards recognition.[62]

Meanwhile, on January 27, 1916, the British political officer in Sikkim communicated to the Government of India the presence in Tibet of a Buddhist Kalmyk, a certain 'Khrumche Olienob'.[63] He had left Rgyal-rtse on January 11, together with a friend, 'Jambel' (*Jam dpal*) and a monk from the monastery of Bras-spungs on his way to Russia, passing through China.[64] He had with him a passport issued in Kyakhta on February 10, 1915 and a 'letter from some eminent lama authorising him for religious reasons to visit Dalai Lama', but the real purpose of his trip was not known to the political officer.[65] According to the trade agent in Rgyal-rtse, David Macdonald (who first broke the news to the agent in Sikkim), the Kalmyk was a friend of aeDorzhiyev.[66] 'Khrumche Olienob' had also visited the paṇ-chen bla-ma in Gzhis-ka-rtse.[67]

The opportunity to send a British agent to Lhasa, as decided in the Simla Convention, arose in the early spring of 1916. The Tibetans, in fact, in the framework of the program of modernization of the country and of the army set up by the thirteenth dalai lama, intended to buy machine guns from Japan through the Japanese consul in Calcutta; the Tibetan ministers had written to the political agent in Sikkim that they would in fact send a delegation to Calcutta, but if it was not possible to buy these weapons there, they would go straight to Japan.[68] Tibetans had obtained assurances regarding the sale through the consul in Calcutta from Aoki Bunkyō[69] (1886-1956), a Japanese monk who studied in the Tibetan capital between 1913 and 1916.[70]

There were three options for the Government of India, 'all of which appear objectionable': the British could supply the Tibetans with weapons, thus avoiding the Japanese (however recognizing 'a practical difficulty, viz., that we have no machine guns which we could spare'); they could explain to the Tibetans that it was not possible to allow machine guns purchased in Japan to pass through Indian territory, 'though we hope later on to provide a few ourselves'; the third option was authorizing the Tibetans to do what they required.[71]

However, according to Austen Chamberlain, who had succeeded Crewe-Milnes as secretary of state for the India Office on May 27, 1915,[72] the issue could not be dealt with in writing: it was necessary to send someone to the Tibetan capital to discuss and convince the Tibetan government to renounce.[73] On the basis of the agreements made with Russia and extensively analyzed previously, the consent of the Russian government was needed, but, as far as Chamberlain knew, the Russians had significantly decreased their interest in Tibet after the start of the war and also the Russians were 'probably, on general grounds, no less mistrustful than His Majesty's Government of Japanese activities in outlying portions of the Chinese Empire'.[74] Based on this reasoning, according to the India Office, '[*i*]t would seem possible, therefore, that, if the special circumstances of the case and the purely temporary nature of the action contemplated were fully explained to them', the Russians would have no reason to prevent the sending of a British agent to Lhasa.[75]

Alternatively, the British could write to the Tibetan government, and if it was not possible to convince the ministers of the dalai lama to renounce the purchase, then they had to communicate directly to Japan, in any case a British ally, about the impossibility to allow a passage in India to Japanese machine guns.[76] However, Edward Grey, while agreeing on the problems highlighted by the Government of India and the India Office, did not want to open new questions with the governments of Petrograd or Tokyo at that delicate moment, or risk offending the Japanese.[77] Instead of sending the British agent to Lhasa, a written communication from Charles Bell to the Tibetan government was preferable for Grey.[78]

In any case, if the First World War was redefining certain interests in High Asia, no less so were the Russian Revolutions of 1917, in particular, of course, the October Revolution. The results of the Bolshevik Revolution had, in the following years and decades, direct effects on the political institutions of High, East and Southeast Asia, as well as in the rest of the world, both by contrast and by imitation. The conditions were created for new confrontations and conflicts while the ideology veiled but did not eradicate the geopolitical aspects.

Endnotes

1 This is the name assumed by the Russian capital in the summer of 1914.

2 TNA, FO 535/17, Enclosure in No. 256, Agreement respecting Railway Construction in Mongolia, p. 292.

3 TNA, FO 535/17, Enclosure in No. 257, Telegraph Concessions in Mongolia, p. 293.

4 TNA, FO 535/18, No. 3, Mr. Macleay to Sir Edward Grey, December 10, 1914, p. 2.

5 Ulaan Üde (in Russian: Ulan Ud·e) is the current capital of the Republic of Buryatia (Russia).

6 TNA, FO 535/18, No. 8, Sir J. Jordan to Sir Edward Grey, Peking, January 11, 1915, p. 5; TNA, FO 535/18, Enclosure 1 in No. 8, Extract from the "Harbinski Viestnik" of December 14 (27), 1914, p. 5; TNA, FO 535/18, Enclosure 2 in No. 8, *Construction of the Verkhneudinsk-Urga Railway*, Extract from the "Novosti Zizni" of December 16 (29), 1914, p. 6.

7 Ch'ing-tao 青島 is better known in the West with the transcription of the postal romanization system (郵政式拼音 *yu-cheng-shih p'in-yin*): Tsingtao.

8 On the concession see J. E. SCHRECKER, *Imperialism and Chinese Nationalism: Germany in Shantung*, Cambridge, MA 1971.

9 TNA, FO 535/18, No. 8, Sir J. Jordan to Sir Edward Grey, Peking, January 11, 1915, p. 5; TNA, FO 535/18, Enclosure 2 in No. 8, *Construction of the Verkhneudinsk-Urga Railway*, Extract from the "Novosti Zizni" of December 16 (29), 1914, p. 6.

10 TNA, FO 535/18, No. 8, Sir J. Jordan to Sir Edward Grey, Peking, January 11, 1915, p. 5; TNA, FO 535/18, Enclosure 2 in No. 8, *Construction of the Verkhneudinsk-Urga Railway*, Extract from the "Novosti Zizni" of December 16 (29), 1914, p. 6.

11 TNA, FO 535/18, No. 8, Sir J. Jordan to Sir Edward Grey, Peking, January 11, 1915, p. 5.

12 TNA, FO 535/18, Enclosure in No. 12, *Russian Affairs in Mongolia*, Extract from "Novosti Zizni" of January 4 (17), 1915, p. 9.

13 TNA, FO 535/18, Enclosure in No. 12, *Russian Affairs in Mongolia*, Extract from "Novosti Zizni" of January 4 (17), 1915, p. 9.

14 In Mongolian: Khövsgöl nuur. The word *nuur* means «lake» in Mongolian.

15 TNA, FO 535/18, Enclosure in No. 12, *Russian Affairs in Mongolia*, Extract from "Novosti Zizni" of January 4 (17), 1915, p. 9.

16 TNA, FO 535/17, No. 218, Foreign Office to Board of Trade, July 17, 1914, p. 218.

17 TNA, FO 535/17, No. 259, Board of Trade to Foreign Office, December 11, 1914, p. 294.

18 TNA, FO 535/17, No. 202, Board of Trade to Foreign Office, July 7, 1914, p. 199.

19 TNA, FO 535/17, No. 218, Foreign Office to Board of Trade, July 17, 1914, p. 218.

20 TNA, FO 535/17, No. 218, Foreign Office to Board of Trade, July 17, 1914, p. 218.

21 TNA, FO 535/17, No. 259, Board of Trade to Foreign Office, December 11, 1914, p. 294.

22 TNA, FO 535/17, No. 259, Board of Trade to Foreign Office, December 11, 1914, p. 294.

23 TNA, FO 535/17, No. 260, Foreign Office to India Office, December 19, 1914, pp. 294-295.

24 TNA, FO 535/18, No. 4, India Office to Foreign Office, January 26, 1915, pp. 2-3.

25 TNA, FO 535/18, No. 6, Sir Edward Grey to Sir G. Buchanan, February 5, 1915, pp. 3-4.

26 TNA, FO 535/18, No. 5, Sir G. Buchanan to Sir Edward Grey, January 13, 1915, p. 3; TNA, FO 535/18, Enclosure in No. 5, Memorandum respecting National Bank of Mongolia, January 13, 1915, p. 3. The source is the Russian official *Trade Gazette*.

27 TNA, FO 535/18, Enclosure in No. 5, Memorandum respecting National Bank of Mongolia, January 13, 1915, p. 3.

28 TNA, FO 535/18, Enclosure in No. 5, Memorandum respecting National Bank of Mongolia, January 13, 1915, p. 3.

29 TNA, FO 535/18, Enclosure in No. 5, Memorandum respecting National Bank of Mongolia, January 13, 1915, p. 3.

30 TNA, FO 535/18, No. 11, Sir G. Buchanan to Sir Edward Grey, February 20, 1915, pp. 8-9.

31 TNA, FO 535/18, No. 11, Sir G. Buchanan to Sir Edward Grey, February 20, 1915, p. 8.

32 The full text of the treaty in French is in TNA, FO 535/18, Enclosure in No. 30, Treaty signed at Kiatkta, June 7, 1915, pp. 40-43; TNA, FO 535/18, No. 21, Sir J. Jordan to Sir Edward Grey, June 7, 1915, p. 34.

33 In Mongolian: Hölönbuyr. In Chinese: Hu-lun-pei-erh 呼倫貝爾.

34 TNA, FO 535/18, Enclosure in No. 28, Note verbale, le 27 mai (9 juin), 1915, p. 38.

35 TNA, FO 535/18, Enclosure in No. 28, Note verbale, le 27 mai (9 juin), 1915, p. 38.

36 TNA, FO 535/18, Enclosure in No. 28, Note verbale, le 27 mai (9 juin), 1915, p. 38.

37 TNA, FO 535/18, No. 34, Foreign Office to India Office. (Also to Board of Trade, *mutatis mutandis*), July 23, 1915, p. 45.

38 TNA, FO 535/18, No. 34, Foreign Office to India Office. (Also to Board of Trade, *mutatis mutandis*), July 23, 1915, p. 45.

39 TNA, FO 535/18, No. 34, Foreign Office to India Office. (Also to Board of Trade, *mutatis mutandis*), July 23, 1915, p. 45.

40 TNA, FO 535/18, No. 34, Foreign Office to India Office. (Also to Board of Trade, *mutatis mutandis*), July 23, 1915, p. 45.

41 TNA, FO 535/18, No. 34, Foreign Office to India Office. (Also to Board of Trade, *mutatis mutandis*), July 23, 1915, p. 45.

42 TNA, FO 535/18, No. 38, Board of Trade to Foreign Office, September 10, 1915, pp. 46-47.

43 TNA, FO 535/18, No. 54, Sir J. Jordan to Sir Edward Grey, November 8, 1915, p. 63.

44 TNA, FO 535/18, No. 54, Sir J. Jordan to Sir Edward Grey, November 8, 1915, p. 63.

45 TNA, FO 535/18, No. 54, Sir J. Jordan to Sir Edward Grey, November 8, 1915, p. 63.

46 TNA, FO 535/18, No. 54, Sir J. Jordan to Sir Edward Grey, November 8, 1915, pp. 63-64.

47 TNA, FO 535/18, No. 54, Sir J. Jordan to Sir Edward Grey, November 8, 1915, p. 64.

48 TNA, FO 535/18, No. 54, Sir J. Jordan to Sir Edward Grey, November 8, 1915, p. 64.

49 TNA, FO 535/18, No. 54, Sir J. Jordan to Sir Edward Grey, November 8, 1915, p. 64.

50 TNA, FO 535/18, No. 54, Sir J. Jordan to Sir Edward Grey, November 8, 1915, p. 64.

51 TNA, FO 535/18, No. 54, Sir J. Jordan to Sir Edward Grey, November 8, 1915, p. 64.

52 TNA, FO 535/18, No. 54, Sir J. Jordan to Sir Edward Grey, November 8, 1915, p. 64.

53 TNA, FO 535/18, No. 54, Sir J. Jordan to Sir Edward Grey, November 8, 1915, p. 64.

54 TNA, FO 535/18, No. 54, Sir J. Jordan to Sir Edward Grey, November 8, 1915, p. 64.

55 TNA, FO 535/18, No. 54, Sir J. Jordan to Sir Edward Grey, November 8, 1915, p. 64.

56 TNA, FO 535/19, No. 8, Sir Edward Grey to Sir G. Buchanan, May 29, 1916, p. 7.

57 TNA, FO 535/19, No. 8, Sir Edward Grey to Sir G. Buchanan, May 29, 1916, p. 7.

58 TNA, FO 535/19, No. 8, Sir Edward Grey to Sir G. Buchanan, May 29, 1916, pp. 7-8.

59 TNA, FO 535/19, No. 8, Sir Edward Grey to Sir G. Buchanan, May 29, 1916, p. 8.

60 P'ENG TSE-CHOU 彭澤周, *Chin tai Chung kuo chih ke ming yü Jih pen* 近代中國之革命與日本, T'ai pei 臺北 78 [1989], p. 171.

61 TNA, FO 535/19, No. 2, Sir J. Jordan to Sir Edward Grey, February 23, 1916, p. 3; the full text of the agreement is in *Treaties and Agreements with and concerning China, 1894-1919*, Vol. II: Republican Period (1912-1919), compiled and edited by J. V. A. MacMurray, New York 1921, pp. 1259-1265.

62 *The Correspondence of G. E. Morrison* 2013, n. 809, G. E. Morrison to F. E. Taylor, March 31, 1916, p. 504.

63 TNA, FO 535/19, Enclosure in No. 3, Political Officer, Sikkim, to the Government of India, January 27, 1916, p. 4. The communication was forwarded by the India Office to the Foreign Office on March 18, TNA, FO 535/19, No. 3, India Office to Foreign Office, March 18, 1916, p. 3.

64 TNA, FO 535/19, Enclosure in No. 3, Political Officer, Sikkim, to the Government of India, January 27, 1916, p. 4.

65 TNA, FO 535/19, Enclosure in No. 3, Political Officer, Sikkim, to the Government of India, January 27, 1916, p. 4.

66 TNA, FO 535/19, Enclosure in No. 3, Political Officer, Sikkim, to the Government of India, January 27, 1916, p. 4.

67 TNA, FO 535/19, Enclosure in No. 3, Political Officer, Sikkim, to the Government of India, January 27, 1916, p. 4.

68 TNA, FO 535/19, Enclosure in No. 4, Government of India to Mr. A. Chamberlain, March 24, 1916, p. 5.

69 TNA, FO 535/19, Enclosure in No. 4, Government of India to Mr. A. Chamberlain, March 24, 1916, p. 5.

70 See R. KOBAYASHI, *The Tibet-Japan Relations in the Era of the 1911 Revolution: Tibetan Letters from the Aoki Bunkyō Archive*, in: チベット・ヒマラヤ文明の歴史的展開 *The Historical Development of Tibeto-Himalayan Civilization*, edited by Iwao Kazushi 岩尾一史 and Ikeda Takumi 池田巧編, Kyōto 京都 2018, p. 103.

71 TNA, FO 535/19, Enclosure in No. 4, Government of India to Mr. A. Chamberlain, March 24, 1916, p. 5.

72 *The India Office List for 1928, compiled from official records by direction of the Secretary of State for India in Council*, London 1928, p. 118.

73 TNA, FO 535/19, No. 4, India Office to Foreign Office, March 31, 1916, p. 4.

74 TNA, FO 535/19, No. 4, India Office to Foreign Office, March 31, 1916, p. 4.

75 TNA, FO 535/19, No. 4, India Office to Foreign Office, March 31, 1916, p. 4.

76 TNA, FO 535/19, No. 4, India Office to Foreign Office, March 31, 1916, p. 4.

77 TNA, FO 535/19, No. 5, Foreign Office to India Office, April 7, 1916, p. 5.

78 TNA, FO 535/19, No. 5, Foreign Office to India Office, April 7, 1916, p. 5.

Conclusions

Twentieth-Century Geopolitical Notes

Much of the historical-political and diplomatic dynamics that I have tried to examine in this work are reflected in a contemporary framework, which, although changed on an ideological and international level, has been structured during the twentieth century, and then until today, on the same geopolitical scenario. One of the main reasons for the historical reconstruction of this research is precisely to provide an interpretative key for the analysis of contemporary phenomena of the geopolitics of High Asia and, in a broader system, of relations between China and India. The point of view of the British, the most important European political and economic power in Asia, was chosen as the backbone of the work. After the end of the Second World War and the subsequent Indian independence, as well as the Communist victory in China, the institutional structures underwent a radical metamorphosis, but the same geopolitical logics survived, on the basis of the indisputable principle explained by Morgenthau: 'the most stable factor upon which the power of a nation depends is obviously geography'.[1]

Choices made at the beginning of the twentieth century had their effects on events following the independence of India from the British Empire and the defeat of Chiang Kai-shek[2] in 1949, with the proclamation of the People's Republic of China by Mao Tse-tung and the flight of nationalists on the island of T'ai-wan where they tried to preserve their political legitimacy. As for Bhutan, in 1949, the Kingdom signed another treaty with India and the guide of Bhutanese foreign policy passed from London to New Delhi.[3] In 2007 a new treaty was signed between the two South Asian countries where the Indian guide is no longer recognized.[4] In 1950, Sikkim became ('shall continue to be') a protectorate of (independent) India, in accordance with Article II of the Gangtok Treaty of December 5, 1950 ('Sikkim shall continue to be a Protectorate of India and, subject to the provisions of this Treaty, shall enjoy autonomy in regard to its internal affairs'[5]). Article VI of the Treaty provided, among other things, that '[t]he Government of India shall have the exclusive right of constructing, maintaining and regulating the use of railways, aerodromes and landing grounds and air navigation facilities, posts, telegraphs, telephones and wireless installations in Sikkim'. In 1975, after a difficult and failed democratization process, the small Himalayan state was annexed by India.

Through the lens of the interests of the British Empire in Asia, this work has tried to define the political dimension of Tibet in the early twentieth century, its role in international relations of the time and its institutional reality. London remained the center of this research because the British were certainly the most interested in the actual independence of Lhasa from Peking. Therefore, through the British archival sources it has been possible to reconstruct a picture of High Asia that provides a meditated view of political aspects still at the center of the debate on the Tibetan question today. The intention was to contribute to the political and historical analysis while expanding the framework of the role of the People's Republic of China on the Roof of the World, by participating in the debate on the effective independence of Tibet in that period.

De facto independence, in the Tibetan and Mongolian case, can be effectively translated in terms of legitimacy, although only Mongolia was lucky enough to be able to retain its status after the Communist victory in China. It was essentially the different geopolitical role, and not a matter of international law, that allowed Outer Mongolia to maintain its independence while Tibet was conquered by Mao Tse-tung. In the first case, the presence of the Soviet Union prevented any Chinese claims, while Tibet was in fact abandoned by the British. The unenviable status of Soviet satellite at the time of the birth of the People's Republic of China in 1949, proved to be much more favorable for Mongolia than the real autonomy, the substantial independence, which Tibet enjoyed in the first half of the twentieth century and which instead decreed the invasion by the People's Liberation Army. When the Tibetan question reached the United Nations in 1959, the British government, chaired by Harold Macmillan, had to face an obvious embarrassment, forced to abstain 'despite our sympathy with the present plight of the Thibetan people'.[6] In fact, given their own history and the still present colonial dimension, the British had prevented the United Nations, in the course of previous years, from taking a position on human rights.[7] The British government, therefore, chose abstention.[8] However, the United Kingdom still voted in favor of the other two resolutions on Tibet in 1961[9] and 1965.[10]

The British position regarding the Chinese role in Tibet officially changed only in 2008, when the then foreign secretary, David Miliband, in a Written Ministerial Statement explained that:

> Our interest is not in restoring an order that existed 60 years ago and that the Dalai Lama himself has said he does not seek to restore.
>
> We are also concerned about more immediate issues arising directly from the unrest of this spring, including the situation of those who remain in detention following the unrest, the increased constraints on religious activity, and the limitations on free access

to the Tibetan autonomous region by diplomats and journalists. These issues reinforce long-held unease on the part of the Government about the underlying human rights situation in Tibet.

Other countries have made similar points. But our position is unusual for one reason of history that has been imported into the present: the anachronism of our formal position on whether Tibet is part of China, and whether in fact we harbour continued designs to see the break-up of China. We do not.

Our ability to get our points across has sometimes been clouded by the position the UK took at the start of the 20th century on the status of Tibet, a position based on the geopolitics of the time. Our recognition of China's "special position" in Tibet developed from the outdated concept of suzerainty. Some have used this to cast doubt on the aims we are pursuing and to claim that we are denying Chinese sovereignty over a large part of its own territory. We have made clear to the Chinese Government, and publicly, that we do not support Tibetan independence. Like every other EU member state, and the United States, we regard Tibet as part of the People's Republic of China. Our interest is in long-term stability, which can only be achieved through respect for human rights and greater autonomy for the Tibetans.[11]

Only in 2008 was the line that had characterized the British approach – namely the recognition of Chinese suzerainty, but not of full sovereignty, over the territory of Tibet – to Tibetan affairs finally set aside.

The work, therefore, tried to give an interpretation of the geopolitical dimension of Tibet and Mongolia, as well as a necessary comparison between the political and cultural elements of the period under examination. However, some of these elements lived on, even after the birth of a People's Republic of China which continues to maintain, at the base of its actions, the same motivations of the Empire, further highlighting the importance of studying the end of the Manchu dynasty. Those same motivations are translated into concrete actions, such as the attempt to appoint religious offices, using traditional methods for their identification on a formal level. If this could have some logic in the imperial framework of the Ch'ing dynasty, any criterion of rationality is lost within a communist system, which should, therefore, try to redefine its relationship with Tibet by not mimicking past customs and institutions, but in an honest political and legal confrontation.

The fundamental problem for the Chinese communist leadership today, however, is that the only source of legitimation of its presence in Tibet lies precisely in those imperial institutions that the Chinese Communist Party – albeit with its numerous and extravagant ideological evolutions – should instead deny. In a broader vision, Peking must rely on imperial history to give a foundation to its power over Lhasa and thus obtain its own geopolitical and economic advantage over a huge region, with very few inhabitants, but with the sources of the rivers that then flow in the areas of the planet with the highest population density. And, after geography, the other factor of relative stability indicated by Morgenthau in his book is represented precisely by natural resources.[12] It would be impossible not to consider the subsequent history of Tibet, China and Mongolia and the political and cultural space of the Tibetan question, but this very question, in my opinion, also has its roots in that precise historical moment, in those few years that I have tried to delineate in this work. The border that passes between autonomy and independence is repeated today in the space of confrontation between the Central Tibetan Administration and the Government of the People's Republic of China in an attempt by the fourteenth dalai lama to find a satisfactory agreement that should guarantee substantial self-government for the Tibetan plateau, even within the Chinese system.

Endnotes

1 H. J. MORGENTHAU, *Politics Among Nations: The Struggle for Power and Peace*, New York 1948, p. 82.

2 Again, as with Sun Yat-sen, I use the transcription of his Cantonese name. The transcription of the name in Mandarin Chinese is Chiang Chieh-shih.

3 For the full text of this treaty see *Documents on Sikkim and Bhutan*, edited by S. K. Sharma and U. Sharma, New Delhi 1998, pp. 224-226.

4 The text of the 2007 treaty is available on the website of the Indian Ministry of Foreign Affairs (https://mea.gov.in/Images/pdf/india-bhutan-treaty-07.pdf).

5 Full text of the treaty: TNA, DO 133/124, Deputy High Commissioner for the United Kingdom Frank K. Roberts to the Commonwealth Relations Office, December 15, 1950 (Treaty between India and Sikkim, December 5, 1950).

6 TNA, CAB 128/33/54, Cabinet - Conclusions of a Meeting of the Cabinet held at 10 Downing Street, S.W. 1, on Tuesday, 20th October, 1959, at 11.15 a.m., p. 3.

7 TNA, CAB 128/33/54, Cabinet - Conclusions of a Meeting of the Cabinet held at 10 Downing Street, S.W. 1, on Tuesday, 20th October, 1959, at 11.15 a.m., p. 3.

8 TNA, CAB 128/33/54, Cabinet - Conclusions of a Meeting of the Cabinet held at 10 Downing Street, S.W. 1, on Tuesday, 20th October, 1959, at 11.15 a.m., p. 3; General Assembly of the United Nations (GA), Resolution 1353 (XIV).

9 GA, Resolution 1723 (XVI).

10 GA, Resolution 2079 (XX).

11 House of Commons Daily Debates, Vol. 481, Tibet, 29 Oct 2008, col. 31WS.

12 MORGENTHAU 1948, p. 82.

Annexes

In Mongolia. The journey of Gerald Charles Binsteed

A communication from Beilby Alston, from the British Embassy in China, to Sir Edward Grey informed him that a British officer, Lieutenant Gerald Charles Binsteed,[1] had made a journey from Haylaar, to Urga, then continued to Kyakhta.[2] The extract of the Binsteed report is transcribed here.[3] The document is in fact particularly interesting: it is a careful analysis of the economic and political conditions of Outer Mongolia and a precious source for the reconstruction of the dramatic situation of the country in 1913.

COMMERCE in Khalkha and Western Barga during my journey may be said to be rapidly becoming non-existent. The usual routes from the south by which Mongolia is wont to be supplied with the vast mass of her requirements have been completely closed by the predatory warfare of the Mongol bands. No goods have come through across the Gobi from China this year. If the now well-known fact be borne in mind that the Russian merchant cannot be persuaded to be content with moderate profits, and also that the Chinese traders, handicapped with the 5 per cent. *ad valorem* duty exacted from Chinese alone by the new Mongol Government, are hardly able to compete with the Russians if they import goods by the expensive route viâ Manchuria Station, it is obvious that the blocking of the southern roads could not fail to lead to a great rise in prices. But this great rise in prices is of comparative unimportance when placed side by side with a further and most unusual consequence of the Mongol policy. Instead of seizing the magnificent opportunity, created for it by the Russian-guided Mongol policy, of making large profits by supplying all the wants of a population who would have no alternative but to accept the high prices demanded, the Russian trading community has done almost nothing to meet the situation. In the area I traversed, the actual number of Russian traders, and its increase since last year, are both infinitesimal. Between Hailar and Urga, a distance of 700 to 300 miles along the chief arteries of life and communication, I found only four Russian trading establishments. Last year there was one. Of the four only two could boast of a house, the total stock of the other two firms being contained in one, or at most two, yurts. The numerous Chinese traders have either decamped altogether and returned to China, or else are remaining on in the somewhat pitiable condition of waiting to see what is going to happen next. In all but one or two rare cases they have no goods left for sale. To illustrate the situation better, let us survey the details at the important centre of San Peitzo Urgo. Last year there were here one Russian and thirty Chinese trading houses. This year there are three Russian shops, of which one is only an off-shoot from the old firm of last year; of the thirty Chinese firms only six remain, of which four are without goods ; one of the remaining two manages to buy goods somehow at Manchuria Station, brought round by the expensive railway route, and, though paying 5 per cent. *ad valorem* duty at Manchuria Station to the Bargut authorities, sells them at San Peitzu Urgo at a price which is able to compete with the Russians; lastly, the sixth Chinese firm is merely a partnership of coolies trying to raise enough money to buy railway tickets back to China.

Almost without exception every Mongol I met in the vicinity of his own home between Urga and Hailar asked me the question, "Have you brought anything to sell?" Already buda ("hsiao mi tzu," millet) and brick tea are getting scarce. Clothes are slowly being worn out. There is no means of replacing the deficit except by journeying perhaps hundreds of miles to Urga or some other great centre where a shop exists. Even there everything will be much dearer than it was formerly, and there is also to be considered the expense of the journey. Lastly the poorest classes have not the wherewithal, or perhaps the leisure, to make these long journeys to buy their requirements.

To quote some more details: Russian traders from Manchuria Station admitted to me that they made from 50 to 60 per cent. clear profit on most of the goods they sold. Again, it must be borne in mind that even the goods sold by the Russian traders are for the most part what are loosely termed "Chinese goods," that is to say, goods that come from China and of identically the same origin as those formerly sold by the Chinese. As a matter of fact, a great proportion of these "Chinese goods," especially the piece goods, are of English and other European or American origin. The new Russian traders retail a great many of these "Chinese goods," which are the only kinds which the conservative Mongol will use ; but there remain a great many articles which the Mongol requires and which Russia does not produce, and which the Russian merchants do not stock. Of such articles the Mongol is now wholly deprived. It will only be with the greatest difficulty and delay that he will be persuaded to make use of Russian substitutes for such "Chinese goods" to which he has been accustomed.

Another example of the inertness of the Russian trading community is the fact that at the time of my visit Urga was and had been for some time absolutely bereft of all oil for lighting purposes and all spirit. In general it is extremely difficult to obtain many most ordinary requirements in Urga. Prices are very high (oats 1·80 to 2 roubles per 36 lb.; flour, third class quality, 4 roubles per 36 lb.) Earlier in the year prices were even higher. Many goods were unobtainable. Many Russian firms sent agents to report on conditions at Urga during the past year, and most of these agents have reports adversely with the result that very few new firms have appeared there. The Russian consul has tried to impress upon firms the necessity for sending proper business men to look after the branches in Urga, and not mere moujiks like the mass of the present Urga tradesmen.

I will next consider the reason why the Russian commercial world has failed to profit by the opening made for it by the Russian diplomatic world. As a preliminary it should be pointed out that the word failure would probably only be used by a Russian official; the Russian trader admits no failure because he admits no effort made by him. To the Russian trader and to many other Russians the idea of Russia being able to supply Mongolia with her requirements is simply ridiculous, the ill-considered fantasy of bureaucratic officials who are utterly out of touch not only with Mongolian conditions of trade but also with the conditions of Russian traders in Mongolia and of Russian industry generally. It is argued, and, I am of opinion, with good reason, that the production of Russian industry is not yet far enough advanced to supply the needs even of the Fatherland. Russia still imports vast quantities of manufactured goods. Only in years of bad harvest does the purchasing power of the Russian masses fall so low that there remains a surplus of the products of home industries which can be exported. The last three years have seen excellent harvests in Russia. Consequently there is no reason why manufacturers should seek a market in a country like Mongolia, where hitherto goods from "China" have almost exclusively been used. To win such a market would necessitate the manufacture of special patterns to suit Mongol tastes. The Mongol yields to no one in bigoted insistence upon getting that to which he has become accustomed, irrespective of whether the new article is better or worse, cheaper or dearer. It is a notorious fact that the Moscow manufacturers have hitherto paid very little attention to the demands of local traders for the manufacture of goods suited to the Mongol taste.

Next to pass to the question, is Russian diplomacy really so badly informed as to Mongolian trade conditions, and if so, why? I am of opinion that the complaints of the Russian trading community against their consular representatives on this score are well founded. (This does not alter the fact that the Russian consuls are in their turn quite right in looking upon the Russian subjects in Mongolia as representative of the scum of Siberia. As I have pointed out formerly no good feeling is lost between Russian officials and civilians in Mongolia).

The reasons for the ill-informedness of Russ an officialdom are twofold:

1. The consuls never travel (unlike Shishmaryoff, the first consul at Urga, which position he filled for fifty years). They know nothing of conditions outside their own post. This is a constant charge against them in Russian literature, and it is a fact of which I have personal experience.

2. Almost without exception no Russian official in Mongolia can talk Mongol. M. Miller himself, in conversation with me, deplored the fact that he had no Russian under him in Urga of official rank who could talk well enough to act as an interpreter. There were such as could make out documents and could write, but no one who could talk well. The reason for this extraordinary fact is that until last year almost all consular and diplomatic work was conducted in Chinese with the Ta Ch'ing's representatives. The result now is that the Russian officials are dependent upon interpreters, chiefly Buriats. These people are avowedly regarded as most unsatisfactory even by the consuls, and judging by the hatred with which they are looked upon by the civilian Russian element and Urga opinion in general, they are mostly persons of a self-seeking and unscrupulous character.

Abolition of 50-Verst Trade Zone

Before passing on to the political situation which as it were forms a sequel to the above described economic starvation of Mongolia, we must note under the heading " commercial " the fact that the decision of the Russian Government to abolish 50–Verst Free Trade Zone along the Russo-Ta Ch'ing frontier has been applied not only to the frontier conterminous with the territory of the hated Chinese Republic but also to that conterminous with the pseudo-friendship State of Outer Mongolia. Thus there have either already been introduced or will shortly be introduced duties on the carriage across the frontier of such commodities as timber, flour (0·45 roubles per 36 lb.), fish (2·50 roubles per pond or 36 lb.). This chiefly affects the Russian inhabitants along both sides of the frontier who hitherto have been in the habit of freely using and trading with commodities such as the above, which can be acquired either gratis or very cheaply in Mongolia. Russian colonists in Mongolia who would like to see a further increase of Russians on the Mongolian side of the frontier complain that the new duties still further discourage the achievement of their wishes. The Russian Government undoubtedly has no desire to see emigration into Mongolia until such time as Siberia is sufficiently Russified.

Political and Politico-Economic

The three main facts in the political situation in Khalkha to-day are:

1. Russia, owing to the dearness of commodities and the economic starvation caused by the policy pursued under her guidance, has already lost the sympathy of the Khalkha princes and is fast losing that of the common people.

2. Having lost faith in Russia, the Khalkha princes, some openly, some only secretly, desire to see the autonomy and economic development of their country maintained and furthered by its being thrown open to the trade of all nations on an equal footing. They realise that the advent of western traders will be followed by that of consuls, whose mutual jealousies will prevent the prolongation of the present situation, whereby the representatives of a single strong Power are able to impose their will in all cases upon the Mongol Cabinet, who without any armed force and without any advisers except such as Russia herself provides, have no alternative, but eventually to carry out the Russian proposals.

3. Russia, aware of the desire to attract foreign interests other than her own, is bent upon frustrating this plan by the systematic isolation of all the powerful Khalkhas. By careful surveillance the Mongol Ministers are prevented from having any relations with foreigners except through Russian channels. For the same reason the Russians refuse to allow the Mongols to accept the Chinese proposal for a conference at Udes, insisting that it should be held either at Urga or Verkhua-Udinsk.

To amplify the above facts:

In addition to the economic situation, other causes which have led to the anti-Russian revulsion are:

(a) Chinese intrigues. Biritu Wang, it seems certain, was sent as the emissary of Peking to bring over the Khalkha princes to the Chinese cause. As is well known, his mysterious and sudden death is popularly suspected of having been caused by poison administered by his political enemies. Hai San charges the Russian officials with instigating the murder, and believes that it will not be long before he himself is got rid of in the same way.

(b) The (in Mongol eyes) high-handed means employed by Russia to prevent the Mongols having any relations with the outer world except Russia. Han Ta Ch'ing Wang, during his recent visit as special emissary to the Tsar, was very anxious to continue his journey into Western Europe. This he was prevented from doing on the ground that he had not the requisite passports. His complete ignorance of all foreign countries, and the fact that the Prince and his suite were dependent solely upon the interpreters provided by the Russian Government made it impossible to insist upon proceeding out of Russia. Similarly, the Ta Lama has long desired to make a tour abroad viâ Peking, but is so carefully guarded that he cannot get away from Urga. Han Ta Ch'ing Wang and Sain Noin lately determined by a sudden visit to the representative of the British American Tobacco Company to make known, without the presence of the Russian interpreters, their secret desire for the arrival of foreign traders and consuls. Before they had succeeded in having more than a few minutes conversation, an almost unacquainted and totally uninvited Russian gaily entered the room and sat down expressing his great pleasure at having quite by chance dropped into so congenial a gathering. Russian and Mongol custom by which the merest acquaintance can walk unushered into one's private apartments, make such methods as the above very difficult to counteract.

The anti-Russian revulsion, besides being obvious from popular complaints as to the dearness of goods, was testified to by the comparatively unbiassed Sheng Yun, who has a healthy contempt for the backward northern branch of his race, and was also admitted to me both by Colonel Mitrovo and M. Miller. The latter, in answer to my question, said he could not name a single Khalkha prince upon whom he would care to rely as belonging truly to the so-called pro-Russian party. They all have either pro-Chinese tendencies or else desire western intervention to counteract Russian influence.

While the above must be borne in mind, it may nevertheless be said that two parties exist in political circles in Urga. The first is that led by the Ta Lama, a man who wields immense influence with the people of Khalkha. His party may be best termed " Nationalist," though the Russians often call it the pro-Chinese party. It includes Hai San. Its programme includes the peaceful settlement by compromise of differences with China, the attraction of western European trade and consuls, the maintenance of Lamaism and of the pacific tendencies of Mongol life.

The other party may be termed the military and outwardly pro-Russian party. It includes those who, from ideas of sound expediency or less worthy motives, support the Russian proposals, especially the foundation of a Mongol army. This party includes Dalai Wang, Han Ta Ch'ing Wang, and Sain Noin. Tushetu Wang and Erdeni Wang (the former Namsarai Kung, a great personal friend of the Urga Hutukhtu) are regarded as caring for nothing except their own pockets. Everywhere I heard testimony as to the corruption of the new Mongol officials. Sain Noin's secret pro-Chinese sympathies were attributed by M. Miller to his vanity and personal ambition, which caused him to be attracted by the glitter of coveted titles and distinctions bestowed from Peking. The list of Ministers in Urga is as follows:

>Premier (a post created last autumn by Russian advice, specially to overrule the Ta Lama) : Sain Noin.

>Minister of Interior : The Ta Lama.

>Minister of Foreign Affairs : Han T'a Ch'in Wang (Han Ta Dorji).

>Minister of War : Dalai Wang (formerly Dalai Peitzu).

>Assistant Minister of War : Sait Südjict Kung.

>Minister of Justice : Erdeni Wang.

>Minister of Finance: Tushetu Wang.

In general, the political outlook, from the Mongol point of view, can only be regarded post pessimistically. The Mongols have no men who are not utterly ignorant. The Khalkhas as a whole have little national feeling upon which to found a State. There is much evidence in support of the view that the Mongol race is fast dying out altogether. The Russian, no less than the Chinese, really entertains the greatest contempt for the Mongol, and the latter is beginning to realise this. In my opinion this contempt is thoroughly well deserved because of the extraordinary laziness, lack of enterprise and all ambition, and the moral and physical filthiness of the Mongol race.

Before passing on to consider the conclusions to be drawn from the above political and commercial situation and the relation it has to British interests, it is necessary to note some facts in regard to three special areas, Barga, Kobdo, and Urianghai.

1. In Barga, in addition to the discontent at the dearness and scarcity of goods, there was evident a decided feeling in favour of the restoration of the Ta Ch'ings. This is to be attributed to the following circumstances. Under the Ta Ch'ings the Barguts constituted bannermen and received allowances as such. Since the *coup d'État* these allowances have naturally ceased to be paid and instead of receiving money, Barga is now called upon to contribute her share to the expense of the new Mongol Government.

Again, suspicions are entertained with regard to Russian sincerity. It is pointed out that for 200 years the Barguts lived in peace under the Ta Ch'ings. The Russians never had much dealing with the Barguts until 1911 when they suddenly proclaimed themselves the devoted friends of Barga.

I may add:

I. I have heard plenty of evidence confirming the already reported accounts of the active part taken by Russia in the secession of Barga in January 1912; and

II. That Colonel Baranoff's pamphlet on Barga, the only existing work on this area, contains a great deal that is not correct;

III. At the time of my visit to Hailar, the Amban Sheng-fu was engaged in trying to obtain from the Russians control over the Chinese in the railway settlements, who, he complained, acted as spies for Peking and over whose persons he has at present no power.

2. Kobdo district: From Sait Südjict Kung I learnt the following:

The three chief men in Kobdo are Jahantza Lama (evidently the same as Cha (I) (Ja Lama), spoken of in a letter written by a German traveller shown last summer by the German military attaché to the British military attaché), Danbei Jantsang Lama, and Bayir Taiji.

All the Kobdo leaders, except Bayir Taiji are pacifist and inclined to settle matters with China by compromise. Bayir Taiji alone stands for the military policy. He is watching with his troops the passes through the Mongolian Altai. This confirms former information.

3. With reference to the Urianghai district, which I have formerly pointed out would be almost wholly annexed to Siberia, it is interesting to note:

- a) That on a map by the Irkutsk General Staff which I saw in the cabinet of M. Miller, the broad red line marking the Imperial boundary passed to the south of the Urianghai area, an alternative line of equal prominence passing along the former Imperial frontier to the north ; and

- b) That a Russian merchant exploiting the fisheries in Urianghai said that the administration there had already been taken over by Russian officials. After cross-questioning this merchant, I convinced myself that the statement was not true, but it probably indicates that the transfer is imminent ;

- c) M. Pokrovsky told me that he believed that it was already definitely settled that Urianghai was to be recognised as Russian territory.

Finally, a word as to the Japanese.

Throughout my route I saw no signs of Japanese activity except at Hailar where there were some fifty to sixty Japanese including the usual quota of prostitutes, chemists, dentists, and doctors. From Russian sources I learnt that in the Cherim league of Eastern Mongolia the Japanese had quite failed to make any headway in trade against the Chinese.

In September a Japanese highly posted in the employ of the South Manchurian Railway Company visited Urga. Sheng Yun, who received a visit from him, told me that he came to reconnoitre as to the possible development of Japanese economic interests in Mongolia.

The Relation of the Politico-Economic Situation to British Interests

Chinese trade having been dealt a very serious blow and Russian trading circles being incapable of filling the place vacated by the Chinese, there remains a splendid opportunity for the extension of the trade of those Powers who already have large businesses in North China.

The advent of Western European trade in Mongolia may almost be said to be expected by the Russians. As explained above, it is earnestly desired by all the Mongol princes. Russian minor officials, struggling with small salaries to contend with the exorbitant prices demanded by their own tradesmen, would gladly see the opening of European shops. Even serious agents of Russian manufacturing firms said to me that foreign competition would be a blessing to them, as it might wake the Urga tradesmen up to fresh efforts. On the other hand, Russian officials consider that the advent of European competitors would mean the decisive and final collapse of all Russian trade. Colonel Mitrovo, fearing this event, is strongly advocating that the Government should itself take steps to have imported free of all duties viâ Vladivostok and Kiakhta those same English and American piece goods which have hitherto held sway in the Mongolian market and which it has been found impossible to oust with the products of Moscow. Colonel Mitrovo told me frankly that he believed for many years to come Russian manufacturers cannot possibly supply Mongolia.

Again, another scheme which is mooted by the Russians as a means for themselves trading with our goods as Urga is to open up a new commercial highway from Manchuria station to Urga viâ the Kerulen valley. This would avoid passing the Russian Customs. But there would be the freight charges by railway from Tien-tsin or wherever the goods were acquired, and then a cart journey perhaps even slightly longer than that from Kalgan. It is persistently reported that a company (called "Lloyd") is about to open automobile communication from Manchuria station to Urga both for goods and passenger traffic. Having regard to the fact that new means of communication are always "about to be commenced " for decades before they really are, this plan is not likely to be realised soon.

Again, M. Miller regarded the economic situation as hopeless, and it was evident that he expected foreign competition from the fact that the first question he put to me was: "When is a British consul coming to Urga?" Speaking of the Grant incident, M. Miller is reported to have said: " Another incident like this, and we shall have an English consul here."

In my own opinion, the scheme whereby Russians are to conquer the Mongolian market with English and American goods may be classed together with the already exploded plan for supplying Mongolia with Russian manufactures. The Russification and development of Siberia is too vast a task to allow of the Russian people being able to do much elsewhere in Mongolia. Russia will insist on remaining politically paramount in Mongolia, but she cannot insist upon preventing others from doing that which she herself is unable to do, namely, to develop and exploit Mongolia economically. There are only two possibilities in the future, which are:

1. A complete reversion to the old state of things, whereby the Chinese will control all the trade, possibly with the innovation of reasonable customs dues; or

2. The exploitation of the Mongolian market by English, American, German, or Japanese firms, working probably through Inner Mongol or Chinese servants.

Both Russians and Mongols would certainly prefer the latter alternative.

It is not the intention here to prove how well worth contending for is the Mongolian market, but I may quote the opinion of the Kiakhta frontier commissioner, who believes that when with patience Europeans have taught the Mongols how to improve the quantity and quality of their already vast wealth in live-stock and raw products, Mongolia will certainly be one of the world's chief markets for the purchase of these most important requirements of mankind. In the Russian Altai great success has attended the blending of Mongolian and Caucasian breeds of sheep. Already Russia has made a start in teaching the Mongols how to improve their stock and protect it from disease by the despatch of numerous flying and stationary veterinary parties into Mongolia.

I would also point out that the future value of the Mongolian market must not be judged by the present thinness of population. The greater part of Mongolia is a land fully suited to economic development and settled habitation, and later on, whatever may become of its present degenerate inhabitants, it will be peopled by one or other of the more virule and more industrious races which surround it.

The present scattered distribution of the population need not deter the trader, because the mobile Mongol has always been accustomed to go comparatively long distances in buy his requirements. This feature, however, makes the keeping trading establishment unsuited for Englishmen in person. But there are excellent opportunities for Indian British subjects as the actual serving personnel for British or British Indian firms.

It should be noted that the anti-Chinese dues levied by the Mongols affect our trade. They diminish the sale of our goods in Mongolia, and they increase the price at which our merchants in North China buy from the Chinese the raw produce which is obtained in exchange for our manufactured goods. The Chinese have to pay a tax of 1 tael on the purchase or sale of every ox or horse, 2 taels per camel, and 3 ch'ien of silver per sheep.

N.B. – I may add that, if required, I can supply any intending traders with lists of goods in use among the Mongols and much other detailed information as to Mongol trading customs and Mongol tastes, means of transport in Mongolia, wages, &c. Trade in Mongolia possesses quite peculiar characteristics, which must be understood to achieve success.

Endnotes

1 Gerald Charles Binsteed, born in Cairo in 1885, died in Le Gheer, Belgium, in April 1915 (*The Bond of Sacrifice: A Biographical Record of All British Officers who Fell in the Great War*, Vol. II: January-June 1915, London s.d., 'Captain Gerald Charles Binsteed. M.C., 2nd Battn, The Essex Regiment').

2 TNA, FO 535/16, No. 429, Mr. Alston to Sir Edward Grey, November 1, 1913, p. 403.

3 TNA, Extract from a Report by Lieutenant Binsteed on a Journey from Hailar to Urga, and thence to Kiakhta, FO 535/16, Enclosure in No. 429, p. 405-411.

Anglo-Russian Convention of August 31, 1907

(TNA, Convention, FO 535/10, Enclosure 1 in No. 49, pp. 31-35)

Convention

SA Majesté le Roi du Royaume-Uni de la Grande-Bretagne et d'Irlande et des Territoires Britanniques au delà des Mers, Empereur des Indes, et Sa Majesté l'Empereur de Toutes les Russies, animés du sincère désir de régler d'un consentement mutuel différentes questions touchant aux intérêts de leurs États sur le Continent Asiatique, ont résolu de conclure des accords destinés à prévenir toute cause de malentendus entre la Grande-Bretagne et la Russie par rapport aux dites questions et ont nommé à cet effet pour leurs Plénipotentiaires respectifs, savoir:

Sa Majesté le Roi du Royaume-Uni de la Grande-Bretagne et d'Irlande et des Territoires Britanniques au delà des Mers, Empereur des Indes, le Très Honorable Sir Arthur Nicolson, son Ambassadeur Extraordinaire et Plénipotentiaire près Sa Majesté l'Empereur de Toutes les Russies;

Sa Majesté l'Empereur de Toutes les Russies, le Maître de sa Cour Alexandre Iswolsky, Ministre des Affaires Etrangères;

Lesquels, après s'être communiqué leurs pleins pouvoirs, trouvés en bonne et due forme, sont convenus de ce qui suit:

Arrangement concernant la Perse.

Les Gouvernements de la Grande-Bretagne et de Russie, s'étant mutuellement engagés à respecter l'intégrité et l'indépendance de la Perse, et désirant sincèrement la préservation de l'ordre dans toute l'étendue de ce pays et son développement pacifique, aussi bien que l'établissement permanent d'avantages égaux pour le commerce et l'industrie de toutes les autres nations ;

Considérant que chacun d'eux a, pour des raisons d'ordre géographique et économique, un intérêt spécial au maintien de la paix et de l'ordre dans certaines provinces de la Perse contiguës ou voisines à la frontière russe d'une part, et aux frontières de l'Afghanistan et du Béloudjistan de l'autre; et étant désireux d'éviter tout motif de conflit entre leurs intérêts respectif dans les provinces Persanes dont il a été fait mention plus haut ;

Se sont mis d'accord sur les termes suivants:

I.

La Grande-Bretagne s'engage à ne pas rechercher pour elle-même et à ne pas appuyer en faveur de sujets Britanniques, aussi bien qu'en faveur de sujets de Puissances tierces, de Concessions quelconques de nature politique ou commerciale, telles que les Concessions de chemins de fer, de banques, de télégraphes, de routes, de transport, d'assurance, &c., au delà d'une ligne allant de Kasri-Chirin par Isfahan, Iezd, Kakh, et aboutissant à un point sur la frontière Persane à l'intersection des frontières Russe et Afghane, et à ne pas s'opposer, directement ou indirectement, à des demandes de pareilles Concessions dans cette région soutenues par le Gouvernement Russe. Il est bien entendu que les localités mentionnées ci-dessus entrent dans la région où la Grande-Bretagne s'engage à ne pas rechercher les susdites Concessions.

II.

La Russie de son côté s'engage à ne pas rechercher pour elle-même et à ne pas appuyer en faveur de sujets de Puissances tierces de Concessions quelconques de nature politique ou commerciale, telles que les Concessions de chemins de fer, de banques, de télégraphes, de routes, de transport, d'assurance, &c., au delà d'une ligne allant de la frontière Afghane par Gazik, Birdjand, Kerman, et aboutissant à Bender Abbas, et à ne pas s'opposer, directement ou indirectement, à des demandes de pareilles Concessions dans cette région soutenues par le Gouvernement Britannique. Il est bien entendu que les localités mentionnées ci-dessus entrent dans la région où la Russie s'engage à ne pas rechercher les susdites Concessions.

III.

La Russie s'engage pour sa part à ne pas s'opposer, sans s'être préalablement entendue avec l'Angleterre, à ce que des Concessions quelconques soient données à des sujets Britanniques dans les régions de la Perse situées entre les lignes mentionnées dans les Articles I et II.

La Grande-Bretagne prend un engagement identique en ce qui concerne des Concessions à donner à des sujets Russes dans les mêmes régions de la Perse.

Toutes les Concessions existant actuellement dans les régions désignées dans les Articles I et II sont maintenues.

IV.

Il est entendu que les revenus de toutes les douanes Persanes, à l'exception de celles du Farsistan et du Golfe Persique, revenus garantissant l'amortissement et les intérêts des emprunts conclus par le Gouvernement du Schah à la Banque d'Escompte et de Prêts de Perse, jusqu'à la date de la signature du présent Arrangement, seront affectés au même but que par le passé.

Il est également entendu que les revenus des douanes Persanes du Farsistan et du Golfe Persique, aussi bien que ceux des pêcheries sur le littoral Persan de la Mer Caspienne et ceux des postes et télégraphes, seront affectés comme par le passé au service des emprunts conclus par le Gouvernement du Schah à la Banque Impériale de Perse jusqu'à la date de la signature du présent Arrangement.

En cas d'irrégularités dans l'amortissement ou le paiement des intérêts des emprunts Persans conclus à la Banque d'Escompte et de Prêts de Perse et à la Banque Impériale de Perse jusqu'à la date de la signature du présent Arrangement, et si la nécessité se présente pour la Russie d'instituer un contrôle sur des sources de revenus garantissant le service régulier des emprunts conclus à la première des dites banques et situées dans la région mentionnée dans l'Article II du présent Arrangement, ou pour la Grande-Bretagne d'instituer un contrôle sur des sources de revenus garantissant le service régulier des emprunts conclus à la seconde des dites banques et situées dans la région mentionnée dans l'Article I du présent Arrangement, les Gouvernements Anglais et Russe s'engagent à entrer préalablement dans un échange d'idées amical en vue de déterminer d'un commun accord les mesures de contrôle en question et d'éviter toute ingérence qui ne serait pas conforme aux principes servant de base au présent Arrangement.

Arrangement concernant l'Afghanistan

Les Hautes Parties Contractantes, en vue d'assurer la parfaite sécurité sur les frontières respectives en Asie Centrale et le maintien dans ces régions d'une paix solide et durable, ont conclu la Convention suivante:

ARTICLE I

Le Gouvernement de Sa Majesté Britannique déclare qu'il n'a pas l'intention de changer l'état politique de l'Afghanistan.

Le Gouvernement de Sa Majesté Britannique s'engage, en outre, à exercer son influence en Afghanistan seulement dans un sens pacifique, et il ne prendra pas lui-même en Afghanistan et n'encouragera pas l'Afghanistan à prendre des mesures menaçant la Russie.

De son côté, le Gouvernement Impérial de Russie déclare qu'il reconnaît l'Afghanistan comme se trouvant en dehors de la sphère de l'influence Russe, et il s'engage à se servir pour toutes ses relations politiques avec l'Afghanistan de l'intermédiaire du Gouvernement de Sa Majesté Britannique ; il s'engage aussi à n'envoyer aucuns Agents en Afghanistan.

ARTICLE II

Le Gouvernement de Sa Majesté Britannique ayant déclaré dans le Traité signé à Kaboul le 21 Mars, 1905, qu'il reconnaît l'Arrangement et les engagements conclus avec le défunt Émir Abdur Rahman et qu'il n'a aucune intention de s'ingérer dans l'administration intérieure du territoire Afghan, la Grande-Bretagne s'engage à ne pas annexer ou occuper, contrairement au dit Traité, une partie quelconque de l'Afghanistan, ni à s'ingérer dans l'administration intérieure de ce pays, sous réserve que l'Emir remplira les engagements déjà contractés par lui à l'égard du Gouvernement de Sa Majesté Britannique en vertu du Traité susmentionné.

ARTICLE III

Les autorités Russes et Afghanes, spécialement désignées à cet effet, sur la frontière ou dans les provinces frontières, pourront établir des relations directes réciproques pour régler les questions locales d'un caractère non politique.

ARTICLE IV

Les Gouvernements de la Grande-Bretagne et la Russie déclarent reconnaître, par rapport à l'Afghanistan, le principe de l'égalité de traitement pour ce qui concerne le commerce, et conviennent que toutes les facilités qui ont été ou seront acquises à l'avenir au commerce et aux commerçants Anglais et Anglo-Indiens seront également appliquées au commerce et aux commerçants Russes. Si le développement du commerce vient à démontrer la nécessité d'agents commerciaux, les deux Gouvernements s'entendront sur les mesures à prendre, eu égard bien entendu aux droits souverains de l'Émir.

ARTICLE V

Les présents Arrangements n'entreront en vigueur qu'à partir du moment où le Gouvernement Britannique aura notifié au Gouvernement de Russie le consentement de l'Emir aux termes ci-dessus stipulés.

Arrangement concernant le Thibet

Les Gouvernements de la Grande-Bretagne et de Russie, reconnaissant les droits suzerains de la Chine sur le Thibet et considérant que par suite de sa situation géographique la Grande-Bretagne a un intérêt spécial à voir le régime actuel des relations extérieures du Thibet intégralement maintenu, sont convenus de l'Arrangement suivant:

ARTICLE I

Les deux Hautes Parties Contractantes s'engagent à respecter l'intégrité territoriale du Thibet et à s'abstenir de toute ingérence dans son administration intérieure.

ARTICLE II

Se conformant au principe admis de la suzeraineté de la Chine sur le Thibet, la Grande-Bretagne et la Russie s'engagent à ne traiter avec le Thibet que par l'entremise du Gouvernement Chinois. Cet engagement n'exclut pas toutefois les rapports directs des agents commerciaux Anglais avec les autorités Thibétaines prévus par l'Article V de la Convention du 7 Septembre, 1904, entre la Grande-Bretagne et le Thibet, et confirmés par la Convention du 27 Avril, 1906, entre la Grande-Bretagne et la Chine ; il ne modifie pas non plus les engagements assumés par la Grande-Bretagne et la Chine en vertu de l'Article I de la dite Convention de 1906.

Il est bien entendu que les Bouddhistes tant sujets Britanniques que Russes, peuvent entrer en relations directes sur le terrain strictement religieux avec le Dalaï-Lama et les autres représentants du Bouddhisme au Thibet; les Gouvernements de la Grande-Bretagne et de Russie s'engagent, pour autant qu'il dépendra d'eux, à ne pas admettre que ces relations puissent porter atteinte aux stipulations du présent accord.

ARTICLE III

Les Gouvernements Britannique et Russe s'engagent, chacun pour sa part, à ne pas envoyer de Représentants à Lhassa.

ARTICLE IV

Les deux Hautes Parties s'engagent à ne rechercher ou obtenir, ni pour leur propre compte, ni en faveur de leurs sujets, aucunes Concessions de chemins de fer, routes, télégraphes et mines, ou autres droits au Thibet.

ARTICLE V

Les deux Gouvernements sont d'accord qu'aucune partie des revenus du Thibet, soit en nature, soit en espèces, ne peut être engagée ou assignée tant à la Grande-Bretagne et à la Russie qu'à leurs sujets.

Annexe à l'Arrangement entre la Grande-Bretagne et la Russie concernant le Thibet

La Grande-Bretagne réaffirme la déclaration signée par son Excellence le Vice-Roi et Gouverneur-Général des Indes et annexée à la ratification de la Convention du 7 Septembre, 1904, stipulant que l'occupation de la Vallée de Chumbi par les forces Britanniques prendra fin après le paiement de trois annuités de l'indemnité de 25,00,000 roupies, à condition que les places de marché mentionnés à l'Article II de la dite Convention aient été effectivement ouvertes depuis trois ans, et que les autorités Thibétaines durant cette période se soient conformées strictement sous tous les rapports aux termes de la dite Convention de 1904. Il est bien entendu que si l'occupation de la Vallée de Chumbi par les forces Britanniques n'aura pas pris fin, pour quelque raison que ce soit, à l'époque prévue par la Déclaration précitée, les Gouvernements Britannique et Russe entreront dans un échange de vues amical à ce sujet.

La présente Convention sera ratifiée et les ratifications en seront échangées à Saint-Pétersbourg aussitôt que faire se pourra.

En foi de quoi les plénipotentiaires respectifs ont signé la présente Convention et y ont apposé leurs cachets.

Fait à Saint-Pétersbourg, en double expédition, le 18 (31) Août, 1907.

(L.S.) A. NICOLSON.

(L.S.) ISWOLSKY.

Treaty between Mongolia and Tibet of December 29, 1912 (January 1913, 11)

(TNA, Mongol-Thibetan Treaty, concluded at Urga December 29, 1912 (January 11, 1913), FO 535/16, Enclosure 1 in No. 88, pp. 66-67)

(Translation)

MONGOLIA and Thibet, having freed themselves from the dynasty of the Manchus and separated from China, have formed their own independent States, and, having in view that both States from time immemorial have professed one and the same religion, with a view to strengthening their historic and mutual friendship the Minister for Foreign Affairs, Nikta Biliktu Da-Lama Rabdan, and the Assistant Minister, General and Manlai baatyr beiseh Damdinsurun, as plenipotentiaries of the Government of the ruler of the Mongol people, and gudjir tsanshib kanchen Lubsan-Agvan, donir Agvan Choinzin, director of the Bank Ishichjamtso, and the clerk Gendun Galsan, as plenipotentiaries of the Dalai Lama, the ruler of Thibet, have made the following agreement:

ARTICLE 1

The ruler of Thibet, Dalai Lama, approves and recognises the formation of an independent Mongol State, and the proclamation, in the year of the pig and the ninth day of the eleventh month, of Chjebzun Damba Lama of the yellow faith as ruler of the country.

ARTICLE 2

The ruler of the Mongol people, Chjebzun Damba Lama, approves and recognises the formation of on [*sic*] independent (Thibetan) State and the proclamation of the Dalai Lama as ruler of Thibet.

ARTICLE 3

Both States will work by joint consideration for the well-being of the Buddhist faith.

ARTICLE 4

Both States, Mongolia and Thibet, from now and for all time will afford each other assistance against external and internal dangers.

ARTICLE 5

Each State within its own territory will afford assistance to the subjects of the other travelling officially or privately on affairs of religion or State.

Article 6

Both States, Mongolia and Thibet, as formerly, will carry on a reciprocal trade in the products of their respective countries in wares, cattle, &c., and will also open industrial establishments.

Article 7

From now the granting of credit to anyone will be permitted only with the knowledge and sanction of official institutions. Without such sanction Government institutions will not consider claims.

As regards contracts made previous to the conclusion of the present treaty, where serious loss is being incurred through the inability of the two parties to come to terms, such debts may be recovered by (Government) institutions, but in no case shall the debt concern " shabinars " or " khoshuns."

Article 8

Should it prove necessary to supplement the articles of the present treaty, the Mongolian and Thibetan Governments must appoint special delegates, who will conclude such agreements as the conditions of the time shall demand.

Article 9

The present treaty shall come into force from the date of its signature.

Plenipotentiaries from the Mongolian Government for the conclusion of the treaty:

Nikta Biliktu Da-Lama Rabdan, Minister for Foreign Affairs; and General and Manlai baatyr beiseh Damdinsurun, Assistant Minister.

Plenipotentiaries from the Dalai Lama, the ruler of Thibet, for the conclusion of the treaty:

Gudjir tsanshib kanchen Lubsan-Agvan, Choinzin, the Director of the Bank of Thibet Ishichjamtsa, and the clerk, Gendun-Galsan.

Signed (by Mongol reckoning) in the fourth day of the twelfth month of the second year of the "Raised by the Many," and by Thibetan reckoning on the same day and month of the year of the "water-mouse."

Foreign Office to India Office, March 29, 1913

(TNA, Foreign Office to India Office, March 29, 1913, FO 535/16, No. 168, pp. 140–141)

Foreign Office, March 29, 1913

Sir,

I AM directed by Secretary Sir E. Grey to acknowledge the receipt of your letter of the 25th instant, recommending that amended instructions should be sent to His Majesty's Ambassador at St. Petersburgh with regard to the reception of the Mongolian Mission.

Sir E. Grey has given his careful attention to the considerations advanced by the Marquess of Crewe, and is fully alive to the desirability of losing no opportunity of obtaining a lever for counteracting the spread of Russian influence into Thibet through Mongolia.

He is not, however, convinced that this end will be best attained by Great Britain acquiring a footing in Mongolia. Though it may be possible for her to establish her right to equal commercial treatment in that country, yet she cannot hope to compete effectively with Russia at Urga, or to counteract there any influence which Russia may exert through the Mongolians upon Thibet. Sir E. Grey is rather of the opinion that the more effective way of counteracting that influence lies in the exertion of British influence upon Thibet, either directly in the negotiations between the Chinese and Thibetans in India, or indirectly through the Nepalese, while at the same time His Majesty's Government, in their discussions with the Russian Government, make use of the action of the latter in Mongolia to justify any British action that it may be desirable to take in Thibet.

Sir E. Grey further thinks that a reversal of the decision that Sir G. Buchanan should decline to receive the Mongolian Mission would merely expose His Majesty's Government to the suspicion of Russia and the hostility of China with very little compensating advantage.

Sir E. Grey trusts that Lord Crewe will appreciate the force of these arguments, and agree that it would be better to let matters remain as they are.

I am, &c.

W. LANGLEY

References

PRIMARY SOURCES

The National Archives, London, Kew (TNA)

FO 17 Foreign Office: Political and Other Departments: General Correspondence before 1906, China: FO 17/1746, FO 17/1751.

FO 405 Foreign Office: China and Taiwan Confidential Print: FO 405/208, FO 405/211, FO 405/212.

FO 535 Foreign Office: Confidential Print Tibet and Mongolia: FO 535/3, FO 535/4, FO 535/10, FO 535/11, FO 535/12, FO 535/13, FO 535/15, FO 535/16, FO 535/17, FO 535/18.

FO 800 Foreign Office, Private Offices: Various Ministers' and Officials' Papers: FO 800/72.

CAB 128 Cabinet: Minutes (CM and CC Series): CAB 128/33/54.

DO 133 Commonwealth Relations Office and successors: High Commission and Consular Archives, India: Registered Files (1946-1971): DO 133/124 *Events in Sikkim* (1948 Nov 15-).

British Library, London (BL), India Office Records

IOR/L/PS Political and Secret Department Records.

IOR/L/PS/18 Political and Secret Department Memoranda (1840-1947): IOR/L/PS/18/C69/5, IOR/L/PS/18/C69/6, IOR/L/PS/18/C69/7, IOR/L/PS/18/C32, IOR/L/PS/18/C78, IOR/L/PS/18/C41/5, IOR/L/PS/20/RUS/3.

IOR/L/PS/20 Political and Secret Department Library (1757-1952): IOR/L/PS/20/150, IOR/L/PS/20/211, IOR/L/PS/20/D4, IOR/L/PS/20/RUS1.

IOR/L/MIL/17 Military Department Library.

IOR/L/MIL/17/12 India, Bhutan & Sikkim, Ceylon: IOR/L/MIL/17/12/60.

IOR/L/MIL/17/14 Afghanistan, Central Asia, Tibet: IOR/L/MIL/17/14/4.

IOR/R/12 The records of the British Legation at Kabul, 1923-48.

IOR/R/12/LIB Kabul Library: IOR/R/12/LIB/106.

British and Foreign State Papers (BSP)

Vol. 49, Vol. 67, Vol. 70.

House of Commons Daily Debates

Vol. 481.

Command papers

C. 7312, *Convention between Great Britain and China relating to Sikkim and Tibet. Signed at Calcutta, March 17, 1890. With Regulations appended thereto, signed at Darjeeling, December 5, 1893*, London 1894.

C. 919, *Correspondence respecting Central Asia*, London 1874.

Cd. 914, *Agreement between the United Kingdom and Japan relative to China and Corea. Signed at London, January 30, 1902*, London 1902.

Cd. 1920, *East India (Tibet). Papers relating to Tibet*, London 1904 (BL reference: Mss Eur F197/103).

Cd. 3088, *Convention between Great Britain and China respecting Tibet. Signed at Peking, April 27, 1906*, London 1906.

Cd. 4450, *Regulations respecting Trade in Tibet (amending those of December 5, 1893) concluded between the United Kingdom, China, and Tibet. Signed at Calcutta, April 20, 1908*, London 1908.

Cd. 2735, *Agreement between the United Kingdom and Japan. Signed at London, August 12, 1905*, London 1905.

Cd. 5240, *East India (Tibet). Further papers relating to Tibet* [In continuation of Cd. 2370], London 1910 (BL reference: IOR/L/PS/20/259).

Cd. 5735, *Agreement between the United Kingdom and Japan. Signed at London, July 13, 1911*, London 1911.

Cd. 2383, *Convention between the United Kingdom and France respecting Newfoundland, and West and Central Africa, Signed at London, April 8, 1904*, London 1905.

Cd. 2384, *Declaration between the United Kingdom and France respecting Egypt and Morocco. Signed at London, April 8, 1904*, London 1905.

Cd. 2385, *Declaration between the United Kingdom and France concerning Siam, Madagascar, and the New Hebrides, Signed at London, April 8, 1904*, London 1905.

Cd. 2534, *Treaty between the British Government and the Amir of Afghanistan, Dated 21 March 1905, with papers relating thereto*, London 1905 (BL reference: Mss Eur F131/5).

Cmd. 1786, *Treaty between British and Afghan Governments. Signed at Kabul, November 22, 1921*, London 1922.

Other primary sources

AITCHISON, C. U., *A Collection of Treaties, Engagements, and Sanads relating to India and Neighbouring Countries*, Vol. I, Calcutta 1892.

BELL, C., *Portrait of the Dalai Lama*, London 1946.

BELL, C., *Tibet Past and Present*, Oxford 1924.

British Documents on the Origins of the War: 1898–1914, edited by G. P. Gooch and H. Temperley, Vol. IX: The Balkan Wars – Part I: The Prelude ; The Tripoli War, London 1933.

BULSTRODE, B., *A Tour in Mongolia*, London 1920.

Chung kuo Hsi tsang she hui li shih tzu liao 中国西藏社会历史资料, edited by Chin Hui 金晖, Jen I-nung 任一农 and Ma Nai-hui 马鼐辉, Pei-ching 北京 1994.

Documents on Sikkim and Bhutan, edited by S. K. Sharma and U. Sharma, New Delhi 1998.

DU HALDE, J. B., *Description géographique, historique, chronologique, politique, et physique de l'empire de la Chine et de la Tartarie chinoise, enrichie des Cartes générales et particulieres de ces Pays, de la Carte générale et des Cartes particulieres du Thibet, & de la Corée ; & ornée d'un grand nombre de Figures & de Vignettes gravées en tailledouce*, Tome Quatrième, La Haye 1736.

Foreign Office, Historical Section, Peace Handbook, *Mongolia*, No. 68, London 1920.

Handbook for the Diplomatic History of Europe, Asia, and Africa, 1870-1914, by F. M. Anderson – A. S. Hershey (with the assistance of 50 contributors), prepared for the National Board for Historical Service, Government Printing Office, Washington 1918.

Historical and Political Gazetteer of Afghanistan, Vols 1-6, edited by L.W. Adamec, Graz 1972-1985.

Intelligence Branch Army Head-Quarters, India (produced in the), *The Second Afghan War, 1878-1880: Abridged Official Account*, London 1908.

JOHNSTON, R. F., *Twilight in the Forbidden City*, New York 1934.

Lin shih kung pao 臨時公報, 辛亥年十二月二十六日 (February 13, 1912), Pei-ching 北京 1912.

MARKHAM, C.R., *Narratives of the Mission of George Bogle to Tibet, and of the Journey of Thomas Manning to Lhasa*, London 1876.

MOLESWORTH, G. N., *Afghanistan 1919. An Account of operations in the Third Afghan War*, Bombay 1962.

Official history (naval and military) of the Russo-Japanese war, Vols I-III, prepared by the Historical section of the Committee of imperial defence, London 1910-1920.

PEASLEE, A. J., *Constitutions of Nations*, Vol. I, Concord 1950.

PRICE, E. B., *The Russo-Japanese Treaties of 1907-1916 Concerning Manchuria and Mongolia*, Baltimore 1933.

The Bond of Sacrifice: A Biographical Record of All British Officers who Fell in the Great War, Vol. II: January-June 1915, London s.d.

The Correspondence of G. E. Morrison, Vol. II: 1912-1920, edited by H. Lo, New York 2013.

The India Office List for 1893, London 1893.

The India Office List for 1928, compiled from official records by direction of the Secretary of State for India in Council, London 1928.

The Mongols and Tibet: A Historical Assessment of Relations Between the Mongol Empire and Tibet, Department of Information and International Relations (DIIR), Central Tibetan Administration, Dharamsala 1996.

Traités et conventions entre l'Empire du Japon et les puissances étrangères, Première Partie - Traités, Ministère des affaires étrangères, Tokyo 1908.

Treaties and Agreements with and concerning China, 1894-1919, Vol. I: Manchu Period (1894-1911), compiled and edited by J. V. A. MacMurray, New York 1921.

Treaties and Agreements with and concerning China, 1894-1919, Vol. II: Republican Period (1912-1919), compiled and edited by J. V. A. MacMurray, New York 1921.

Treaties, Conventions, etc., between China and Foreign States, Vol. I, Second Edition, published by Order of the Inspector General of Customs, Shanghai 1917.

TRIEPEL, H., *Nouveau Recueil Général de Traités et autres actes relatifs aux rapports de droit international*, Troisiéme Série, Tome VII, Leipzig 1913.

United Nations Department of Economic and Social Affairs/Population Division, *World Population Prospects: The 2010 Revision*, Vol. I: Comprehensive Tables, New York 2011.

United Nations, General Assembly, Resolutions: GA Resolution 1353 (XIV), GA Resolution 1723 (XVI), GA Resolution 2079 (XX).

WANG CHIA-WEI 王家伟 – NI-MA-CHIEN-TSAN 尼玛坚赞, *Chung kuo Hsi tsang te li shih ti wei* 中国西藏的历史地位, Pei-ching 北京 1997.

WHITE, J. C., *Sikhim & Bhutan: Twenty-One Years on the North-East Frontier. 1887-1908*, London 1909.

YOUNGHUSBAND, F., *India and Tibet. A history of the relations which have subsisted between the two countries from the time of Warren Hastings to 1910; with a particular account of the mission to Lhasa in 1904*, London 1910.

Договоры Россіи съ Востокомъ: Политическіе и торговые, Собралъ и издал Т. Юзефовичь, С. Петербургъ 1869.

Извѣстія Министерства иностранныхъ дѣлъ, Третій годъ изданія, 1914, К. I, С.-Петербургъ 1914.

НИКОЛАЕВИЧ КРЫЛОВ-ТОЛСТИКОВИЧ, А., *Придворный календарь на 1915 год. Комментарии*, Москва 2015.

Полное собраніе законовъ Россійской имперіи, Томъ: III, 1828, Санктпетербургъ 1830.

官報 Kanpō, August 15, 1907.

韓國ニ關スル條約及法令 / 統監府編纂, カンコク ニ カンスル ジョウヤク オヨビ ホウレイ, [京城] 1906.

SECONDARY SOURCES

Books and papers

AFARY, J., *The Iranian Constitutional Revolution, 1906-1911: Grassroots Democracy, Social Democracy and the Origins of Feminism*, New York 1996.

ANDREYEV, A., *Soviet Russia and Tibet: the debacle of secret diplomacy, 1918-1930s*, Leiden 2003.

ANDREYEV, A. I. –YUSUPOVA, T. I., *Petr Kuzmich Kozlov (1863–1935)*, in: *The Quest for Forbidden Lands: Nikolai Przhevalskii and his Followers on Inner Asian Tracks*, edited by A. Andreyev, M. Baskhanov and T. Yusupova, Leiden – Boston 2018, pp. 212-254.

ARIS, M., *Bhutan: The Early History of a Himalayan Kingdom*, Warminster, England 1979.

ARIS, M., *The Raven Crown: The Origins of Buddhist Monarchy in Bhutan*, Chicago 2005.

ATKIN, M., *Russia and Iran: 1780-1828*, Minneapolis 1980.

BADDELEY, J. F., *The Russian conquest of the Caucasus*, London – New York – Bombay – Calcutta 1908.

BAREJA-STARZYŃSKA, A., *The Mongolian Incarnation of Jo nang pa Tāranātha Kun dga' snying po: Öndör Gegeen Zanabazar Blo bzang bstan pa'i rgyal mtshan (1635-1723): A case study of the Tibeto-Mongolian Relationship*, in: The Tibet Journal, Vol. 34/35, No. 3/2, Special Issue: The Earth Ox Papers, Autumn 2009-Summer 2010, pp. 243-261.

BAUSANI, A., *Religion in Iran: From Zoroaster to Baha'u'llah*, translated by J. M. Marchesi, New York 2000.

BAWDEN, C. R., *The Modern History of Mongolia*, London – New York 2009.

BAYAT, M., *Iran's First Revolution: Shi'ism and the Constitutional Revolution of 1905-1909*, New York 1991.

BERGÈRE, M.-C., *Sun Yat-sen*, translated by J. Lloyd, Stanford, California 1998.

BERTON, P., *Russo-Japanese Relations, 1905-17: From Enemies to Allies*, London – New York 2012.

BOLDBAATAR, J. – HUMPHREY, C., *The Process of Creation of National Symbols and Their Adoption in the 1992 Constitution of Mongolia*, in: Inner Asia, Vol. 9, No. 1, 2007, pp. 3-22.

BOSE, M. L., *History of Arunachal Pradesh*, New Delhi 1997.

BULAG, U. E., *Introduction: The 13th Dalai Lama in Mongolia, or the Dawn of Inner Asian modernity*, in: *The Thirteenth Dalai Lama on the Run (1904-1906): Archival Documents from Mongolia*, edited by S. Chuluun and U. E. Bulag, Leiden – Boston 2013, pp. 1-25.

BURNES, A., *Cabool: a personal narrative of a journey to, and residence in that city, in the years 1836, 7, and 8*, London 1843.

BURNES, A., *Travels into Bokhara ; Being an account of a journey from India to Cabool, Tartary and Persia ; Also, narrative of a voyage on the Indus from the sea to Lahore*, 3 vols, London 1834.

CHENG, A., *Storia del pensiero cinese*, Vol. I: Dalle origini allo «studio del Mistero», Italian translation by A. Crisma, Torino 2000.

CROSSLEY, P. K. – RAWSKI, E. S., *A Profile of The Manchu Language in Ch'ing History*, in: Harvard Journal of Asiatic Studies, Vol. 53, No. 1 (Jun., 1993), pp. 63-102.

CROSSLEY, P. K., *A Translucent Mirror: History and Identity in Qing Imperial Ideology*, Berkeley 1999.

CROSSLEY, P. K., *The Wobbling Pivot: China since 1800; An Interpretive History*, New York 2010.

DAM CHOS LHUN GRUB, *'Brug brgyud 'dzin gyi rgyal mchog dang pa mi dbang o rgyan dbang phyug mchog gi rtogs brjod*, Thimphu 2008.

DARGYE, N. L., *La biografia segreta del Sesto Dalai Lama, 1683-1706 (1746)*, edited by E. Rispoli, Milano 1999.

DE BULMERINCQ, M. [*August von Bulmerincq*], *Le passé de la Russie depuis les temps les plus reculés jusqu'à la paix de San-Stefano 1878*, Bruxelles 1881.

DEB, A., *George Bogle's Treaty with Bhutan (1775)*, in: Bulletin of Tibetology, 8, 1, 1971, pp. 5-14.

DEY, K. P., *The Life and career of Major Sir Louis Cavagnari, C.S.I., British envoy at Cabul, together with a brief outline of the Second Afghan War*, Calcutta 1881.

DILLON, M., *China: A Modern History*, London – New York 2012.

DUBGYUR, L., *The Wheel of Laws: An Insight into the Origin of Buddhist Kingship, Constitution and Judicial Independence in Bhutan*, Thimphu 2015.

ELLIOTT, M. C., *The Manchu Way: The Eight Banners and Ethnic Identity in Late Imperial China*, Stanford 2001.

Encyclopedia of the Age of Imperialism, 1800-1914, edited by C. C. Hodge, Westport, Connecticut – London 2008.

EWING, T. E., *Between the Hammer and the Anvil? Chinese and Russian Policies in Outer Mongolia 1911-1921*, Uralic and Altaic Series, Vols 138-139, London – New York 2006.

FORBES, A., *The Afghan Wars: 1839-42 and 1878-80*, London 1892.

FRENCH, P., *Younghusband: The Last Great Imperial Adventurer*, London 2004.

GOLDSTEIN, M. C., *A History of Modern Tibet, 1913-1951: The demise of the Lamaist State*, Berkeley – Los Angeles – London 1989.

HATTERSLEY, R., *Campbell-Bannerman*, London 2006.

HEISSIG, W., *The Religions of Mongolia*, translated by G. Samuel, Berkeley – Los Angeles 1980.

HENSMAN, H., *The Afghan War of 1879-80*, London 1881.

ICHIKO, C., *Political and institutional reform, 1901-11*, in: *The Cambridge History of China*, edited by D. Twitchett and J. K. Fairbank (general editors), Vol. 11: Late Ch'ing 1800-1911, Part 2, edited by J. K. Fairbank and K. Liu, New York 1980.

ICHINNOROV, S., *The biography of Öndör Gegeen*, translated by Baasanjav, in: *The History of Mongolia*, Vol. III, edited by D. Sneath and C. Kaplonski, Folkestone 2010, pp. 674-682.

IMAEDA, Y., *Histoire médiévale du Bhoutan: établissement et évolution de la théocratie des 'Brug pa*, Tokyo 2011.

ISHIHAMA, Y., *On the Dissemination of the Belief in the Dalai Lama as a Manifestation of the Bodhisattva Avalokiteśvara*, in: *The History of Tibet*, Vol. II, edited by A. McKay, London – New York 2003, pp. 538-553.

JAGOU, F., *Le 9e Panchen Lama (1883-1937): enjeu des relations sino-tibétaines*, Paris 2004.

JAGOU, F., *The Thirteenth Dalai Lama's Visit to Beijing in 1908: In Search of a New Kind of Chaplain-Donor Relationship*, in: *Buddhism Between Tibet and China*, edited by M. T. Kapstein, Boston 2009.

JOHNSON, R., *Spying for Empire: The Great Game in Central and South Asia, 1757-1947*, London 2006.

KAKAR, M. H., *A political and diplomatic history of Afghanistan, 1863-1901*, Leiden 2006.

KAO LAO 高勞, *Hsin-hai ke-ming shih* 辛亥革命史, Shang-hai 上海 12 [1923].

KAPLONSKI, C., *Truth, History and Politics in Mongolia: Memory of Heroes*, London 2004.

KAPSTEIN, M. T., *Early Twentieth-Century Tibetan Encounters with the West*, in: *Sources of Tibetan Tradition*, edited by K. R. Schaeffer, M. T. Kapstein and G. Tuttle, New York 2013, pp. 703-726.

KHODARKOVSKY, M., *Non-Russian subjects*, in: *The Cambridge History of Russia*, Vol. I: From Early Rus' to 1689, edited by M. Perrie, Cambridge 2006, pp. 520-538.

KLEIN, I., *The Anglo-Russian Convention and the Problem of Central Asia, 1907-1914*, in: Journal of British Studies, Vol. 11, No. 1 (Nov., 1971), pp. 126-147.

KOBAYASHI, R., *An Analytical Study of the Tibetan Record of the Simla Conference (1913-1914): Shing stag rgya gar 'phags pa'i yul du dbyin bod rgya gsum chings mol mdzad lugs kun gsal me long*, in: *Current Issues and Progress in Tibetan Studies, Proceedings of the Third International Seminar of Young Tibetologists, Kobe 2012*, edited by T. Takeuchi, K. Iwao, A. Nishida, S. Kumagai and M. Yamamoto, Kobe 2013, pp. 183-200.

KOBAYASHI, R., The Tibet-Japan Relations in the Era of the 1911 Revolution: Tibetan Letters from the Aoki Bunkyō Archive, in: チベット・ヒマラヤ文明の歴史的展開 *The Historical Development of Tibeto-Himalayan Civilization*, edited by Iwao Kazushi 岩尾一史 and Ikeda Takumi 池田巧編, Kyōto 京都 2018, pp. 101-122.

KOLMAŠ, J., *The Ambans and Assistant Ambans of Tibet (1727-1912). Some statistical observations*, in: *The History of Tibet*, Vol. II, edited by A. McKay, London – New York 2003, pp. 602-614.

KUHN, P. A., *Rebellion and its enemies in late imperial China: militarization and social structure, 1796-1864*, Cambridge, Mass. 1980.

KUNG SHU-TO 龚书铎 ET AL., *Chung kuo chin tai shih kang* 中国近代史纲, ti erh pan 第二版, Pei-ching 北京 1993.

LAMB, A., *Britain and Chinese Central Asia: The Road to Lhasa, 1767 to 1905*, London 1960.

LAN, M., *China's "New Administration" in Mongolia*, in: *Mongolia in the Twentieth Century: Landlocked Cosmopolitan*, edited by S. Kotkin and B. A. Elleman, Armonk – London 1999, pp. 39-58.

LARY, D., *China's Republic*, Cambridge, UK – New York 2007.

LATTIMORE, O., *Pivot of Asia: Sinkiang and the Inner Asian Frontiers of China and Russia*, Boston 1950.

Life and Teachings of Tsong Khapa, edited by R. A. F. Thurman, Dharamsala 2006.

MA LYNN, A., *Muslims in China*, translated by P. Lan Lin and C. Fang, Indianapolis 2004.

MAKSIMOV, K. N., *Kalmykia in Russia's Past and Present National Policies and Administrative System*, translated by A. Yastrzhembska, Budapest – New York 2008.

MATSUI, M., *The Russo-Japanese Agreement of 1907: Its Causes and the Progress of Negotiations*, in: Modern Asian Studies, Vol. 6, No. 1, 1972, pp. 33-48.

MCKAY, A., *Tibet and the British Raj: the frontier cadre, 1904-1947*, Richmond 1997.

MITTER, R., *1911: The Unanchored Chinese Revolution*, in: The China Quarterly, No. 208 (December 2011), pp. 1009-1020.

WHEELER, G., *Epilogue*, in: G. MORGAN, *Anglo-Russian Rivalry in Central Asia: 1810-1895*, London 1981, pp. 215-224.

MORGENTHAU, H. J., *Politics Among Nations: The Struggle for Power and Peace*, New York 1948.

MORSE, H. B., *The international relations of the Chinese Empire*, Vol. [I]: The period of conflict, 1834-1860, London 1910.

NAUMOV, I. V., *The History of Siberia*, edited by D. N. Collins, London – New York 2006.

New Qing Imperial History: The Making of Inner Asian Empire at Qing Chengde, edited by J. A. Millward, R. W. Dunnell, M. C. Elliott, P. Forêt, London 2004.

NORRIS, J. A., *The First Afghan War: 1838-1842*, Cambridge 1967.

ONON, U. – PRITCHATT, D., *Asia's First Modern Revolution: Mongolia proclaims its Independence in 1911*, Leiden 1989.

P'ENG TSE-CHOU 彭澤周, *Chin tai Chung kuo chih ke ming yü Jih pen* 近代中國之革命與日本, T'ai pei 臺北 78 [1989].

PERDUE, P. C., *China Marches West: The Qing Conquest of Central Eurasia*, Cambridge – London 2005.

PETECH, L., *Asia Centrale*, in: *Le civiltà dell'Oriente. Storia, letteratura, religioni, filosofia, scienze e arte*, Vol. I: Storia, under the direction of G. Tucci, Firenze – Roma 1965, pp. 919-960.

PETECH, L., *Central Tibet and the Mongols: The Yüan-Sa-skya Period of Tibetan History*, Roma 1990.

PETECH, L., *China and Tibet in the early 18th century*, Leiden 1950.

PETECH, L., *Il Tibet*, in: *Le civiltà dell'Oriente. Storia, letteratura, religioni, filosofia, scienze e arte*, Vol. I: Storia, under the direction of G. Tucci, Firenze – Roma 1965, pp. 1123-1141.

PETECH, L., *Il Tibet*, in: *Nuova storia universale dei popoli e delle civiltà*, Vol. XX: Asia Centrale e Giappone, edited by M. Bussagli, L. Petech and M. Muccioli, Torino 1981, pp. 235-306.

PETECH, L., *The Dalai-Lamas and Regents of Tibet: A Chronological Study*, in: T'oung Pao, Vol. 47, Livr. 3/5, 1959, pp. 368-394.

PETECH, L., *The Kingdom of Ladakh: C. 950-1842 A.D.*, Roma 1977.

PHUNTSHO, K., *The History of Bhutan*, Noida 2013.

POMMARET, F., *Ancient Trade Partners: Bhutan, Cooch Bihar and Assam (17th to 19th centuries)*, in: Journal of Bhutan Studies, Vol. 2, No. 1, Summer 2000, pp. 30-53.

POULLADA, L., *Reform and rebellion in Afghanistan, 1919-1929: King Amanullah's failure to modernize a tribal society*, Ithaca 1973.

POWERS, J., *Introduction to Tibetan Buddhism*, Ithaca – Boulder 2007.

RAWSKI, E. S., *The Last Emperors: A Social History of Qing Imperial Institutions*, Berkeley – Los Angeles – London 1998.

RHOADS, E. J. M., *Manchus and Han: ethnic relations and political power in late Qing and early Republican China, 1861-1928*, Seattle – London 2000.

RICHARDSON, H. E., *Tibet and Its History*, Boulder – London 1984.

RICHARDSON, H., *The Dalai Lamas*, in: *The History of Tibet*, Vol. II, edited by A. McKay, London – New York 2003, pp. 554-566.

RIZVI, J., *Ladakh: Crossroads of High Asia*, Delhi 1996.

ROBBINS, K., *Sir Edward Grey: A Biography of Lord Grey of Fallodon*, London 1971.

RUEGG, D. S., *Mchod yon, yon mchod and mchod gnas / yon gnas: On the historiography and semantics of a Tibetan religio-social and religio-political concept*, in: *Tibetan History and Language: Studies dedicated to Uray Géza on his seventieth birthday*, edited by E. Steinkellner, Wien 1991, pp. 441-454.

SA SKYA BSOD NAMS RGYAL MTSHAN, *Rgyal rabs gsal ba'i me long*, Pe cin 2002.

SAGASTER, K., *The History of Buddhism among the Mongols*, in: *The Spread of Buddhism*, edited by A. Heirman and S. P. Bumbacher, Leiden – Boston 2007, pp. 379-432.

SAHADEO, J., *Russian Colonial Society in Tashkent: 1865-1923*, Bloomington – Indianapolis 2007.

SANDERS, F., *The Life and Lineage of the Ninth Khalkha Jetsun Dampa Khutukhtu of Urga*, in: Central Asiatic Journal, Vol. 45, No. 2, 2001, pp. 278-286.

SCHRECKER, J. E., *Imperialism and Chinese Nationalism: Germany in Shantung*, Cambridge, MA 1971.

SCHWIEGER, P., *The Dalai Lama and the Emperor of China: A Political History of the Tibetan Institution of Reincarnation*, New York 2015.

SHAKAPA, W. D., (Tsepon), *The Rise of Changchub Gyaltsen and the Phagmo Drupa Period*, in: Bulletin of Tibetology, 1, 1981, pp. 23-33.

SIEGEL, J., *Endgame: Britain, Russia and the Final Struggle for Central Asia*, New York 2002.

SINGH, N., *Bhutan: A Kingdom in the Himalayas*, New Delhi 1972.

SINHA, N. C., *Chhos Srid Gnyis Ldan*, in: Bulletin of Tibetology, V, 3, 1968, pp. 13-27.

SINHA, N. C., *The Simla Convention 1914: A Chinese Puzzle*, in: Bulletin of Tibetology, No. 1, 1977, pp. 35-39.

SKRINE, C. P. – NIGHTINGALE, P., *Macartney at Kashgar: New Light on British, Chinese and Russian Activities in Sinkiang, 1890-1918*, London 1973.

SKRINE, F. H. – ROSS, E. D., *The Heart of Asia: A History of Russian Turkestan and the Central Asian Khanates from the Earliest Times*, London 1899.

SMITH, R. J., *The Qing Dynasty and traditional Chinese culture*, Lanham 2015.

SNELLGROVE, D. L. – RICHARDSON, H. E., *A Cultural History of Tibet*, Boulder 1980.

SONI, S. K., *Mongolia-China Relations: Modern and Contemporary Times*, New Delhi 2006.

SONI, S. K., *Mongolia-Russia Relations (Kiakhta to Vladivostok)*, New Delhi 2002.

SPERLING, E., *The Chinese Venture in K'am, 1904-1911, and the Role of Chao Erh-feng*, in: The History of Tibet, Vol. III, edited by A. McKay, London – New York 2003.

SUNDER, D. H. E., *Survey and Settlement of the Western Duars in the District of Jalpaiguri, 1889 – 1895*, Calcutta 1895.

SYKES, P., *A History of Afghanistan*, Vol. II, London 1940.

TACHIBANA, M., *The 1911 Revolution and "Mongolia": Independence, Constitutional Monarchy, or Republic*, in: Journal of Contemporary East Asia Studies, 3:1, 2014, pp. 69-90.

TEICHMAN, E., *Travels of a Consular Officer in Eastern Tibet, Together with a History of the Relations between China, Tibet and India*, Cambridge 1922.

TENG, S., *The Taiping rebellion and the Western powers*, Oxford 1971.

TENPA, L., *An Early History of the Mon Region (India) and its Relationship with Tibet and Bhutan*, Dharamshala 2018.

The Anglo-Japanese Alliance, 1902-1922, edited by P. P. O'Brien, London – New York 2004.

The New Russo-Persian Frontier East of the Caspian Sea, in: Proceedings of the Royal Geographical Society and Monthly Record of Geography, Vol. 4, No. 4 (Apr., 1882), pp. 213-219.

TSÀN-YAN-GHIA-TSÒ (VI Dalai Lama), *Canti d'amore*, edited by E. Lo Bue, Palermo 1993.

TUCCI, G., *Indo-Tibetica*, Vol. II: Rin c'en bzaṅ po e la rinascita del buddhismo nel Tibet intorno al Mille, Roma 1933.

TUCCI, G., *Le religioni del Tibet*, Roma 1976.

TUCCI, G., *Tibetan painted scrolls*, Vol. I, Roma 1949.

TUTTLE, G., *Tibetan Buddhists in the Making of Modern China*, New York 2005.

VAN SCHAIK, S., *Tibet: A History*, New Delhi 2012.

VAN WALT VAN PRAAG, M. C., *The Status of Tibet: History, Rights, and Prospects in International Law*, Boulder 1987.

WANG, D., *China's unequal treaties: narrating national history*, Lanham 2005.

WANG, G., *To Reform a Revolution: Under the Righteous Mandate*, in: Dædalus, Vol. 122, No. 2, 1993, pp. 71-94.

WHITECROSS, R. W., *Buddhism and Constitutions in Bhutan*, in: *Buddhism and Law: An Introduction*, edited by R. R. French and M. A. Nathan, New York 2014, pp. 350-367.

WILLIAMS, B., *Great Britain and Russia, 1905 to the 1907 Convention*, in: *British Foreign Policy under Sir Edward Grey*, edited by F. H. Hinsley, Cambridge 1977, pp. 133-147.

WINDISCHGRAETZ, M. – WANGDI, R., *The Black-Slate Edict of Punakha Dzong*, Thimphu 2019.

WYLIE, T. V., *Lama Tribute in the Ming Dynasty*, in: *Tibetan Studies in Honour of Hugh Richardson: Proceedings of the International Seminar on Tibetan Studies, Oxford 1979*, edited by M. Aris and A. S. S. Kyi, Warminster, England 1980, pp. 335-340.

YA HAN-CHANG 牙含章, *Ta lai la ma chuan* 达赖喇嘛传, Pei-ching 北京 1984.

ZHWA SGAB PA DBANG PHYUG BDE LDAN, *Bod kyi srid don rgyal rabs*, Vol. I, Kalimpong 1976.

ZHWA SGAB PA DBANG PHYUG BDE LDAN, *Bod kyi srid don rgyal rabs*, Vol. II, Kalimpong 1976.

Tools

DICTIONARIES AND OTHER LINGUISTIC TOOLS

'A. DEHKHODĀ, *Loghat-nāmeh*, Tehrān 1998; H. A. GILES, *A Chinese-English Dictionary*, London 1892; Ḥ. 'AMĪD, *Farhang-e 'Amid*, Tehrān 1342 [1962-1963]; H. A. JÄSCHKE, *A Tibetan-English dictionary: with special reference to the prevailing dialects*, London 1881; the dictionaries and glossaries available online within the THL Tibetan to English Translation Tool (www.thlib.org); S. C. DAS, *A Tibetan-English Dictionary with Sanskrit Synonyms*, Calcutta 1902; C. O. HUCKER, *A Dictionary of Official Titles in Imperial China*, Stanford, California 1985; L. W. ADAMEC, *Historical Dictionary of Afghanistan*, Lanham – Toronto – Plymouth 2012; W. SMITH, *A dictionary of Greek and Roman geography*, London 1873-1878; F. STEINGASS, *A comprehensive Persian-English Dictionary*, London 1963; X. ZHAO, *Il dizionario di cinese*, Bologna 2013; A. SCHUESSLER, *ABC Etymological Dictionary of Old Chinese*, Honolulu 2007; H. A. GILES, *A Chinese-English dictionary*, London 1912 (3 vols); W. F. MAYERS, *The Chinese Government: a manual of Chinese titles, categorically arranged and explained with an appendix*, second edition with additions by G. M. H. Playfair, Shanghai – Hongkong – Yokohama – London 1886; *Dictionary of National Biography*, edited by S. Lee, Vol. XXXV, New York – London 1893; T. V. WYLIE, *A Standard System of Tibetan Transcription*, in: Harvard Journal of Asiatic Studies, Vol. 22, 1959, pp. 261-267; S. E. MARTIN, *A reference grammar of Korean*, Rutland, Vermont – Tokyo 1992.

MAPS AND ATLASES

E. STANFORD, *Atlas of the Chinese Empire*, London 1908; E. STANFORD, *Complete Atlas of China*, London 1917.

TNA, FO 535/16, Russian map to show the tribes of Inner Mongolia, compiled in 1912 by the Staff of the Trans-Amur Section of Frontier Guards from the latest Russian, Japanese and Chinese sources, edited by Maj.-General Volodchenko, Tribes from data supplied by Colonel Baranov, attached to: TNA, FO 535/16, Enclosure in No. 470, Report by Major Robertson on the Military Situation in Inner Mongolia, pp 456-460.

U.S. Army Map Service (AMS):

Series 1301 (GSGS 4646), edition 4-AMS, sheet NI 41, Herāt, scale: 1:1,000,000;
Series 1301 (GSGS 2555), edition 5-AMS, sheet NI 42, Kābul, scale: 1:1,000,000;
Series 1301, edition 5-AMS, sheet NJ 43, Su-Fu, scale: 1:1,000,000.

Note on Indexing

Our books do not have indexes due to the prohibitive cost of assembling them. If you are reading this book in paperback and want to find a particular word or phrase you can do so by downloading a free PDF version of this book from the E-International Relations website. View the e-book in any standard PDF reader and enter your search terms in the search box. You can then navigate through the search results and find what you are looking for. If you are using apps (or devices) to read our e-books, you should also find word search functionality in those.

You can find all of our books here: http://www.e-ir.info/publications

www.ingramcontent.com/pod-product-compliance
Lightning Source LLC
Chambersburg PA
CBHW071608080526
44588CB00010B/1060